EVANSTON
ITS LAND AND ITS PEOPLE

DR. JOHN EVANS
From portrait painted about 1850

EVANSTON
ITS LAND AND ITS PEOPLE

By

VIOLA CROUCH REELING

EVANSTON, ILLINOIS

PUBLISHED BY FORT DEARBORN CHAPTER
DAUGHTERS OF THE AMERICAN REVOLUTION
1928

PRINTED IN U. S. A.
BY W. B. CONKEY CO., HAMMOND, IND.

FOREWORD

IN 1923, during the regency of Mrs. Warren Williams, the Board of Management of FORT DEARBORN CHAPTER OF THE DAUGHTERS OF THE AMERICAN REVOLUTION was asked by Miss Edith Moon, librarian in the Evanston Public Library, to sponsor the publication of a history of Evanston, as there was no book on early Evanston, and the library was frequently receiving calls for one. As the preserving of records is part of the work of the Society, the Board decided to act upon Miss Moon's suggestion.

Mrs. Julian G. Goodhue, who followed Mrs. Williams in office, appointed a committee with Mrs. John A. Briggs as chairman, to do the research work for the book. In April of 1924 a member of this committee was asked to write the book, and she consented on condition that she be allowed to do her own research work. The writing of the book went forward under the regency of Mrs. Wilbur Helm, and was completed after Mrs. Harry Ward became regent.

The book is not a history in the accepted sense of the word, but is intended to be a narrative with historic value, citing great events and small happenings, and, except in a few instances, is carried only to the year of 1900. Various persons, who are recognized authorities on the chapter subjects, have been consulted—among them being Professor U. S. Grant, Head of the Geology and Geography Department of Northwestern University; Professor Fay-Cooper Cole, Ethnologist, of the University of Chicago; Joseph Thompson, Editor of the *Illinois*

Catholic Historical Review; J. Seymour Currey, President Emeritus of the Evanston Historical Society; the late William C. Levere, and many residents of long standing. The author hereby expresses her appreciation for all helpful suggestions and kindly criticisms.

V. C. R.

CONTENTS

LIST OF ILLUSTRATIONS

Only by looking backward can we appreciate today and look forward with an open mind

CHAPTER I

DEVELOPMENT OF THE TOPOGRAPHY OF EVANSTON

E VANSTON, the gem suburb of one of the greatest cities in the world, owes much of its wonderful development and rapid growth to its location along Lake Michigan, and Lake Michigan owes its chief characteristics to the great ice-sheets of the glacial period, which moved over and covered for thousands of years a large portion of North America, the glacial period taking its turn with other periods in preparing this continent for our habitation. The last and greatest ice-sheet, 4,000,000 square miles in area and over a mile in thickness, disappeared, it is estimated, about 25,000 years ago. It is evident that prior to the glacial period, many millions of years ago, the sea covered this region.

In the geography of a region, in its stones and rocks, in the material that goes to make up its surface and the various strata beneath the surface — in these, all of these, the trained eye of the geologist reads the history of that region, for each successive period leaves its trace; and so, in order to learn how the present topography of Evanston developed, we, too, must consider these things.

The trend of the ridges in Evanston was the deciding factor in the shaping of the town, as the ridges were the places of location of the first settlers of this region. These ridges had their beginning in the glacial period;

therefore it is necessary to go back thousands of years
to find how they were built.

THE CHICAGO PLAIN AND ITS BORDERING MORAINE

Evanston is situated on part of the great Chicago
Plain, which is an imperfectly shaped crescent. This
plain extends from Lake Michigan on the east to a ridge
or belt of high land running from Winnetka on the
north, southwest through Galewood and La Grange, then

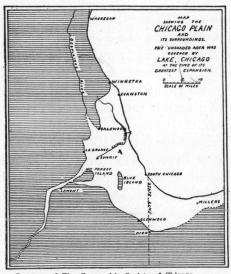

Courtesy of The Geographic Society of Chicago

CHICAGO PLAIN AND ITS
SURROUNDINGS

on southeast through Dyer, Indiana. There it takes a
northeasterly direction. The plain's greatest width is
fifteen miles, in the direction southwest from the city of
Chicago.

As the plain leaves the shoreline of the lake, it rises gradually to the west and southwest, until it reaches a nearly uniform height of sixty feet above the lake, the level of the lake being 581 feet[1] above mean tide level in the New York harbor. At this height of sixty feet the plain ends, as there is an abrupt rise in the land to the west and southwest, where the topography is rolling. The surface of this higher land continues to rise until it reaches an altitude of about two hundred feet above the level of the lake, where it begins to slope downward toward the west, southwest and south. This high, rolling land forms the broad, ridgelike belt, which encloses the plain on its west, southwest and south border, and is a great glacial moraine, formed by glacial drift. It is named Valparaiso Moraine, after the city of Valparaiso, Indiana, which is situated upon it.

THE GLACIAL PERIOD

The Glacial Period was the time when ice covered a large portion of North America and it left proofs of its existence in its drift deposits, which are found in the Chicago Plain. The bordering moraine of the plain is composed entirely of glacial drift.

As a considerable portion of the drift deposits in the plain consists of material too coarse and too heavy to have been carried by water, it must have been deposited by another agent, and that agent, we find, was ice, and that ice — glacial ice. We are told further that deposits made by water differ from glacial deposits, being stratified and assorted, whereas glacial

---

(1)   The average level of the State of Illinois is 600 feet above sea level; the entire valley of the Illinois river, with all its towns and cities, is considerably below *lake* level.

deposits are, for the most part, a heterogeneous mixture.

The Glacial Period came into existence through climatic changes to arctic conditions, and consisted of several epochs, glacial and interglacial. During the interglacial epochs, the climate was less severe and the

PLATE SHOWING AREA COVERED
BY THE GREATEST ICE-SHEET
Black portion shows driftless area

ice diminished in area, or it may have disappeared entirely.

Geologists explain the forming of a glacier in somewhat the following manner. The snowfall of a region might become so great winter after winter that each summer's warmth could not melt all of the winter's snowfall. In this way, the depth of the snow would increase from year to year. The pressure of the weight of the overlying mass of snow would compact the lower portion into ice. Moreover, there would be a tendency on the part of the overlying portion of snow to push out the lower portion of the mass, which would, of necessity, spread in all directions, encroaching on the surrounding areas. Ice moving in this manner is called glacial ice, and the manner of moving, glacial motion.

As bits of timber, vegetable mold, beds of peat and even large trees have been found in the drift, it is evident that, as the glacier advanced, it incorporated these things in its mass and carried them along. It also carried with it and deposited bowlders and clay irregularly over the land, filling in valleys and building up dams; digging into the rock, broadening river-valleys and depositing drift around their sides, thus modifying the great basins, which the Great Lakes now occupy; leaving irregular smaller basins, wherein lie the smaller lakes to the north, northeast and northwest of Evanston. In its course, it carried millions of tons of rock and clay, grinding together bowlders and small stones, and also rubbing them against the solid rock, making grooves which show plainly the direction from which the glacier came. In this way, in its southward journey, it wrote its own autograph, proving just how far it reached in different parts of the country — as far south as the Ohio river, and New York City in the east, and nearly to the Missouri river and to northeastern Kansas in the west.

The ice covered the highest mountains in the northeastern United States. Therefore the depth of the glacier must have been, at least, a little over a mile.

The great bowlders found in such abundance in Wisconsin, and less abundantly in this region are similar to formations of rock found around Lakes Superior and Huron and other points to the north and northeast, a condition which proves the great distances these bowlders were transported by the glacier.

Small stones carried and deposited by a glacier are often found to be grooved or "striated" in several directions on the same side. This is the result of their having been held firmly by the weight above them against the hard surface of the bed-rock and grooved, then turned and marked by the making of fresh "striae." The bed-rock, being stationary, has grooves running in one direction only, the direction of the glacier's motion. Stones of glacier transporting may also be found that are perfectly rounded and polished.

In the regions over which the glacier passed, there is abundant water power to-day, such as water-falls and rapids. These are less common in regions not glaciated.

SIZE OF LAKE MICHIGAN'S BASIN DUE TO THE ICE SHEETS

We learn that the development of the basin of Lake Michigan was, in part, the result of the work of the ice-sheets.

It is believed that long ago a north-south river-valley extended along the axis of the basin of Lake Michigan, which the ice-sheets broadened and deepened; on melting, they left great deposits of drift along its eastern and western sides and a few miles to the south of the southern end of the lake, thus helping change the river-valley into a basin great enough for a lake.

THE BEDROCK OF THE CHICAGO PLAIN AND ITS DRIFT MANTLE

Solid rock forms the whole outer shell of the earth; therefore, it follows that rock forms the sub-structure of the Chicago Plain.

The loose earth made up of sand, clay, gravel and bowlders lying on the bed-rock or sub-structure of the plain is called drift and is of glacial origin.

The composition of the bed-rock of the plain is limestone, called Niagara limestone, as it is believed to be of the same age as the limestone at Niagara Falls, which, we learn, belongs to the later part of the Silurian Period, the third of the seven long periods that make up the Paleozoic Era. This was the first era, so far as is known, when there was abundant marine life.

Wherever limestone is seen in the Chicago area, imperfect shells, parts of shells, corals, and crinoid stems are found, thus proving that the sea covered this region when they were formed, as they are somewhat similar to those being formed in the ocean to-day. Furthermore, the sea was probably shallow, as corals do not flourish in deep waters.

If we could look on the surface of the rock beneath the drift on the Chicago Plain, we would find this surface very uneven; that is, high in some places and low in others. We would also find the top very irregular, showing the effects of erosion by atmosphere and water. The lowest level of the rock surface is a half mile north of the juncture of the North Branch of the Chicago river with the South Branch, this level being one hundred twenty-four feet below the surface of the lake. From this point the rock surface rises gradually toward the borders of the plain, with many undulations, and continues rising under the moraine belt to the north, west and south, with some exposures of the rock surface through the drift mantle, until it reaches an elevation of one hundred to one hundred ten feet above the level of the lake.

The thickness of the drift mantle varies, averaging in the plain fifty feet, and in the bordering moraine one hundred fifty feet. Therefore the elevation of the land around the Chicago Plain is due both to the rise in the surface of the rock and to the greater thickness of its drift mantle.

Good exposures of drift may be seen along the lake bluff from Evanston northward.

DRAINAGE

The drainage of the Chicago Plain is in a southwesterly direction from Chicago. Traversing the broad moraine belt is the Des Plaines valley, through which the Des Plaines river flows. Here, too, are the Illinois-Michigan canal and the Drainage canal. This valley is from thirty to one hundred feet deep, with abrupt slopes, which are one-half mile to one and a quarter miles wide. The floor of the valley is nearly flat and is joined by another valley southwest of the city of Chicago, which is known as the Sag. The floors of the two valleys join the floor of the Chicago Plain, forming the outlet for drainage from the plain southwest across the moraine belt to the Mississippi river system and thence to the Gulf of Mexico.

There was a rise of less than fifteen feet, before the Drainage canal was made, from the level of the lake to the *divide,* which separated the waters that flowed into the great St. Lawrence from the waters that flowed into the Gulf of Mexico. The lake, therefore, barely escaped drainage into the Mississippi river system.[2]

During spring floods or heavy rains the Des Plaines river discharged its waters through both the South Branch of the Chicago river into Lake Michigan through the St. Lawrence system, and down its own normal channel, to the Illinois river, then on to the Mississippi River.

LAKE CHICAGO

We can scarcely realize that where our beautiful city of Evanston now stands, there was once nothing but water, a great lake of water that covered not only our region, but where Chicago and some of the towns to the north, west, southwest, and south stand to-day. This great body of water has been given the name of Lake Chicago.

The basin of Lake Chicago had the Valparaiso moraine on one side and the ice-front on the other. The last ice-sheet, or continental ice-sheet as it was called, remained thousands of years. When climatic conditions became such that the edge of the ice melted faster than the ice advanced, the ice-sheet began its final retreat. When the edge of the ice-sheet retreated northeast of the Valparaiso moraine, the water from the melting snow and ice and from rain-fall flooded the basin or depression between the ice edge or ice-front and the Valparaiso

---

(2)   Joliet, over two centuries ago, considered the Chicago Portage of great importance and said a canal cut through from the Lake of the Illinois (Lake Michigan) to the river that empties into the Mississippi, half a league in length, would make it possible to go from Lake Erie to the Mississippi by water.

moraine and made Lake Chicago. As the ice-front melted — that is, retreated to the north — Lake Chicago increased in size.

The waters in this depression rose until they reached the lowest point in the Valparaiso moraine, sixty feet above the level of Lake Michigan, and then overflowed to the southwest through the region which the Des Plaines valley and the Sag now occupy. This is known as the Chicago outlet. The sides of this valley, near Lemont, rise forty to sixty feet above the valley floor, this height being about on a level with the waters of Lake Chicago, when they were at their greatest height. It is probable that at this time the discharge of waters through the Chicago outlet caused rapids similar to the rapids in the Niagara River to-day.

STAGES IN THE HISTORY OF LAKE CHICAGO

There are several stages in the history of Lake Chicago. A ridge was formed by the waves washing up sand and gravel toward the outer edge of the lake, when the water stood a great length of time at any one level, and this debris remained after the water had receded. While the waters stood at the east base of one ridge, the waves were washing up debris, building up bars or spits in the lake, which, when the waters receded, formed the next ridge further east. In this manner the ridges in Evanston were formed.

The stages of Lake Chicago were as follows: First, Glenwood Stage, leaving Glenwood Beach, *Dutch Ridge,* west of Evanston; second, beach not visible, as the water receded beyond the present shoreline of Lake Michigan, but excavations made in 1923 show an old beach line at the north end of the city, about twenty feet below lake level; third, Calumet Stage, forming Calumet beach, which, in Evanston, is *Ridge Avenue;* fourth, Tolleston Stage, forming Tolleston beach, which is *Chicago* and *Hinman Avenues* in Evanston.

GLENWOOD STAGE

During the Glenwood Stage, the waters are estimated to have stood at sixty feet above the present lake level. The waves washed debris toward the west and south sides, leaving a well defined beach. This is called the Glenwood beach.

A shoreline corresponding to the Glenwood beach is present in Wisconsin, but is not to be found between Waukegan and Winnetka, where Lake Michigan has advanced westward and cut away the Glenwood beach, as well as the Calumet and Tolleston beaches. The Glenwood beach again makes its appearance at the edge of the present bluff, just south of Tower Road in Winnetka, and Sheridan Road crosses this beach line on the little hill on which stands the Episcopalian church; then the beach swings southwest for several miles. From the Sag, the Glenwood shoreline runs southeastward, along the inner slope of the moraine, and then east through Dyer, Indiana.

SECOND STAGE, NO BEACH VISIBLE

The beach of the second stage in the history of Lake Chicago was below the present level of Lake Michigan and so we cannot see it. The waters are thought to have been too low to discharge through the Chicago outlet. At this time it is evident they did not cover the whole of the Chicago Plain, as vegetation flourished, and where there were marshes, peat beds formed over the plain. Deposits of peat were found a few years ago on the campus of Northwestern University, underlying deposits of a later stage. It is probable that the ice had retreated so far to the north, that an outlet was formed in that direction lower than the one by the way of the Des Plaines valley.

At Waukegan, where excavation was being made for the large electric power plant at the north edge of the city in 1923, an old beach line was found about twenty feet below the present lake level. Round masses of clay, water-worn tree trunks and the bones of a deer showed the location of the beach line.

THE CALUMET STAGE

The third stage was the Calumet Stage. Either returning glacial ice blocked the northern outlet, or else a rising of the land lifted the outlet and prevented the waters from draining at this point. One of these possible changes caused the waters to alter their flow and discharge through the southwest outlet, submerging again the Chicago Plain.

The second or Calumet beach, which marks the third stage in the history of Lake Chicago, shows that the waters rose to forty feet above the level of Lake Michigan. This beach lies west of the Chicago and Northwestern tracks from the state line south to Waukegan. Here the waves cut it away as far as Wilmette, where it appears again at the present shoreline between Wilmette and Evanston. At Gross Point the bluff is forty feet high and shows the deposits of that stage. From this point it runs south through Evanston to Rose Hill, swings west and terminates at the North Branch of the Chicago river near Bowmanville. This beach we know as Ridge Avenue. Geologists call it Rose Hill Bar.

TOLLESTON STAGE

During the fourth or Tolleston stage, the waters stood twenty feet above the level of Lake Michigan, and the outlet was still to the southwest through the Des Plaines and the Sag. A third beach was thus developed, called the Tolleston beach. It appears in several places in Wisconsin, lying east of the Calumet beach, and follows closely the Chicago and North Western railway, between the state line and Waukegan. The advance of the waves of Lake Michigan has washed the beach away from this point to the bluff on the grounds of Northwestern University, at the present shoreline. This bluff is twenty feet high and is capped by beach deposits of this stage. From here the beach runs south along Chicago and Hinman Avenues in Evanston, through Lake View, and ends at Lincoln Park in Chicago.

As the ridges were the places of location of Evanston's first citizens, the trend of these ridges or beaches left by the waters of Lake Chicago was the remote deciding factor in the shaping of Evanston.

LAKE CHICAGO BECOMES LAKE MICHIGAN

When the ice melted entirely from the basin of Lake Chicago and uncovered the present outlet through the Straits of Mackinac, which is lower than the Chicago outlet — that is, the Drainage Canal outlet — the waters of Lake Chicago fell to the present lake level. Lake

Chicago passed into history, and Lake Michigan came into existence — Lake Michigan in all its grand and glorious beauty.

As the city-proud Evanstonian stands on the shore of Lake Michigan, and looks out over the vast expanse of its blue waters, he feels a great joy, and a distinctly patriotic thrill in the thought that Lake Michigan is the *only one* of the Great Lakes that is entirely surrounded by United States territory.

Before artificial means were resorted to for preserving the shoreline of the lake, the shore was being washed away in places at the rate of sixteen feet a year.

Lake Michigan is truly a great lake, being third in order of size among the fresh water lakes of the globe, Lake Superior holding first place and Lake Nyanza, in Africa, second.

CHAPTER II

VARIOUS TRIBES OF INDIANS THAT OCCUPIED THIS TERRITORY

THE Indians, in all probability, came into this country from the northwest through Bering Strait, some going southward, others to the Atlantic coast and elsewhere over the United States and over Canada, forming in groups in various localities, and developing cultures often quite distinct.

There are legends in the Winnebago tribes which prove that some of their ancestors were Mound Builders. There are Mound Builders today, in some parts of the country.

The shores of Lake Michigan and the various rivers in Illinois yield rich evidence of the former occupation of these regions by the Mound Builders. In the northern part of Illinois and on toward the west, along Rock River, many mounds were emblematic, representing tribal totems, formed on an immense scale. Near Galena, Illinois, there is a mound in the form of a huge snake, 911 feet long. One in the form of a lizard was formerly on the site that the Wellington Elevated Station occupies. There were other mounds left by the Mound Builders in the forms of birds and reptiles, and some that were not clearly defined.

The curious earth-works left by this people were built for various purposes — signal stations, military defenses, places of worship, and tombs for the dead.

The Mound Builders' system of barter extended over hundreds of miles, exchange being made from tribe to tribe. Their cultivation of corn proved they were not nomadic. In mounds along the Illinois River were found shells from the Gulf of Mexico, mica from the Carolinas, catlinite from Minnesota, galena from southeastern Missouri, and copper from the Lake Superior region, traces which show how extensively trade was carried on.

Various tribes of Indians, mostly of Algonquian stock, occupied the region on the west side of Lake Michigan in successive periods of time, one tribe after another being driven out by other, stronger tribes who coveted the land, and who, in turn, were warred upon and driven away. These were the Illinois, Miami, Foxes, Maskoutens, Kickapoo, Potawatomi, Chippewa and Ottawa—all Algonquins, and the Winnebago of Dakotan stock and the Shawnee "from the Sunny Southland."[1] These tribes inhabited this territory at different times, between the warring Iroquois on the east and the Siouan Indians on the west, which were bitter enemies to all Algonquin speaking tribes. The French called the latter Indians "the Iroquois of the West."

No one knows how many centuries the Indians[2] had occupied the whole of the United States before the white man came. They were divided into several great

---

(1)   The spelling of Dr. William Duncan Strong is followed in Indian tribe names.

(2)   Although Columbus never reached our main land, he was responsible for the name of Indian being applied to the red man.   Every school child has read that when Columbus and his crew landed on one of the Bahama islands, the natives, who were gentle and friendly, ran to the water's edge laden with gifts for their visitors; and Columbus, thinking he had reached the Indies straightway called the islands Indies; the island on which they landed, San Salvadore (Holy Savior); and the natives Indians.   With the exception of prefixing West to Indies, these names have ever since been used.

linguistic groups, according to the similarity of their languages. Tribes speaking similar languages belong to the same linguistic family and are usually related by blood. The Algonquins and the Iroquois were two great family groups covering a large part of Canada and the United States east of the Mississippi River and to the south as far as, and including, Virginia.

The great Algonquin family occupied New England, Pennsylvania, Virginia, New Jersey, Michigan, Ohio, Indiana, Illinois and other districts further west; part of Canada, including New Brunswick and Nova Scotia. This family was composed of the following tribes: the Lenape or Delaware, Ottawa, Chippewa, Potawatomi, Menominee, Sauk and Fox, Maskoutens, Illinois, and Kickapoo.

Although the Iroquois occupied a region far removed from our own, they must be mentioned, as their war parties roamed over half of North America and wrought terror from the Atlantic to the Mississippi; or, as one historian very ably puts it, "From Canada to the Carolinas and from Maine to the Mississippi, Indian women shuddered at the name of 'Ho-de-no-sau-nee' (meaning people of the long house), while even the bravest warriors went far out of their way in the wintry forests to avoid an encounter with them."

In the seventeenth century the Iroquoian family occupied the region that lay like an island in the very heart of the territory occupied by the Algonquian family; that is, around Lakes Erie and Ontario, within the present limits of New York and a large tract of land to the south. This family was originally five separate nations. Naming them from east to west, they were:

Mohawks, Oneidas, Onondagas, Cayugas and Senecas, the Senecas being the largest tribe. These tribes, while nearest kin[3] and neighbors, were always making war on each other and had already wiped out the Hurons, of their own family stock, in 1649. One wise and good Onondaga chief, Hayenwathe, thinking this was a sad state of affairs, and realizing that individually each tribe was weak and could be greatly harmed by a foe, decided that if a confederacy were formed, the tribes would be strong enough to resist the fiercest enemy. This consolidation was accomplished only after promising the chieftaincy of the confederacy to Atotarho, another chief of the same tribe, who had opposed the plan, and who was the very opposite in character to Hayenwathe.[4] The confederacy was then called the Five Nations, and continued to be The Five Nations until some time in the eighteenth century, when the Tuscaroras of North Carolina moved northward and joined the confederacy, after which time it was known as The Six Nations.

The Iroquoian Indians were well built, strong and energetic, and regarded themselves as men surpassing all others. One great Iroquois chief, when he fell wounded among Algonquins, exclaimed, "Must I, who have made the whole earth tremble, now die by the hands of children?"

Indian tribes are made up of several clans or gentes.

Clans are groups of persons related by blood on the maternal side. (Clan is sometimes used in place of gens — singular of gentes.)

Gentes are groups of persons related by blood on

---

(3)   In the Iroquoian tribes, kinship is traced through the female line.
(4)   Each tribe of the Iroquois had two war chiefs of equal power. In the Pine Tree tribes the chiefs were elected.

the paternal side. Tribes are composed of several clans or gentes.

Each clan or gens usually takes its name from a certain animal, supposed to be the friend or protector of all members of that clan or of that gens. This animal — wolf, bear, turtle, or whatever animal it is — is the animal totem of the clan or gens. All members of the same clan or gens are regarded as brother and sister, and none may marry one of his own clan or gens; that is, a wolf may not marry a wolf, but may marry a turtle. In the clan, the name comes down through the mother, and in the gens, the name comes down through the father.

The totem of the man of the house, inherited from his mother, is drawn on bark at the door of his lodge, or carved at the top of the totem pole. Beneath this drawing or carving of the totem animal are drawings or carvings to show his wealth and the brave deeds he has done; and lastly comes the totem of his wife, which will be the totem of the children when they set up housekeeping.

Clans or gentes are much like the fraternities and societies of the white man, in that totem-fellows are expected to help one another. An Indian stranger coming into a village would look for his own totem, being sure of a welcome at the lodge before which he finds his totem.

Figures representing various animals, totems of the chiefs, may be found on Indian treaties, being the sign-manuals of the chiefs.

Each tribe has one or more chiefs. In a matriarchal family the office is hereditary, coming through the female line; that is, the son of a sister and not the chief's son inheriting the office.

The chiefs advise, rather than rule, consulting the minor chiefs and the principal men on all important matters, which are settled by councils. The war chief must be a very able man, with strong personality; he must have personal merit, wisdom and bravery, and must possess eloquence; he should be capable of rallying the young men to follow him into war. If he is disqualified in any way, another may be elected in his place.

The Illinois Indians were here in the early seventeenth century, as early as 1615, five years before the landing of the Mayflower. The maps show that Champlain had heard of them and of the country further west, when he led the Hurons and the Ottawa in an unsuccessful attack against the Iroquois at Lake Huron.

Lake Michigan, from the Algonquin "Michigamea," meaning Great Water, was called by the French "Lac des Illini," because the Illinois Indians lived on its shores.

At the time the French came into the region the Illinois Confederacy consisted of the following tribes: Tamaroa, Michigamea, Kaskaskia, Moingwena, Peoria and Cahokia. The Illinois called themselves Iliniwek, which meant men, and considered themselves superior to their neighbors. The French early changed the name to Illinois.

The principal cities of the Illinois were Kaskaskia on the Illinois River, seven miles west of the present site of Ottawa; two villages of the Peoria and Moingwena, six miles up the river later named Des Moines; and Michigamea, further south on the west bank of the Mississippi. The largest of these villages was Kaskaskia on the Illinois River, and at the time of Marquette's visit, it consisted of seventy-four lodges, each containing several families. Henepin says in 1679 this village contained 460 lodges, with fires in each for two or three families, and that it extended a mile along the river, with a population of from six thousand to eight thousand. This village was transferred to the Kaskaskia River. The Peoria moved later from the Des Moines River to the Illinois River, near Lake Peoria.

In *Jesuit Relations* for 1671, it is stated that at a very early date the Illinois almost destroyed the Winnebago. One writer puts the Illinois-Winnebago war about 1640. There is a tradition that all the Winnebago were taken captive or killed, with the exception of one man, who was shot through the body with an arrow, but escaped and lived. After a time the Illinois sent all the captive Winnebago back. The one man who had escaped was then honored for never having been a slave by being made captain of the Winnebago. Some time later, the Winnebago bent on revenge, sent 600 warriors to attack the Illinois. While they were sailing down Lake Michigan, a furious storm arose and the boats capsized, drowning every man.

The Winnebago tribe encroached on the territory of the Illinois, and the result was continuous warfare, which kept the disputed boundary line shifting north or south, according to which nation was victorious. The Illinois, being braver and having greater numbers, finally drove the Winnebago north into Wisconsin. The Winnebago were unlike the Illinois in disposition, being fiercer and more inclined to war. They wore pieces of pole-cat fur on their ankles, to let it be known that they emulated that animal's movements in self-possession and deliberateness.

According to *Jesuit Relations* for 1671, the Winnebago always lived in the Green Bay region. This tribe is of the Siouan linguistic family.

In 1660 the Illinois were said to have sixty villages and a population of seventy thousand, with twenty thousand warriors. This was probably an extravagant estimation.

In 1665, the Illinois sent a delegation to the Great Chippewa village on Lake Superior, in regard to war with the Sioux. Here Claude Allouez addressed them, assuring them of French protection.

In 1681, LaSalle made a speech at a grand council in the lodge of the chief of the Miami, when trying to seal the friendship between the Miami and the Illinois, an address which has come down in history on account of its fine forest rhetoric. Parkman says there were few who were "so skilled in the art of diplomacy and forest rhetoric as LaSalle." He punctuated his speech on this occasion with presents, a custom in which the white man imitated the Indian. He began with a gift of tobacco, "to clear the brains. . . . " Next he gave them cloth, "to cover their dead, coats to dress them, hatchets to build a grand scaffold in their honor, and beads, bells and trinkets of all sorts to decorate their relatives at a grand funeral feast." All this was to gain the good will of the Indians, who, while accepting the gifts for their own use, were pleased at the compliment offered their dead. La Salle succeeded in making peace between the two tribes. He ended his harangue with a present of two wampum belts and the words, "Let us obey the Great King

[French] and live together in peace under his protection. . . ." The next day the chiefs made their reply in form (the Indian seldom gives an immediate reply), and it was all that La Salle could have wished. "The Illinois is our brother, because he is the son of our Father, the Great King. . . . We make you master of our beaver and our lands, of our minds and our bodies."

The confederacy that La Salle was planning at the time of various Indian tribes to be gathered together for French protection against the Iroquois, was formed in 1682 around Fort St. Louis. Here LaSalle and Tonti gathered an Indian colony, which at one time numbered 20,000. Of the 3,800 warriors, 1,200 were Illinois Indians.

Fort St. Louis was abandoned in 1702 by Tonti, fifteen years after LaSalle's death.

In 1750, it was estimated that there were still about 2,000 left of the Illinois, whereas years previous, there had been prosperous villages of this nation, and their hunting grounds had covered two-thirds of the state.

The Illinois became involved in the Conspiracy of Pontiac, but were unwilling to take active part. Pontiac came to them and made an appeal, but they still refused to act when he told them that if they hesitated longer, he "would consume their tribes, as fire consumed dry grass on the prairies." This great chief of the Ottawa was killed in 1769 by an Indian at Cahokia, and the act was laid to the Illinois Indians. Other Indian tribes swarmed down on the Illinois to avenge the death of their beloved chief, and nearly annihilated them. One band of the Illinois fled for refuge to a high rock, the former site of Fort St. Louis. This rock, situated across the river from

3

Utica in LaSalle county, was 125 feet high, rising straight up from the River Illinois and accessible only from the rear, where there was a steep and narrow passage. Here the Illinois Indians were cruelly and overwhelmingly besieged by a force of Potawatomi and Ottawa in 1770. The food of the little party soon gave out, and the besieging Indians cut the cord attached to vessels for drawing water, the prisoners' only means of obtaining it. The few who desperately made a dash for liberty were caught and cruelly put to death. This high rock, where almost the last of the Illinois Indians met their death, and on which their bones lay undisturbed for many years, has been given the tragic name of Starved Rock.

The missionaries describe the Illinois Indians as gentle, tractable and of good disposition, before they were changed by the influence of the white man, but slovenly in their habits. They were so fond of the priests that wherever the "black-gowns" went, they had a "goodly following." They were good hunters, using the bow and arrow. Hunting was good and game plentiful. They never used canoes and called the Potawatomi Indians "canoe-men." They were addicted to polygamy, and if a man was jealous of his wife, he would cut off her nose and ears. Marquette saw several who were thus disfigured.

However slack and slovenly they were in their habits, they never suffered from famine, as they always had a good crop of corn. The women dug up the ground with sharp sticks or clam shells and cultivated squash, melons, beans and corn, sowing the beans among the corn for the support that the stalks gave the vines. Squash, corn and berries were dried in the sun for winter use.

They made all their utensils of wood and their ladles from the head bones of buffalo.

Their cabins were large and differed in length. They were roofed and floored with mats made of rushes closely interwoven.

The Illinois women went out in their canoes to gather the rushes for the mats to be used as coverings. From these rushes they wove mats measuring sometimes sixty feet in length. Father Hennepin said of their cabins that a double covering of mats was used, and that neither wind nor rain nor snow could penetrate, they were so well sewed. The frames for the cabins were made of bent saplings, said by Hennepin to be "like the arched top of a baggage-wagon."

Deer-skin was used for clothing, oramented with dyed porcupine quills or with beads. Marquette says that the women dressed very modestly and becomingly, but the men wore scanty clothing.

When the Illinois departed for war, the whole village had to be notified by a runner giving a loud shout at the door of each cabin both night and morning before leaving. The captains of the tribe wore red scarfs, to distinguish them from the warriors. These scarfs were made from the hair of bears and buffalo.

If a stranger came into a village, a runner was sent out to notify the populace, whereupon the cooks prepared their best food and offered it to the visitors. Allouez says of the Illinois: "I find all of those, with whom I have mingled, affable and humane and it is said that whenever they meet a stranger, they give a cry of joy, caress him and show him every possible evidence of affection."

Marquette says that among both the Illinois and the

Sioux Indians there was a certain set of young men, who for some religious significance assumed the garb of women and did the same work. They went to war, but had to use clubs instead of bows and arrows. They had to be present at all important councils and nothing could be decided without them. They did not marry.

At the time the first white man came into the region, the Illinois did not bury their dead immediately. The body was wrapped in a skin and suspended by head and feet in trees. Later the body was buried, stone sepulchers sometimes being used.

In 1850, the last of the Illinois were removed from their old home site in the state that bears their name, to their new home in Indian Territory, beyond the great river, on the west side of which, on the Des Moines River, Marquette and Joliet first saw the villages of these Indians. This last remnant numbered but eighty-four and represented only two tribes, the Kaskaskia and the Peoria. In less than two hundred years, from 1658 to 1850, the Illinois tribe of Indians dwindled from a population of 70,000, so estimated, to less than a hundred, the kindly Illinois, hospitable, faithful and well-beloved by the missionaries, and, so far as we have any record, the first Indian inhabitants of this region.

The Miami, originally from west of the Mississippi, migrated to northern Indiana and eastern Illinois.

St. Cosme and his companions found Miami Indians on the site of Chicago in 1699. These Indians were pushed by the warring Iroquois up into Wisconsin, where they joined the Kickapoo and the Maskoutens on Fox River. Here Marquette and Joliet visited them. From this place they were pushed southward by encroaching tribes, among them the Potawatomi and the Chippewa. In 1678, LaSalle found a band of them on the St. Joseph river at Fort Miami, Michigan. In 1718, the Miami left their village on the site of Chicago, being afraid of the canoe-people, the Potawatomi and the Chippewa, and went around the head of the lake to be near their own people. The Foxes were also warring on them at that time. The Miami soon after emigrated to Ohio, where the Miami and Great and Little Maumee rivers perpetuate their memory. William Henry Harrison[5] says of the Miami that in the eighteenth century they could have mustered more than three thousand warriors in the field and composed the finest light horse troops in the world.[6] [7]

The Miami were conceded to be the most civil of all the tribes of Indians in the Northwest, and their chiefs were more prominent, having more influence and being attended by more guards than the chiefs of any other tribes. Charlevoix speaks of the state and ceremony with which one chief received him; not knowing it was their custom, he thought it was done simply to impress him.

Allouez says, "Their language is in harmony with their dispositions; they are gentle, affable and sedate; they speak slowly." Marquette considered the Maskoutens and the Kickapoo, living with the Miami on the Fox River, mere boors in comparison to the Miami. He

(5) Wm. Henry Harrison was appointed governor in 1800 of the Northwest Territory, which did not include Ohio. This territory was named Indiana Territory. He was later United States president.

(6) *Handbook of American Indians* says it is impossible to give a satisfactory estimate of the numbers of the Miami at any one time, on account of confusion with the Wea and the Piankashaw.

(7) At a great conference on the Maumee River, Ohio, the Miami signed with the turtle totem.

thought the way the Miami wore their hair, two long locks over their ears, gave them a pleasing appearance.

On Henry Popple's map, the Miami are shown occupying this site, Fort Miami, as late as 1733.

The Miami, as did the Maskoutens and the Kickapoo, used rushes for their cabins. The rushes were not much protection against the cold or rain, but could be easily made into compact bundles for transporting.

The Foxes (Outagamies) of Algonquian stock, were driven from their home ground along the St. Lawrence River, around Montreal and Quebec, by the Iroquois Indians. The Foxes called themselves by an Indian name composed of two words, meaning red and earth—"Red Earths," or "They of the Red Earth."

Allouez tells of an Iroquois attack on the Foxes, which occurred near the present site of Chicago, in 1670, when "six large cabins of these poor people [Foxes] were put to flight this month of March by 18 Senecas, [largest tribe of the Iroquois Confederacy] who, under the guidance of two fugitive Iroquois slaves of the Potawatomi, made an onslaught and killed all the people except thirty women, whom they led away as captives. As the men were away hunting, they met with but little resistance, there being only six warriors left in the cabins, besides the women and children, who numbered about a hundred."

The Foxes, in 1680, settled on the Fox River, named for this tribe, and sent word to the Sauk, their old neighbors along the St. Lawrence, to join them, notwithstanding the fact that the Fox villages were still new and their people very poor. According to the missionaries, these Indians were half famished and gaunt looking, following the priests around, hoping for food to be given them. The Sauk came and joined the Foxes. These two tribes lived so many years as close neighbors that by long association and intermarriage they became practically one people and an alliance was formed in 1733, after which they were known as one tribe, the Sauk and the Foxes.

The name of the Sauk (Osaukee) came from two Indian words meaning yellow and earth or land, which give the name, "They of the Yellow Land." Judge Hall, who had a long and personal acquaintance with the members of the Sauk and Fox tribe, says they were remarkable for symmetry of form and fine personal appearance, and that few equal them in intrepidity. Their history abounds with daring and desperate adventures and romantic incidents.

Their chief village was near the mouth of the Rock River, occupying a high bluff overlooking the present city of Milan, called Blackhawk's Tower. Blackhawk was chief of the Sauk and Foxes and led his people against the United States in what was known as Blackhawk's War in 1832.

In 1825, the total number of persons in the two tribes was 4,600. When they were removed to Indian Territory, they numbered but 1,600.

The Sauk and Foxes had a peculiar custom. The mother marked each male child at birth with either black or white paint, the colors being applied to the male children alternately. Thus the whole tribe was divided into two nearly equal divisions. In games, hunts, or public ceremonies, one color was ranged against the other. This division also caused keen competition in war time, in obtaining the greater number of scalps. Dr. Strong says the Potawatomi also had this custom.

The Sauk and Foxes hated the beards of the Frenchmen so much, that if they found a Frenchman "alone and unprotected" they would kill him.

This tribe made mat cabins for its journeyings, but had cabins made of heavy bark in the villages.

The habitat of the Maskoutens seems to have been in the vicinity of Michilimackinac, as there is an Ottawa tradition that they were driven from there at an early date by the Ottawa into the southern peninsula of Michigan. About the middle of the seventeenth century, they migrated around the head of the lake into Wisconsin. Here Marquette found a large village of them on the Fox River, with two other tribes, the Kickapoo and the Miami. The Maskoutens were of Algonquian stock, and are described as tall, big and strong. They, too, were astonished to see beards on the faces of the Frenchmen, as they plucked the hair from their own faces as soon as any appeared.

Moll's map shows the Maskoutens in the Chicago area in 1720, and also indicates villages of them on the St. Joseph River. De L'Isle's map shows them on this site in 1703. In the eighteenth century these Indians migrated to the Wabash and dwindled in numbers until they were almost extinct as a tribe. Parrish says they were absorbed by the Foxes, and General Clark speaks of them in 1778 as the Meadow Indians.

The Kickapoo were in the Chicago area in 1703, according to De L'Isle's map. The *Handbook of American Indians* gives the name Kickapoo as being derived from an Indian word meaning, "He moves about, standing now here, now there." The name, according to one interpreter, means Rabbit's Ghost, coming from "Wah-boos," which means rabbit. This tribe of Indians skipped half over the continent, to the despair of various ethnographers. In 1718, they had villages both on the Rock River and in the vicinity of Chicago. On some French maps, made about that time, the Rock River is called the Kickapoo River.

These Indians were industrious, intelligent and clean in their habits. They were well armed and well clothed. The men were tall, sinewy and active. The women were lithe and not lacking in beauty. Their language was soft and liquid, in strong contrast to the language of the Potawatomi, which was harsh and gutteral.

The Kickapoo were not good mixers and in this way they escaped demoralization by the whites, for it is a known fact the Indians learned quickly the bad traits, but were slower to emulate the virtues of the white people.

Beckwith tells us that the Kickapoo preferred to make war going in small groups, rather than in great numbers. A small group of from five to twenty would go hundreds of miles to swoop down on a feeble settlement, or a lone cabin, burn the property, kill the cattle, steal the horses, capture the women and children and make off before an alarm could be given. There is no record of their joining with either the English or French, or other white nations in warfare. Beckwith treats the Kickapoo and the Maskoutens as one tribe.

They were not pliant in the hands of the missionaries. It was a band of the Kickapoo that carried Father Gabriel Ribourde away and broke his head, when he had gone a short distance from his party to meditate and pray (1688). This happened along the Des Plaines River, called by the early French writers Illinois River.

The Sioux Indians, while they never occupied this territory, must be mentioned here, as they warred upon all the tribes who had villages in northern and central Illinois. The Siouan family was the most populous linguistic family, next to the Algonquian, north of Mexico. The name means snake or adder, and by metaphor, enemy. This tribe lived originally on both sides of the Mississippi River, its home site extending north as far as Canada and south to the Gulf states. These Indians were the wildest and most savage of all the Northwest tribes. Notwithstanding this, they "stood abashed and motionless as statues" in the presence of the early white men. Their cabins were covered with deer-skin, carefully and neatly sewed together.

The Potawatomi, as well as the Chippewa (Ojibway) and the Ottawa, with whom they were closely associated, are supposed to be the original people, according to Andreas, who lived at the "village of the Falls at St. Mary's Strait (Sault Ste. Marie) and on the northern bank of Lake Huron." In 1639, John Nicollet[8] visited the Potawatomi at Potawatomi Islands on Green Bay, where they had been driven by the Iroquois. They gradually spread along the western shore of Lake Michigan, occupying the sites of both Milwaukee and Chicago. In the early part of the eighteenth century, a portion of the tribe had migrated into northern Indiana and on around the head of the lake to southeastern Michigan. These In-

---

(8)   Jean Nicollet was Indian agent and interpreter for 25 years and was well loved by the Red Man.

dians were called the Potawatomi of the Woods, while
those that remained in northern Illinois were known as
the Potawatomi of the Prairies.

The three tribes, the Potawatomi, the Chippewa and
the Ottawa, were originally one nation.   The name Potawatomi means in their language, ''We are making a fire.''
The three nations alluded to themselves as ''We of the
Three Fires.'' They had one council fire and spoke one
language.

According to legend, the name, Potawatomi, was bestowed on this tribe by reason of the following incident,
related by Joseph Barron, Interpreter for General Harrison.   A Miami, having wandered from his cabin, met
three Indians, whose language he could not understand.
He made signs for them to follow him; they did so, and
he took them to his cabin and entertained them until dark.
During the night, two of the strange Indians took embers
from the fire and placed them outside the door.   These
were seen by the host and the remaining Indian stranger,
and were understood to imply a council fire between the
two nations.   Ever after this, this tribe of Indians was
known as the Potawatomi.

The Potawatomi were tall, fierce and haughty, and
the most energetic and powerful of all the Northwest
tribes.   The Ottawa were thick-set, good-natured and industrious.   The Chippewa were warlike and daring. All
three nations had the same general lineaments.

The Potawatomi early formed an attachment for the
French that remained unbroken. They were called squatters by other tribes, as they never had lands of their own,
but were always intruding on lands to which other tribes
had prior claim.   They were foremost in all treaties

ceding lands, and wanting the lion's share of presents and annuities, especially where the sale was of land of other tribes, according to Beckwith.

The women did all the work, the men's entire occupation being hunting and dressing. The men were well clothed and made use of a great deal of vermilion. In the winter they wore buffalo robes, richly painted; in the summer, cloth of either red or blue. The women and young girls painted with vermilion and dressed in whatever they possessed, but they were always tidy. At night they did a great deal of dancing, always in perfect time and never losing a step.

The beds of this tribe were of buffalo skins, over which deer-skins were laid. Their portable wigwams consisted of a frame-work of poles, fastened together at the top, and a mat of interwoven rushes fitted over it. Mats of flags or rushes were laid on the floor around the fire. The Potawatomi winter houses were round, covered with birch bark or rush mats; their summer houses were rectangular in shape and larger, and mat-covered. Before a lodge could be occupied, either in winter or summer, there was a ceremony, with offerings of tobacco and a feast of dog meat. The chief's wife was always the first to enter the new lodge. The dog used for the feasts was carefully raised and was never allowed to run with other dogs, and many formalities had to be observed before killing it.

The Potawatomi were divided into four clans, according to Chauvignerie (1736): the Golden Carp, the Frog, the Crab, and the Tortoise. Morgan says the Potawatomi had fifteen totems. The Prairie Potawatomi reckoned descent in the father's line.

In 1846, the Potawatomi, the Chippewa and the Ottawa were united as the Potawatomi nation. They lived along the North Shore for the greater part of two hundred years and theirs was the last native tribe to take its departure, which took place in the years 1835 and 1836.

The Chippewa (Ojibway) were the largest tribe of Indians of Algonquian stock.

Radisson visited the Ottawa at Manitoulin Island in 1658. He called the waters surrounding the islands, "The Lake of the Staring Hairs," as the Ottawa wore their hair "like a brush, turned up." Their ears had five holes in them, each hole large enough to put the end of the finger in it. A hole was bored through the nose, through which a straw a foot long was run.

Charlevoix, sent here by the Canadian government to study the Indians, was a keen observer, as his letters, published in London in 1721, describing "our Indians," as he styles them, prove. He visited camps and villages along the west shore and around the head of Lake Michigan, as well as villages along the Mississippi River.

He thought well of the Indians. He said of the Potawatomi of Canada that they were the finest men in all Canada and had the sweetest natural temper. "The nearer we view our Indians," he said, "the more good qualities we find in them. In the principles that regulate their conduct, the maxims by which they govern themselves, we discover nothing of the barbarian."

He found the cabins in the villages placed without order or design, fifteen to twenty feet broad and some of them one hundred feet in length, each fire serving a space of thirty feet. Some were like "cart houses, others like tubs built of bark, supported by poles, sometimes plastered on the outside with clay, but with less neatness than beavers use.'' When the floor was not large enough for bedding the family, the young people slept on beds in a kind of loft, five or six feet from the floor, running the length of the cabin. Household goods and provisions were placed on shelves above this improvised sleeping loft. Most of the cabins contained a lobby before the entry where the young people slept in summer and where wood was stored in winter. There were no chimneys or windows, but a hole was made in the middle of the roof for the smoke to escape. This had to be stopped up in bad weather, and the fire put out, if the occupants would not be blinded by smoke.

Smoke continually filled the upper part of the cabin, a condition which the Indian did not seem to mind. If one stood up, his head was in a thick cloud of smoke; the eyes watered and it was impossible to see more than two or three feet away. Sometimes it was necessary to lie flat on the earth and press the mouth close to the ground to get a free breath of air not filled with smoke.

The Indian forts were constructed in a manner far surpassing the way their villages were built. A fort was surrounded by two and sometimes three palisades, interwoven with branches of trees, leaving no spaces between.

In putting up the cabins in a village, each squaw knew exactly the place intended for her cabin and there was never any argument about location.

The men's wearing apparel for cold weather consisted of smoke-dried deer skin for the feet, hose of skin or ''stuff'' wrapped around the feet, waistcoat of skin, robe of bear-skin, and several skins of beaver or otter, hairy side in. Men were so fond of shirts, they wore them, Charlevoix said, until they dropped off from rottenness, as they never troubled to wash them.

Women wore bodices that reached below the knee, as did also their skirts of skin. When traveling, they wore little bonnets or leather caps, sewed to the bodices.

Some of the men painted their whole bodies, as they said it was protection against the cold, wet and gnats. The women seldom painted themselves.[9] Some of the young and vain men "spent half their time daubing themselves up, afterward going from door to door and returning well pleased with themselves, though not a word had been spoken."

The men, although they spent many hours in absolute idleness, made everything necessary for hunting, fishing and for war. The making of the canoes and snowshoes was their work, although the women sometimes assisted in this work.

The women were never idle. It was their work to put up the cabins, carry the burdens — and no burden was so great that the papoose could not be added — cultivate the fields, take care of the meat after the hunt, stretch the skins, and do the cooking.

The Indians treated one another with a gentleness and respect unknown to common people in the most polite nations. They never disputed another's word, and for this reason, the Missionaries often thought they had converts, as the Indian listened to their teaching in respectful silence; accordingly the priests were often times disappointed.

---

(9)   Beckwith differed from Charlevoix in this.

In some groups, the Indians did not use a person's name in addressing him, as that would seem too familiar, but would call him instead Brother, Cousin, or an appellation that told the relation in which he stood to the

CHIPPEWA SQUAWS
Painted by J. O. Lewis, 1826

speaker. Neither would an Indian speak his own name, if he were asked, but would turn to some one nearby and wait for him to give it. They had a superstition that speaking one's name was an ill omen; if a child spoke his name, it would stunt his growth. They gave the white man a name that told some dominant quality of him.

One could go into a cabin where there were ten or twelve persons and no sound would be heard.

In very early spring, as soon as the snow was melted, the women, with the assistance of boys too young to hunt, commenced to burn the old corn stalks from over the ground and stir the soil slightly with shells and crooked pieces of wood, with long handles. The babies were carried to the fields, strapped to the mothers' backs, and then deposited conveniently near. Each baby was bound in its cradle neatly and firmly from the waist down, but the upper part of the body, above the waist, was not held in any way, dangling and flopping around loosely in an alarming fashion, when the cradle was in an upright position; but, according to Charlevoix, this seemed to be beneficial rather than hurtful, to judge from the looks of the strong-limbed youngsters beyond the cradle age.

No mothers of any nation gave more care and attention to their babies than the Indian mothers, nor less care to children over three years of age. After attaining the age of three or thereabouts, the children were under no confinement and were absolutely free to go where they would, through woods or water or mire. In the summer, as soon as they arose in the morning, they went to the nearest stream or lake and played there most of the day, oftentimes being in water above the waist, which was the cause of much lung and stomach weakness. Their food was simple and wholesome; they ate to capacity, and then would rest, and eat, or rather stuff themselves, again.

The Indian mother had no fear of her young child getting lost, as Indian children have an almost perfect sense of direction; once having been to a place, a child was always able to find its way back. The Indian's sense of hearing and smell exceeded the white man's. They could smell fire at a great distance and could endure no smell but that of edibles. This was due to their training, and not to innate ability.

According to Charlevoix, the Indian children were seldom corrected. The Indian argued that before they reached the age of discretion they had no reasoning powers, and after that their actions were their own affairs and they were accountable to no person but themselves. Girls were known to strangle themselves after a slight reprimand from the mother, such as a few drops of water thrown in the face, so unusual was a reprimand.

Corn, squash, beans and melons were cultivated. Corn, squash, beans and berries were dried in the sun for winter use. Corn was roasted in the ear on coals. This corn was often sent to persons of distinction to show respect, very much as the keys of a city would be presented today. The corn was hung up to dry, or it would sometimes be threshed out and put away in bark baskets, in which holes were bored to keep it from heating. If the Indians had to leave home, the corn would be buried.

Boasting was the surest mark of a coward and anyone could put ashes on a boaster's head, an act which meant, "If you meet an enemy, you will turn as pale as ashes." Besides putting ashes or earth on the head, one could smear the boaster's face with black. Even the greatest chief was not exempt from this treatment and he, too, must "take all without murmuring."

In going on a hunt, everything needed for five or six months had to be carried on the back.[10]   The Indians traveled single file through thick underbrush and wild country, through which it seemed impossible even for beasts to make their way. They provided themselves with pieces of bark for shelter against rain and snow. Arriving at their destination, all set to work, the missionaries in the party as well as the Indians, to put up the cabins. These were round, consisting of poles tied together at the top and bark arranged thereon, poorly joined together, allowing the cold and snow to penetrate between the pieces. A cabin took less than half an hour to build.[11]   Branches of trees served as mattresses, around which the snow collected, making some protection against the wind.

Each Indian had several dogs for chase, which he took very little trouble to feed. They got what they could catch. As a consequence, the dogs were always hungry and constantly on the watch for a morsel of food, leaping backwards and forwards over a missionary sitting before the fire, if they suspected he had any food in his hand. They had very little hair and so had little protection against the cold. A man would awaken in the night nearly choked, to find two or three dogs lying on him seeking warmth.

Corn was ground in a mortar with a pestle by the women, and bread was made from it which was only a

---

(10)   Charlevoix saw no horses used by the Indians until he reached the southern country around Mississippi far below the Missouri river.   Their first horses were secured from the French and the Spaniards.

(11)   Galinee (missionary) tells of the Algonquins (17th century) carrying on journeys pieces of birchbark split thin and sewed together 6 feet (four fathoms) by 3 feet.   They arranged three of these pieces of bark on twenty or thirty poles lengthwise, touching each other at top, under which eight or nine men could be sheltered comfortably.

mass of ill-kneaded paste, without leaven, and baked under the ashes. It had to be eaten hot, as it would not keep after it grew cold. Sometimes beans, fruits, oil or fat were mixed with it. One had to have a good stomach to digest it. Fat was one of the main ingredients in their dishes.

Women made thread from the interior pellicles of the bark of a tree called white wood, and dyed it. It was manufactured much as hemp is. They made articles of bark and small figures with "hair" of porcupine; they made cups and utensils of wood, and embroidered deer skins and knitted belts and garters from the wool of the buffalo.

Hatchets were made of flint and granite, and were unbreakable. Tomahawks or hatchets differed from axes in having no grooves. The axes were sometimes, though rarely, grooved in two directions — around the top and around the end from the groove on one side to the groove on the other. The method most common of hafting axes was to twist a withe of tough wood around the body of the ax and secure it with rawhide or sinew. Sometimes the tomahawk or hatchet would be hafted by being inserted in the young branch of a tree, split for the purpose, and left there until the wood had grown firmly around it, when the handle would be cut the required length. The only one of this kind in existence, it is claimed, was found at Elizabethtown, Hardin County, Illinois, and is on exhibition at the Missouri Jeffersonian Memorial Museum, at St. Louis.

Some hatchets and axes have a fine cutting edge at each end. Those requiring a fine cutting edge were made of flint. The others were made of granite.

Grooved axes are usually found above ground, seldom in mounds, and were found more abundantly in the central states, diminishing in numbers toward the east. Tomahawks are frequently found in mounds and are found in every part of the country.

CHAPTER III

THE LAST INDIANS OCCUPYING THIS TERRITORY

LESS than a century ago, where now are comfortable homes and compactly built apartment houses, paved streets, well-cared-for parkways and inviting lawns, great trees proudly reared their heads over impassable shrubbery, and shaded well-worn paths — trails over which the Red Man trod for many years.

Of the various tribes of latter day Indians that occupied this region at different times, the Illinois, who were the first of which we have any record, the Miami, and the Potawatomi were the tribes that lived on this site the greatest lengths of time.

It was the Potawatomi Indians that Marquette and Joliet found on the west side of Lake Michigan in 1673. These Indians lived here nearly two hundred years. This tribe had many camps and villages scattered over the territory, which later became the site of Evanston and the adjoining city and villages. The Potawatomi Indian village located at Bowmanville was called "Chicago's greatest Indian Village." This village extended from the site of Rose Hill Cemetery west to the North Branch of the Chicago River and north as far as High Ridge (Kenmore). Judging from the utensils, pottery and copper — over 10,000 articles in number — found on these grounds, this village dated back to the Mound Builders, or earlier.

There were also Indian villages at Niles Center, Forest Glen, the site of Evanston Hospital grounds, and the present site of Glen View Golf grounds. The village on Ridge Trail at Rogers Park was probably a continuation of the Bowmanville village.

Between Clark Street and the lake were two small villages, one of these being within the present limits of Evanston.

At the southwest corner of Davis Street and Wesley Avenue, in 1835, stood a log hut with a straw roof, which was said to have been built by the Indians and occupied by them.

About 1840, James Carney, one of Grosse Pointe's pioneers, visited a village at the foot of Dempster Street. Here lived a roving band of Potawatomi fishermen.

A village consisting of fifteen or twenty wigwams was situated two or three blocks north of the Evanston lighthouse site, fronting the lake shore, on what was later Charles Deering's property. This village was evidently a permanent abode, as the land showed that corn had been cultivated on it. A young son of the Carneys one time visited the village. Five or six Indians followed him home, whereupon he hid in the haystack back of the house, not coming out until the Indians had left. What was his consternation to learn that his mother had given them his much-loved black puppy, to which they had taken a fancy! He told, in after years, of the wigwams built of mats and rushes, and remembered well the Indians, the squaws, the children and the dogs at this village.

An Indian village site was discovered in 1852 by Dr. Henry M. Bannister while he was hunting. This

was just south of Greenleaf Street and east of the present
Sheridan Road; it was also east of an Indian workshop or chipping station. Fire places, utensils and pottery gave mute evidence of former Indian occupation.

Benjamin F. Hill remembered roaming bands of
Potawatomi Indians camping near his father's house and
calling to do their trading. The Hill family occupied
the Mulford house in 1836, on the Ridge, west of Calvary
Cemetery, before the Mulfords occupied it. The site of
Evanston was a hunting ground for the Indians, as deer
were plentiful.

Benjamin F. Hill spoke before the Evanston Historical Society in May, 1902, in regard to his early life
in Evanston and about the Indians. He had lived among
them and understood them well. He said that Shabbona,
one of the chiefs of the Potawatomi, was one of the finest
specimens of American Indian. Shabbona was an Ottawa
Indian, born near the Maumee River in Ohio, in 1775.
After the battle of the Thames, in 1827, where he was
by the side of the great warrior, Tecumseh, when the
latter was killed, Shabbona gave his allegiance to the
United States.

When in 1832 Blackhawk tried to engage every
tribe of Indians against the whites, saying, "Let all our
tribes unite and we shall have an army of warriors equal
in number to the trees of the forest," Shabbona, who
knew the military strength of the white man, replied,
"Your army would equal in number the trees in the
forest, but you would encounter an army of palefaces as
numerous as the *leaves on the trees.*"

At the time Blackhawk and his band were ravaging
the whole northern part of Illinois, Shabbona was the

BLACKHAWK

SHABBONA

Paul Revere of the west, riding his pony a hundred miles or more in twenty-four hours to warn the settlers of their danger, and was a true friend to the white man during the stormy days of the Blackhawk War. He had principle. He was a Christian in his own way; a man of few words, sensible, kind-hearted, always doing a kindness for some one, taking a quarter of venison to a needy person, or doing good in some other way. Shabbona Grove, sixty-five miles west of Chicago, was named after this chief. Here he lived in a wigwam made of blankets woven together, tied and wrapped, making a warm, snug lodge. He had two sons, Shabbona and Smoke.

Shabbona, after returning from California where he had gone on horseback, told to Hill the traits of each tribe of Indians he had met along the way. Hill, going to California later, found that Shabbona had described them accurately. So much could be told of Shabbona, whose "skin was tawny, but his soul was white," to quote J. Seymour Currey. He had always been a friend of the white people. When the Indian tribes moved west, he was urged to go, but he did not wish to leave his white friends. At last he consented to leave. Growing homesick, he returned, only to find his land had been sold. He was told he had forfeited his land by his absence. This discouraged him and he took to intoxicating drinks (he was a teetotaler up to that time), and his mind became affected.

The early settlers were oftentimes annoyed at the manner in which the Indians entered their homes and seated themselves without invitation. This, it seems, was the proper way, according to Indian custom. Mr. Hill said that an Indian would slip into a white man's

house, seat himself as far as possible from any member
of the family and keep his eyes downcast, until some
one in the white man's family would go to him and offer
him food or ask his errand. The Indian wished the white
man to do the same, when the latter went to the Indian's
wigwam. If a white man walked into a wigwam and
looked the host straight in the eyes, the Indian was
offended and felt that the white man was taking advantage of him; but, if he went in and kept his eyes downcast, in a few minutes the Indian would have looked him
over and would be able to describe the white man's dress
exactly, even to the number of buttons on his coat. He
would then approach him and confer any favor that the
white man would ask, even to the dividing of his last
morsel with him, and the white man was welcome to
remain in the wigwam as long as he wished.

At Lake Avenue and Sheridan Road (later the site
of the Westerfield place) in Wilmette, there was a Potawatomi village. The wigwams were made of poles and
mats of rushes. This was evidently a winter home, as
the Indians came late in the fall and left in the spring.
Besides the Indians, French families and half-breeds
occupied this village. Occasionally the Ouilmettes and
Beaubiens lived there. A maple tree sugar tapping gouge
or chisel was found on the Ouilmette Reservation by
Mr. Hill and presented to the Evanston Historical
Society. This implement had evidently been the property of Ouilmette.

Chipping stations or workshops were situated for
miles along the lake shore. There were four of these
south of Indian Boundary Line, in Edgewater and
Rogers Park, and one immediately south of this line.

North of these was one of the largest workshops. This was on land between the present Main and Greenleaf Streets in Evanston, west of an Indian village, which was located east of the present Sheridan Road. Here on the site of this workshop, rejects and arrow-heads were found as late as 1870.

Another chipping station or workshop was located at the present site of Dearborn Observatory, and there were others further north. The implements and weapons manufactured were of great variety, from the most ordinary arrow-head to the finest of polished hatchets and axes. The rejects along the shore proved where the manufacturing was done, and the finished product found further west proved where they were used.

According to Frank Grover, as recently as 1870, there were small bands of Indians, families, and sometimes single Indians traveling through Evanston, occasionally camping over night or stopping a few days. He remembered several bands at various times camped under the oaks at the northeast corner of Sherman Avenue and Lake Street. They were peaceable and went about their business in an orderly way.

The Indians bent trees as markers along a trail; a trail marked in this way was as easy to follow as the white man's figures of today along the highways. The trees were bent while saplings in the direction of the trail to be followed. There is a theory that the Indians had a system of marking their trails by using only one kind of trees on each trail. Over the site of Evanston only oak trees were markers; further north near Wilmette white elms were used; and still further north there were found several years ago eleven markers of white

POTAWATOMI TRAIL TREE THAT GREW
WEST OF THE SITE OF CALVARY
CEMETERY

POTAWATOMI TREE

BASE OF POTAWATOMI TREE

oak trees, in perfect alignment, leading from the site of an old Indian village at Highland Park in a northwesterly direction several miles.

An Indian marker stood in the yard of Dr. Miner Raymond, Davis Street and Hinman Avenue. Another grew west of Calvary Station.[1] This was a red oak tree, whose great trunk lay close to the ground for fifteen feet, with three good sized trees rising straight from it. The head had taken root, thus providing the tree with two sources of sustenance.

The famous Potawatomi Tree, while not an Evanston product, is of sufficient interest to North Shore residents to be mentioned here. Until 1903 this giant cottonwood tree stood on the farm of M. A. Koelpfer, on the Glenview Road, two miles west of Wilmette. This tree was said to be the largest, not only in Illinois, but in the whole Mississippi Valley; it was 165 feet high, 45 feet in circumference at a point three feet from the ground, and had a diameter at the base of 18 feet, its trunk running up 75 feet before putting out a branch.

From the time of the earliest white man in this region, the trunk has been hollow at its base, with an entrance five feet wide by nine feet high, leading into a chamber over twenty feet high, with a smooth floor nearly twenty feet in diameter, on which have stood thirty-one persons at one time. It was estimated by English foresters that this tree was over six hundred years old at the time it was taken down in 1903. It gained the name Blackhawk Tree at the time of the Blackhawk War, when Blackhawk

---

(1)   Fort Dearborn Chapter, Daughters of the American Revolution, had this tree moved in 1926 from its original site to Bell Park, at Davis Street and Forest Place.

and two hundred of his warriors danced around it. It is also said that Indian councils have been held and treaties ratified within its cavity.

In 1832, a forest fire destroyed all the trees in the section where this tree stood, but this tree remained unharmed, giving rise to a superstition among the Indians that it was under the protection of the Great Spirit. This belief was current to the last of its existence, being passed along to the farmers and particularly to the youth of the region, who believed that the tree held a potent spell over their love affairs.

A thirty foot section of the trunk has been moved to and preserved at 1405 Central Street, Evanston, where the public may view it at any time.

Indian graves have been found in many places over the site of Evanston, a condition which authorities say indicates that the Indian population was widely scattered. A mound was discovered and excavated, about 1860, by Evanston pioneers, Joel Stebbins, Paul Pratt and James Colvin, at the intersection of the St. Paul viaduct and Ridge Avenue, disclosing war instruments and skeletons. Two graves were found in 1866, when excavating was going on for the foundation of Heck Hall; one was also found on the property of Dr. Robert D. Sheppard, one about a block north of Charles Deering's property on the shore of the lake, and one during the excavation for the foundation of the Rood building on Davis Street in the nineties. More recently, an Indian skeleton was found buried on Charles Dawes' ground in front of the house.

There was an Indian cemetery four or five blocks northwest of Evanston lighthouse, extending from Evanston hospital to the lake, and along the eastern edge of Evanston golf grounds. The last "burial" in this cemetery was evidently that of a warrior, as the body was placed in a sitting posture above ground. According to Charlevoix, "Burying in a sitting posture is an honor due alone to warriors." The coffin or resting place was like a little pen, six feet long by four feet wide, and was made of poles or saplings laid up like a log house and bound together at the corners with withes of bark. The top was also fastened in a like manner. The skeleton, sitting upright above ground, was facing the east. With him were his dog, gun, pipe, tobacco, and tomahawk. The tomahawk, which has a steel head and wood handle, and probably was of French manufacture, may be seen at the Evanston Historical department, as it was presented to the Historical Society by B. F. Hill, who with his two older brothers saw this grave, and twelve or fifteen years later procured the instrument. These small boys, after viewing the grinning skeleton through the spaces between the poles, fled terror-stricken to their home. The exact site of this last "burial place" was less than fifty feet from the ninth hole or green of the former Evanston Golf Club's course.

The Indians met annually at Gross Point burial ground, the point at the head of the Ridge, to mourn their dead. An Indian cemetery, located north of the Institute, was washed away in 1862.

James H. Hammill, Indianologist of Oak Park, discovered on the Evanston Hospital grounds in 1921, a number of Indian relics that had been ploughed up. Further investigation disclosed the fact that this was the site of an ancient Indian village,[2] as well as a burying ground.

A gravel pit excavated on the Budlong farm in Bowmanville in 1904 disclosed to view a grave containing fourteen skeletons buried in a circle, with their feet toward the center. The bodies were apparently well preserved until exposed to the air, when they crumbled, leaving only the skeletons. This was probably a Potawatomi Indian grave.

Charlevoix says the Indians buried their dead with the head toward the east, that they might look toward the Happy Hunting Ground in the west. This is the reverse of the way B. F. Hill found the Indian buried, above referred to. Charlevoix also tells how surprised the Indians were at the French not burying articles that belonged to the dead, with the dead. They did not consider the white man's way honest, and thought the living had no right to the dead man's possessions.

By 1835, most of the Indians had gone from this site, in accordance with the Treaty of Chicago in 1833. The Indian is not given to showing his emotion, but on the day when the Red Men and their families took their departure, herded by government agents, each one plainly evinced his feelings in regard to leaving his home. The pity of it touched even the most hardened heart, and that leave-taking was one not soon to be forgotten.

---

(2)   Fort Dearborn Chapter, Daughters of the American Revolution, in 1923, placed a bowlder on the Evanston Hospital grounds, with a bronze tablet.

CHAPTER IV

HABITS AND CHARACTERISTICS OF
THE INDIAN

UP to the coming of the white man, this country belonged to the Indian in all its great expanse, from north to south, from east to west. Land was owned, not individually, but in great tracts by clans, or tribes, or great families. Things done were done for the betterment of the whole tribe and not for the betterment of an individual.

It will always be a mooted question, in the minds of some people, whether the Indian is better off since the advent of the white man. The white man came and found the Indian occupying all of this country, its fertile valleys and hills, using the great waterways as his only means of travel — other than on foot; found him friendly and eager to help the white man make a home in his own home land, the land of his forefathers. The pilgrims were kept from starving during their first awful winter, through the kindness of the Indians. According to custom, the Indians burned their prisoners at the stake, but should we judge them, whom we call savages, when our own history tells us of the treatment accorded the so-called witches by civilized men? Let us be fair and judge the red man by the standards to which he has measured, according to the early writers, who lived with the Indian and held communication with him, day after day and month after month.

Charlevoix says of the Indians around Lake Michigan, "Most of them have a nobleness of soul and a constancy of mind, at which we rarely arrive, with all the assistance of philosophy and religion."

We know that the white man took advantage of the Indian's ignorance. We cannot forget that the Indians entered into many treaties under some form of compulsion, but today the United States government is doing all it can for the Indians on the Reservations, and so we like to think that the Indian *is* better off since the advent of the white man. The Indian of today is far advanced in civilization (according to our ideas of civilization), and far removed from the Indian of America's early days, who was superstitious (but so in his way was the white man), brutal, and, at time, cannibalistic, when he thought such a feast would increase his courage. The Indians were taught from their earliest infancy to ignore pain, both in themselves and others. According to Theodore Roosevelt, the Indians east of the Mississippi river were not as brutal as those living west of it.

Had the white man not put in appearance, instead of "the survival of the fittest," it would probably have been "the survival of the most savage" of the Indian tribes, as they were continually making war on each other. Statistics show, by actual count, that the number of Indians in one tribe dropped from 2,300 to 800 in one state in less than 50 years, and during that time none had emigrated. War and disease had caused this reduction in their number.[1]

---

[1] Franklin K. Lane, in the *National Geographic*, for January, 1915, gives the Indian population in United States, in 1860, 254,300; in 1910, 304,950, including mixed blood.

The Iroquois Indians, though numbering 2,500 warriors, made war on all their neighbors, destroying more than thirty nations and causing the death of more than 600,000 persons within eighty years, according to Mason, thus "rendering the country about the Great Lakes a desert."

Parkman tells us that the Miami and the Illinois suffered so much by repeated attacks of the Five Nations (Iroquois) and by other wars, that the population ascribed to them by the early French writers dwindled during the first quarter of the eighteenth century to a few small villages. Parrish puts the remaining number at six hundred fighting men, whereas fifty-seven years previous, they had covered two-thirds of the state of Illinois.

Today the number of deaths from disease is less to the hundred, as the white man has taught and is teaching sanitation among them, thus mitigating the ravage of disease caused by insanitary surroundings. The Indian does not take kindly to indoor sleeping rooms, and it is found that the members of the older generation still use the tepees for sleeping quarters.

Although the "last hatchet was buried" several years ago, a tribe will still travel many miles to seal its friendship with another tribe, holding feasts for several days and exchanging presents.[2]

We usually picture the Indians as of one type — tall and straight, with copper colored skin, high cheek bones, straight, coarse black hair — but there is great variation in physical types. The Fox Indians are tall and well built; the Ottawa are short and squatty. The Indians

---

[2]   The Winnebago and Chippewa held such a ceremony for four days in September, 1921, on the Flambeau reservation in Wisconsin, with a great exchange of presents to prove their friendship.

of some tribes have long, narrow heads; in other tribes heads are short and wide. There are some who have eyes similar to the eyes of the Chinese, narrow and slanting. As to the color of the skin, the shades run from nearly white to copper color, brown, or nearly black.

Nearly all tribes of Indians bear names that signify "men." Marquette says of the Illinois, "When one speaks the word, 'Illinois,' it is as if one said in their language, 'The men,' as if the other savages were looked upon merely as animals."

The Indians all had some kind of religion, but their religion almost defies description. Dr. William Jones says the Sauk and Foxes and the Kickapoo have similar religious rites and ceremonies. The basic principle of the Algonquian religion is pure, naïve worship of nature.

The Sauk and Foxes and the Kickapoo — and perhaps other Algonquian tribes — believed a manitou could exist in either an animate or an inanimate object and that this manitou could be freed and be made to enter a person's body by the person's own desire, expressed in various ways. The word, manitou, in the Algonquian language, would probably correspond very nearly to the word spirit, as the missionaries used the term. Manitou, according to Dr. Jones, is a religious word, and carries with it an idea of solemnity, and kindles an emotional sense of mystery.

The Potawatomi, according to Schoolcraft, believed there were two spirits, the Great Spirit, good and beneficent, and the Evil Spirit, which was wicked. The *Handbook of American Indians* says that this was the result of Christian teaching, and that formerly the Potawatomi worshiped the sun to some extent; at least, they offered sacrifices in honor of the sun, in order that the sick might recover or that some desire might be obtained. According to Dr. William Duncan Strong in his leaflet, *The Indian Tribes of the Chicago Region,* the Potawatomi believed that the human body had but one soul or spirit, which eventually followed the trail over the Milky Way into the western heavens to a land ruled over by the brother of the great culture hero, Wisaka. He says of the Potawatomi religion, that it is hard to reduce to a formula. This is true, also, of the religions of other tribes.

In the Potawatomi tribe, each clan had a sacred bundle, containing various objects supposed to be sacred. The possession of such bundles gave power and success to the clans in their activities. Many of the bundles were supposedly given the clans by the great culture hero, but others were acquired or made as the result of dreams or visions of the people who originated the clan. Each bundle had a special legend attached to it, accounting for its origin.

Parkman was of the opinion that the Indians believed in a Great Spirit only after the advent of the white man. Nicolas Perrot, a ranger in the woods, who spent over thirty-five years with the Indians from 1665 to 1701, says in his memoirs, "Michabous is one form of the name of the Great Spirit, which all Indian tribesmen invoke as their highest deity." Allouez, missionary, writes that the Illinois, Foxes and other tribes toward the south hold "that there is a great and excellent genius, master of all the rest, who made heaven and earth and who dwells, they say, in the east toward the country of the French,"—a belief probably the result of Christian teaching. He says

SIOUX WOMAN

SIOUX MEDICINE MAN

Painting by G. Catlin

the Ottawa and other tribes recognized no sovereign master of heaven and earth, but believed there were many spirits, some good — sun, moon, lakes, rivers and woods; others bad — dragons, cold, and storms. They believed that spirits were all about them, in the trees, in the wind, in the rain, etc., and that the souls of the departed govern the fishes in the lake. Therefore, they never burned fish bones, as that would displease the souls and the fish would not come into their nets. They believed that if a man were ill, a bad spirit had taken away his soul and had entered his body; that a common cause of sickness was the failure to give a feast after successful hunting or fishing, and that small spirits entered the part of the body that was sick. In order to exterminate these spirits, the medicine man, who was also a juggler, would apply his lips to the part of the body that was sick, pretending he was extracting the spirits, then he would triumphantly exhibit small stones, which he claimed to have drawn from the sick man's flesh, but which had been hidden all the while in his mouth. Sometimes the patient was compelled to walk over live embers and he would fall unconscious.

The medicine men had some knowledge of healing, but they added to their treatment of vapor baths and decoctions of herbs and roots horrible incantations and howlings to scare the evil spirit away.

Frederick Starr says, "Some misfortunes were attributed to witchcraft and an Indian would travel hundreds of miles to shoot down the person suspected of being a wizard, and could return without being harmed."

According to Parkman, the Iroquois thought the God of Thunder had his home among the caverns beneath the cataract of Niagara. The Algonquins believed that thunder was a bird, "who built his nest on a pinnacle of towering mountains. Two daring boys once scaled the height and thrust sticks into the eyes of the portentous nestlings, whereupon flashed such wrathful scintillations that the sticks were shivered to atoms."

That the Indians did believe in an after life and thought that inanimate objects had souls, is evidenced by their placing a man's gun, tomahawk, bow and arrow on his grave, or burying them with him. They knew these things stayed where placed, but thought that their souls accompanied the man's soul to the Happy Hunting Ground. Sometimes the things placed on an Indian's grave would be first broken. Whether this was to help their souls to escape or whether they feared the dishonesty of some one passing, it is not known.

Petitions and sacrifices were made to the Great Spirit with a view of receiving benefits during this life and with no thought of benefit to the soul after death. Sacrifices of animals and torturings of the flesh are things of the past, even though the Indian is today permitted freedom of thought in his religion.

Torture of prisoners was due to one of the many Indian superstitions. It was considered an ill omen if a captor failed to make his captive cry out in pain.

In some tribes, if an Indian desired a certain thing to come to pass, he would fast for many days, keeping his thoughts all the time on whatever he wished, whether it was a successful hunt for moose, or the routing of a fierce band of Iroquois. At last he would be rewarded with a dream, depicting the very thing he desired — a natural result where the mind held but one idea for days and the body was exhausted from hunger. Afterward the members of the tribe, considering the dream a message to this favored son, immediately laid their plans for hunting or war, or whatever the dream portrayed. Visions do not come to everyone that fasts.

Potawatomi boys at about the age of ten were urged by their parents to fast all day and seek a vision which would enable them to select a guardian spirit that would bring them success through life. Boys sixteen or more were required to fast from four to eight days. After a boy had had a vision he was considered a man, according to Strong.

The Potawatomi of the Woods retained the ancient customs of the Algonquian Indians, while the Potawatomi of the Prairie were influenced by the Miami, Illinois, Sauk and Foxes, in consequence of which many of their customs were changed.

William Jones, an educated full blooded Sauk, says in one of his articles that there was a tendency among the Potawatomi to elide vowels and syllables, due to the rapidity with which the dialect is spoken, as compared with the speech of the Ottawa and the Chippewa.

The Indian character is, in itself, so contradictory that it is difficult to describe it. The red man has many good traits, and many that are—according to our ideas —not good; traits similar to those belonging to a spoiled child. Colonel Johnson (U. S. Commissioner), says that the Indian was absolutely honest in his dealings in money matters and if one were found who had been dishonest, he was dealt with severely by the chiefs. He was a staunch and faithful friend, but a bitter and cruel enemy. He was a hero worshiper, and had great respect for the heroes and sages of his tribe. It was due to this reverence that members of a tribe lived so harmoniously together, as the word of the elders was always heeded, and quarreling and wrangling in a tribe were unknown.

A parent seldom struck a child and a child seldom cried. An Indian would stalk an enemy rather than face him and give an open blow. For glory he would face the worst torture, enduring cold and hunger, and even brave death itself for it.

An Indian is trained to conceal, rather than subdue his emotions, always repressing any exhibition of tender feelings, scorning them as beneath him; whereas the women in grief, not only give way to their feelings, but join together in dismal howlings and lamentations that, Parkman says, "would put to shame an Irish death-howl." However, if a man has a toothache, it is a very different matter, although toothache in the early Indian days was rather an uncommon thing. "The toothache," says Roger Williams, in his observation on the customs of the New England tribes, "is the only paine which will force their stoute hearts to cry," and states that the Indian women never cry as he has heard "some of their men in this paine."

Referring to the well preserved teeth of the Indians, it may be said that several hundred skulls were examined in the National Museum in Washington and only one decayed tooth was found. This perfect condition of the teeth was due to the primitive diet, as the food of the early Indian contained plenty of lime and phosphates for both body use and the necessary upkeep of the teeth. Within the last few years, five skulls were washed up on the shore of the Menominee River in Wisconsin and every tooth in these skulls was found to be in absolutely perfect condition.

A game the Indian children used to play to learn to bear pain stoically, was to hold live embers between the body and the arm, the winner being the one who held the embers the longest. The children were interested in public affairs from their earliest infancy.

Traditions were passed down from one generation to another by a limited number of young men with excellent memories appointed by the sage to memorize the traditions.

Benjamin Hill says in his recollections: "The Indian will get the pipe and light it and take a puff, and touch the ground with the end that he has put in his mouth and pass the pipe over to you. You take the pipe, take a puff or two, touch it to the ground and pass it back again. You have made a friend of him."

The Indian mother left her papoose in its cradle-board outside the door. One could pat its head or even squeeze it, but it would not cry. Mr. Hill said he had never heard an Indian baby cry.

Dancing and singing formed a very important part in the life of the Indian, and was usually a religious ceremony to benefit the whole tribe. There was a dance for almost every occasion—before a war, and in celebration after; before a hunt, or in the midst of it, if the hunt was proving unsuccessful; when the Indians treated their sick; and when they made treaties. In the war dance, the men painted their faces and bodies as if for war, and had everything around them pertaining to war. The scalp dance was a victory dance, in celebration of a successful battle; the buffalo dance was to compel herds of

CHIPPEWA INDIANS DOING PIPE DANCE AND TOMAHAWK DANCE
Painted by J. O. Lewis at Treaty of Prairie du Chien, 1825

buffalo to appear, when a hunt had been unsuccessful, at which time the dancers were dressed in buffalo skins and wore the horns of buffalo on their heads.

In all these dances, those who took part either used rattles made of dried balls of skin tied on wooden handles, or small gourds with rattlers in them, or they drew bones across notched sticks. Drums and tambourines were used entirely for the beating of time, and the beaters did not take part in the dancing, but sat at one side.

The songs did not have a great range of tone, but the rhythm was perfect.

The dancer had to be cleansed or purified before taking part in one of these ceremonials, if the desired result was to be obtained. The cleansing was done in various ways:—taking a sweat bath, afterward rubbing the body with sweet smelling plants; sitting in smoke from the burning of a sacred herb or wood; or fasting for several days. The dancer was not to touch anything he had used before, nor must he come in contact with another person. Objects to be used during the ceremony were purified by holding them in sacred smoke.

There is a general impression that the Indian woman was a very much imposed upon person, but probably the work was divided in a manner the Indian thought was fair. Although the women were expected to cultivate the soil, carry the burdens, put up the tents for lodges — all of which we consider the man's share of the work — the man had to provide food for the family and be free to kill game the moment any should appear. Moreover, as hostile Indians were always lurking around, the man must be free to protect his family in case of an attack.

Hunting and fishing with him were not pastimes, but a real business to obtain food. The strenuous hours of dancing must have been more tiresome for the man than the same number of hours of toil in the field was for the woman.

The woman was, in some tribes, the real head of the house, and frequently decided momentous questions, such as of peace or war. If the man failed to do his part in providing for the family, the woman could drive him away.

The Indians are great story tellers, and a story is a valuable personal possession. If one sold a story, he must never tell that story again, as it belongs to another. Certain stories must be told only at certain times. Some "old stories" must be told only in the winter, for in the summer, when the leaves are on the trees, the spirits in them would hear, but in the winter with the snow on the ground and the leaves gone from the trees and the trees themselves appearing to be dead, it is safe to tell these stories by the campfire. A myth may be told by the Sauk and Foxes, and the Kickapoo only in winter. To tell a myth out of season is to take chances with something beyond human power. These stories may be of their own brave deeds, the brave deeds of their tribe, of some great hero of the tribe, or of how the earth was created. If a man told a story that seemed improbable, some one handed the medicine man a pipe, who painted the stem red and prayed over it; he then handed it to the man whose story he doubted, bidding him smoke, but to remember, if he did smoke, the story must be "as sure as there is a hole through the stem. So your life shall be long . . . . but if you have spoken falsely, your days are counted."

If the man refused to smoke, all knew that his story was not true. With such a custom, it is probable there were few boasters among the red men.

An Indian never walked around while smoking. He pursued his smoking in silence, as smoking was considered a communion with the Great Spirit. The pipes never left the Indians' mouths, while in council, for "good thoughts come while smoking."

'Picture-writing'' was a custom of the Indians, and a piece of birchbark, with a few pictures hastily scratched

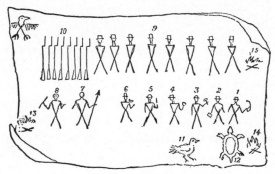

INDIAN LETTER
(Schoolcraft)

on it would take two or three times its space to tell in words all that it conveyed. Even the pole, to which the birchbark was attached, was placed in the ground in a way that had a meaning—the direction of the journey. The number of days that would be required to make the journey was told by the notches on the pole. The Indians in the pictures were represented without hats, while the soldiers and officers wore hats; the soldiers had guns, and the duty of each officer was shown by that which he carried in his hand — sword, book or hammer. Even their food was shown — turtle, prairie hen, or whatever it was, as well as who partook of it. The missionaries tell us that they, too, made their marks in the woods to let the Indian know they had passed.

Wampum was used as a medium of exchange and was originally made from sea shells. After the coming of the white man, porcelain beads were used. A wampum belt sometimes contained five thousand beads.

In the making of the shell wampum, a piece of shell would be ground down to the thickness of a straw, then held stationary in the left hand against a drill rolled over the thigh by the right hand. The drill consisted of a sharp pointed stone stuck in the end of a reed.

The wampums were made with different colors predominating. "The purple," one writer tells us, "was to the Indians as gold is to us, and white as our silver is to us." The prevailing color of the wampum belt sent to summon tribes to war was red and black. The prevailing color, in time of peace, was white.

Perhaps the largest wampum belt ever made was the one Pontiac had his squaws make. It was six feet long and four inches wide, and symbols were woven in it from end to end of the various tribes and villages under his alliance, which numbered forty-seven.

King Philip, the famous chief, had a coat made entirely of "wampampeog" and when he needed money, he would cut a piece from his coat.

Sometimes tobacco was used instead of the wampum belt. Tobacco was considered an emblem of deliberation.

6

There was one person selected as "keeper of the belts" and he was supposed to know what each figure and symbol represented and to give out this information from time to time.

The greatest painter of Indian portraits was George Catlin, born in Philadelphia in 1796, and educated for the practice of law. He traveled all through the Indian country, spending many years making paintings of the red men, the buffalo, the various Indian games, and of the country. He found it no easy task to get the Indians to pose for their pictures, as they held some superstition in regard to having a likeness made. Even today, on the reservations, some hold that death awaits them if their pictures are made.

One fine looking chief desired Catlin to paint his portrait, which Catlin was glad to do. Another chief of the same tribe, a sour tempered man, sneeringly said that Little Bear, the other chief, was but half a man, as his picture (profile) proved it. This led to trouble; the first chief was shot, and Catlin lost no time in getting out of their country.

Many of Catlin's pictures and the Indian things he collected are in the National Museum at Washington.[3]

A murderer was not punished for his crime, because he may have been intoxicated at the time, or he may have struck in self defense. In either case, it was considered his own affair. Often a murderer would be adopted into a family in the place of the man he had killed. He would then assume the dead man's responsibilities and enter into all his rights.

---

(3)   The pipestone found in the quarries in Minnesota has been given the name of catlinite, because George Catlin was the first white man to visit the quarries.

Theft, however, was looked upon as a disgrace, and the thief as a dishonor to the family. That stain was sometimes wiped out by his blood.

The Indians were great gamblers. Platter, or bones, one of the most popular games among the Potawatomi, was sometimes played for several days at a time, the Indians staking everything they wore and all the movables in the cabins and sometimes even their personal liberty, which is the dearest thing on earth to the Indian. In the game La Crosse, a favorite of the Illinois Indians, the female relatives would sometimes be gambled away in the excitement.

Many diseases were unknown until the coming of the white man, such as small pox, measles, gout and apoplexy.

Each Indian had one particular and very much loved friend, whom he hoped to meet and never to part from in the next world.

After liquor had been introduced, the fields at times echoed with the most hideous howlings, which Charlevoix describes as sounding like the howlings of a gang of devils let loose from hell.

Sweating or vapor baths were a grand remedy for every ill. After the sweating the person jumped into cold water, or had cold water thrown over him. This bath would be prepared for visitors as a mark of respect, and the host kept the guest company in the bath. After the vapor bath, the feet would be rubbed with oil. This treatment was for the purpose of calming the mind and refreshing the body.

The vapor bath was used also in a kind of ceremonial rite among the Algonquian Indians.

A Fox Indian would slash the skin on his arms and legs, before entering the bath, believing that the manitou held within the stone would escape with the steam and enter his body through the slashed skin. He claimed to experience great benefit immediately upon the entrance of the manitou into his body. The steam was made by a stone being heated and dropped into the water.

If a man knew he was about to die, he would prepare his own funeral oration, and give orders for his funeral feast. All his dogs were caught, and their throats cut. Then they were thrown into a kettle of boiling water. Possibly this practice was discontinued after the coming of the white man, as sometimes the dog was buried with his master.

An Indian can imitate perfectly the call of a bird or the cry of an animal, and the white men were often lured to their death in this way.

Trees were felled by applying fire near the roots and cutting away the charcoal with flint or heavy shells, as the fire burnt into the wood. A plaster covering of mud was used to prevent the fire from extending higher than it was needed. This method was also used to cut logs into the desired lengths for canoes.

Arrow heads were two inches or less in length, and could be chipped out in one or two minutes. A well formed ax, grooved and polished, was made in sixty-six hours of actual working time recently at the National Museum from a block of nephrite, the hardest and toughest rock known, and the tools used were jasper hammers for shaping, and quartzites for smoothing. From another rock a little softer than granite a grooved ax was completed in two hours. An Indian has been known to make a symmetrical arrow head or flint knife in from five to ten minutes, and a rougher one in a minute or two. Perforators were made of flint and were used as awls to make holes when sewing skins.

An Indian, by examining a footprint, was able to tell to what tribe the one who made it belonged. Radisson,

CHIPPEWA SQUAWS GATHERING RICE
(Schoolcraft)

one of the early priests traveling in the Northwest territory wrote, in 1568, in his quaint style, "All knows one another by their march, for each hath his proper steps, some upon their toes, some on their heels, which is natural to them, for when they are infants, the mother warpeth them to their mode."

It is claimed that the Chippewa, the largest tribe of the Algonquins, made the finest canoes in all the world. Their canoes would, with care, last five or six years, while those of the Iroquois were so poorly built that they lasted only about a month. The Chippewa stripped the bark from the birch trees for their canoes in August, when the sap was going down. The bark for the bottom had to be the full length of the canoe, twenty feet, but the sides could be pieced. The canoes were two feet in width. They were strengthened inside with very thin cedar floors and gunwales, so that one man could carry a canoe with ease. One of these canoes could carry four men and eight or nine hundredweight of baggage. Gallinee said that one was not even a finger's breadth from death in a canoe of the Chippewa, only the thickness of four or five sheets of paper.

The Indian's snow shoes, or rackets, as the missionaries called them, were a source of interest to the early Frenchmen, and were very much admired by them.

Fire was made by twirling one long pointed stick between the hands, with its sharp end in the hollow of another piece of wood. Pieces of burning birch bark were used for lighting purposes.

The Indians of the Plains went on buffalo hunts about twice a year. Often whole villages took part. Valuables would be buried; tents rolled and tied to the ponies (nineteenth century) and looked after by the women. The man must not be burdened as it was his job to kill the game. Dr. Strong says that among the Potawatomi Indians the leaders of the buffalo hunt were chosen from among the principal men of the buffalo clan. The keeper of the sacred clan bundle was usually chosen also. A feast was held which was supposed to attract the buffalo. After the feast, there was an eating contest between representatives of the two tribal divisions. The winners were appointed to carry the sacred buffalo clan bundle on the hunt. Sixteen braves were appointed as police, and no hunting was allowed while traveling west, for fear it might frighten the herds. When the buffalo

Courtesy of Chicago Historical Society

BUFFALO HUNT

(G. Catlin)

were sighted, the hunters were divided into two groups to surround the herd, and the hunt was carried on under the supervision and control of the police.

Bears were hunted in the winter, while they were sleeping in caves. Beaver, otter, mink and muskrat were trapped. Ducks and geese were killed and preserved in brine.   Large parties were sent out to secure deer. (Strong)

The Miami, during buffalo hunts, surrounded the herd with grass fires, leaving only a small opening, where the buffalo were shot, as they stampeded from the fire. (Hennepin)

The buffalo had a peculiar habit. One would go round and round, encompassing an area of two or three acres, gradually making the circle smaller, beating the snow down, until it came to the center, when it would lie down, rising only to eat the tender branches of the trees within reach. It would not go out of this circle until hunger compelled it to do so.

The buffalo hair falls off in summer and the skin becomes as soft as velvet. At this season, the Indians used the hides for making fine robes, which they painted in various colors.

It was the woman's work to stretch the skins of animals and take care of the meat. The skins of both deer and buffalo were stretched on the ground and pegged, hairy side down. Bone scrapers were used to thin the skin and take off the fat. As the skin dried, brains, liver, and fat were applied and rubbed in; the skin was then rolled up and left several days to soften, after which time it was washed like linen and worked until it was soft and pliable.

The meat to be used immediately was put in water in a skin bag, clean side up, in a hole in the ground. Stones were heated and dropped in the water with the meat, and boiling was accomplished in this way. Thus it is evident that the Indian was familiar with the fireless cooker many years before the white man ever thought of it.

The curing of meat was a long and tedious process. It was cut in very thin strips and laid on a grate of small wooden switches, three feet above the fire, and dried over the fire until there was no moisture left in it — as dry as a piece of wood. It was then put up in packages of twenty or forty pieces each, and rolled in pieces of bark. In this way it would keep indefinitely. When it was to be used, it was reduced to a powder by rubbing between stones, and this powder boiled in water for a broth, with Indian corn added. This was called by the frontiersman, "jerked meat."

Pemmican is dried buffalo meat, beaten to shreds, mixed with melted suet or fat and packed in skins which were then sewed up. This was taken on journeys, to be sliced and eaten. A very small strip appeased the appetite, as it was really a condensed food, and antedated the white man's condensed food.

Buffalo grass had a peculiarity worth mentioning here. In the fall a film formed near the ground, preventing part of the sap from going into the roots, so that all during the winter months the buffalo could paw away the snow and graze on the tender, juicy blades of grass above the film. This grass not only kept the animals in good condition, but made them fat.

The beaver skins most desired by the French were those the Indians had worn next to their bodies, as the oil they used on their persons made the fur more supple, and therefore more valuable.

Parkman tells us that the English and the French who were taken prisoners and returned, would go back to the Indians, preferring their mode of living. The Indians who were taken prisoners while young, by the white men, and educated, would return to their own people (when they became of age and were set at liberty), and would become as fond of the Indian way of living as though they had never learned any other.

In the early days the only animal domesticated was the dog and it was probably a tamed wolf. The dog was used as food, and the missionaries tell of roasted dog being a highly prized dish at great feasts.

The horse was introduced by the Spaniards. Previous to the coming of the Spaniards, the red men traveled on foot or by canoe. Though they had no other means of traveling, trade was carried on between tribes living great distances apart.

There are many words of the Algonquian language that we use as freely as we do the English—for instance, the words *wigwam, papoose, squaw, and moccasin.*

CHAPTER V

INDIAN TREATIES

REGARDING the many treaties with the Indians who occupied land in what is now the State of Illinois, there were four that affected directly the Red Men of the Chicago area. These were the Treaty of 1816 at St. Louis, Treaty of Prairie du Chien in 1825, Treaty of Prairie du Chien in 1829, and the Treaty of Chicago in 1833.

At no time or place could an Indian orator display his powers to better advantage than before a council fire, and the execution of the treaties afforded the white man the opportunity of appreciating real Indian oratory. The Indian orator's fire, strength and pathos would have done him honor at any gathering. He never raised his voice to any considerable pitch, nor did he use any gestures, yet he had great persuasive powers. He could speak for four or five hours at a time, neither hesitating nor forgetting. Occasionally he used little sticks, with notches cut thereon, to help his memory.

Just as one tribe of Indians coveting land had warred upon another and weaker tribe and taken possession of the latter's home site, so did the white man come along, coveting, like his red brother, another's land, and by means not always fair pushed the red man further and further to the west.

No government was ever fairer or more honest toward a weaker people than that of the United States, but its agents were, in many cases, unscrupulous, setting out to acquire the land and carrying out their intentions, oftentimes, by methods the government would not have approved. When we consider how the unsuspecting Indian was influenced by the white man, the miserly amounts paid for the land, the use of whiskey, and the cheap, gaudy wares dangled before the Red Man's eyes, that tempted him to part with his birthright—"the land given by the Great Spirit to hunt upon, to make our corn-fields upon, to live upon and to make down our beds upon, when we die. . . . ", every honest man must feel shame that some of our land came to us through such means.

TREATY OF 1816 AT ST. LOUIS

August 24, 1816, Ninian Edwards, William Clark and Auguste Chouteau executed a treaty at St. Louis with the Ottawa, Chippewa and Potawatomi ceding "land 20 miles wide on eastern boundary at Lake Michigan (being ten miles north and ten miles south of the Chicago river in width) and extending generally southwest so as to include the Chicago Portage and a strip of land extending to the mouth of the Fox river." This strip of land was intended to be used for the building of the proposed canal. This cession is bounded on the north by the center line of Indian Boundary Road, beginning at Lake Michigan at a point—in the words of the treaty—ten miles northward of the mouth of Chicago Creek. This boundary line runs southwest, and is known as Rogers Avenue.

This treaty, as did many others, contained a clause to the effect that the Indians might hunt or fish within the tract so long as it continued to be the property of the United States.

TREATY OF PRAIRIE DU CHIEN IN 1825

The Treaty at Prairie du Chien was for the purpose of promoting peace between various tribes of Indians in northern Illinois and vicinity, and establishing boundary lines between them. The Sioux—the Iroquois of the West, as the early Frenchmen were wont to call them— had warred upon the Sauk and Foxes and the Chippewa, and the government, fearing they would extend their war invasions and involve other tribes upon the Missouri, Mississippi and the Lakes, invited the tribes to assemble together, that future trouble might be avoided.

The fifteen articles of the treaty dealt with the fixing of the boundary lines and the respective rights of hunting, provided for peace between the tribes, and acknowledged "the general controlling power of the United States."

We are indebted to Henry S. Schoolcraft in his *Thirty Years with the Indian Tribes,* for vivid descriptions of the scenes and of the various tribes assembled. He came all the way from Mackinac in a canoe to assist in the negotiations, the trip taking 21 days. The following excerpts are from his work.

"We found a very large number of the various tribes assembled. Not only the village, but the entire banks of the river (Mississippi) for miles above and below the town, and the island in the river, were covered with their tents. The Dakotahs, with their high pointed buffalo skin tents, above the town, and their decorations and implements of flags, feathers, skins and personal 'brav-

Menominee Chief with Calumet
(Catlin)

Menominee Indians with Lover's
Flute and War Club
(Catlin)

eries', presented a scene of a Bedouin encampment. Some of the chiefs had the skins of skunks tied to their heels, to symbolize that they never ran, as that animal is noted for its slow and self-possessed movements. The Winnebagoes (of Dakotan stock) were encamped near and resembled them in their style of lodges, arts and general decorations.

"The Chippewas (the best representatives of the Algonquin family) . . . were well represented.

"The Menomonies, Pottowatomies and Ottawas assimilated and mingled with the Chippewas.

"But no tribe attracted as intense a degree of interest as the Iowas and the Sacs and Foxes — tribes of radically diverse languages, yet united in a league against the Sioux. These tribes were encamped on the island, or opposite coast. They came to the treaty ground, armed and dressed as a war party. They were all armed with spears, clubs, guns and knives. Many of the warriors had a tuft of red horse hair tied at their elbows, and wore a necklace of grizzly bears' claws. Their head dress consisted of red dyed horse hair, tied in such a manner to the scalp lock as to present the shape of the decoration of a Roman helmet. The rest of the head was completely shaved and painted. A long iron shod lance was carried in the hand. A species of baldrick (girdle) supported part of their arms. They were, indeed, nearly nude, and painted. Often the print of the hand, in white clay, marked the back or shoulders. They bore flags of feathers. They beat drums. They uttered yells at definite points. They landed in compact ranks. They looked the very spirit of defiance. Their leader stood as a prince, majestic and frowning. The wild, native pride of man, in the savage state, flushed by success of war, and confident in the strength of his arm, was never so fully depicted to my eyes. And the forest tribes of the continent may be challenged to have ever presented a spectacle of bold daring, and martial prowess, equal to their landing.

"Their martial bearing and high tone, and whole behavior during their stay, in and out of council, was impressive and demonstrated, in an eminent degree, to what a high pitch of physical and moral courage, bravery and success in war may lead a savage people. Keokuk, who led them, stood with his war lance, high crest of feathers and daring eye . . . and when he spoke in council, and at the same time shook his lance at his enemies, the Sioux, it was evident that he wanted but an opportunity to make their blood flow like water. Wapelo and other chiefs backed him, and the whole array, with their shaved heads and high crests of red horse hair, told the spectator plainly that each of these men held his life in his hand, and was ready to spring to the work of slaughter at the cry of the chief."

This treaty, which took nearly a month to conclude, spelled peace to the various tribes who had trespassed on each other's territories and so had kept continually at war with each other.

The Indians believed that the commissioners were opposed to the use of spirituous liquor on account of its expense, and not on account of the bad effects it produced. In order to disabuse the Indian of this impression, the commissioners decided to try an experiment which they hoped would prove that the government was above such a petty principle. Accordingly, a row of tin kettles, each holding several gallons of liquor, was placed on the grass from one end of the council house to the other. After suitable remarks, the contents of these kettles were emptied on the ground. This action did not have the desired result, and caused the Indians to be considerably disgruntled by the waste of good whiskey.

TREATY OF PRAIRIE DU CHIEN IN 1829

Three tribes — the Potawatomi, the Chippewa and the Ottawa — ceded to the government in 1829 at Prairie du Chien a large territory in Illinois and Wisconsin between the Rock river and the Mississippi, and another tract of land between Rock river and Lake Michigan, to the west and north of land ceded by Treaty of 1816. On Lake Michigan the tract included in width the site of Evanston and nearly all of Wilmette. Its description in the Treaty reads, "beginning on the Western shore of Lake Michigan at the North East corner of the field of Antoine Ouilmette, who lives at Grosse Pointe, about twelve miles north of Chicago, thence running due west to the Rock river." Antoine Ouilmette had located at Grosse Pointe prior to 1828.

Over 15,000 acres were parceled out by this treaty to sixteen favored and more or less deserving individuals, some of them Frenchmen, some Indian wives of white men, and some actual signers of the treaty, such as Indian chiefs and head men. Archange Ouilmette, wife of Antoine, and her children received two sections of land, later known as the Ouilmette Reservation, covering part of Evanston and most of the Village of Wilmette. Shabbona, a Potawatomi chief friendly to the whites, very deservedly received a reservation.

7

Several other treaties were concluded with other tribes at this time, and by these treaties, for a comparatively insignificant compensation, the Indians parted with their right to eight million acres of land.

Caleb Atwater, one of the government commissioners, tells how, at the conclusion of the treaties, forty-two chiefs and head men sat for two hours on raised benches, admiring the gaudy wares and merchandise, for which they had sold their birthright; wearing in the month of August fur hats "with three beautiful ostrich plumes in each hat"; gowned in ruffled calico shirts and adorned with cheap jewelry and government medals, given them by the commissioners, as supposed tokens of merit and esteem. Before each person, male and female, was a pile of clothes two feet high, such as could be worn during the year. The sight nearly overcame the new owners with joy. All were treated alike, and a gun was fired for the departure of each nation. Mr. Atwater further says: "They one and all invited me to visit them at their new abode. In a few minutes they were off, covering a considerable surface with their canoes, each one of which carried a flag, floating on the gentle breeze, which ruffled the surface of the Mississippi."

TREATY OF CHICAGO IN 1833

The Treaty of Chicago in 1833 gave the white man the title to the last strip of land owned by the Indians in the State of Illinois.

The citizens of Chicago, feeling certain that the Indian title would be extinguished in the vicinity by the treaty about to be negotiated, voted for the incorporation of the town August 5, 1833. There was then a resident population of about 150, the number required to form a corporate town organization. After the treaty, by the close of the year, the population had increased to 250.

By the Treaty of Chicago, concluded September 26, 1833, the Potawatomi ceded to the United States government a vast territory "supposed to contain," according to the treaty, "about five million acres," in southern Wisconsin, in Illinois, and large tracts in Michigan and Indiana not definitely described. This treaty extinguished the Indian title to this fair state of ours, giving the white man the right to the land, where for centuries the Red Man had lived and loved and fought and died. It provided for and resulted in his removal west of the Mississippi, which took place a few years later.

The consummation of this treaty took more than a month, and during this time within a radius of five miles around Chicago five thousand Indians, squaws and children, all accompanied by their dogs, camped and lived well at the expense of the government. No longer were these Indians the powerful and proud men of former times. Whiskey and the white man's influence had turned them into a degraded lot of people for the most part, putting off the council from day to day. Sometimes a few flimsy clouds in the sky — the Indian never performed any important business unless the sky was clear — sometimes a chief was not at hand; these and other petty excuses caused the delays. They and their families and their ponies and their dogs were living exceedingly well without toil or hardship. Why not continue?

Charles J. Latrobe, a highly educated English writer, one-time governor of New South Wales and of another

English colony, says in his *Rambler of North America*: "When within five miles of Chicago we came to the first Indian encampment. Five thousand Indians were said to be collected round this little upstart village for the prosecution of the Treaty, by which they were to cede their lands in Michigan and Illinois.

"The Pottowatomies were encamped on all sides . . .

"You will find horse-dealers and horse-stealers, rogues of every description, white, black, brown and red half-breeds, quarter-breeds and men of no breed at all; dealers in pigs, poultry and potatoes. . . . The little village was in an uproar from morning to night and from night to morning, for during the hours of darkness . . . the Indians howled, sang, wept, yelled and whooped."

There was no national costume, each one dressing as best suited his taste or financial standing. There were coats of every color, mostly gaudy; rich sashes ornamented, and bright colored leggins; embroidered petticoats and highly ornamented head dresses, covered with various trinkets, such as plates of silver, beads, and mirrors.

The greater number of the women were not gaily dressed; "dandyism" seemed to belong more to the men, who spent hours on their toilet, painting themselves in the most fantastic styles. Black and vermilion paint was used in many ways, all more or less "fanciful and horrible." Gambling was the order of the day. "The interior of the village was one chaos of mud, rubbish and confusion . . . "

"Far and wide the prairies teemed with figures, warriors mounted or on foot, squaws and horses. Wrangling and weeping could be heard in many tents, the squaws, as well as the master of the tent, being intoxicated.''

Meanwhile, every flimsy excuse was offered to put off the assemblage of the chiefs. At last, on the twenty-first of September, the Potawatomi decided to meet the commissioners. The Council Fire was lighted under a spacious shed on the green meadow, on the opposite side of the river from that on which the fort stood. This was late in the afternoon. The chief government commissioner arose and asked why he and his colleagues had been called to the council. An old warrior arose and gave answer, the sum and substance of which was that the assembled chiefs wished to know what was the object of the Great Father at Washington in calling his Red Children together at Chicago. This was amusing, as everything had been explained at the opening session, and especially as the Red Children had been feasting sumptuously at the expense of the government during the intervening time. Replying, the commissioner delivered a ''real Jacksonian discourse, amounting to almost a threat not to play with their Great Father, but to come to an early decision.'' The council was then dissolved.

A few days later, September 26, the Treaty with the Potawatomi was concluded, ''the commissioners putting their hands, and the assembled chiefs their paws, to the same,'' and the last of the land in Illinois owned by the Indian passed into the white man's hands.

A couple of years after the signing of this treaty, in 1835 and also in 1836, the Potawatomi, about five thousand in number, were removed west of the Mississippi River to a place near Fort Leavenworth. After a year or two, on account of the hostility of the frontier settlers, they were removed to Council Bluffs and in a few years some were again removed to Kansas and the rest to Indian Territory.

They were gone, the last of the Red Men, from these parts, and the white man settled down in peace and contentment, building his home where the Red Man had roamed and hunted his game, had wooed the dusky maiden, brought up his children, and buried his dead; but ever and anon one of the Red Children, overcome by homesickness, wandered back, unwittingly frightening the housewife and children, as he peered into the window of a pioneer cabin, or strolled in, uninvited and undesired, to throw himself before the fire-place, where he lay deep in thought.

CHAPTER VI

THE FIRST WHITE MEN

ACCORDING to the earliest records, the first white men who coasted the shores and trod the land where later grew Evanston, were men of strong religious tendencies and great intellectual abilities, men not unlike Evanston's own founders, who were God-loving men and women, with keen appreciation of the natural beauty of the place.

There is no more lovely character in history than that of Marquette, missionary, physician and kindly companion, loved by white man and Indian alike; nor is there one stronger in purpose than La Salle, greatest of French adventurers, who set his goal, and, facing it, marched onward through untold difficulties and hardships. He was denounced as a madman, his friends turned against him and he barely escaped death by a poison put in his food. He was finally assassinated by one of his own men. To Marquette and Joliet, we owe the discovery of the Mississippi,[1] gentle Marquette, and

---

(1)   The question very naturally arises, if the Mississippi had already been discovered by De Soto, how, then, could it be said to be discovered by Marquette and Joliet.   The answer is, although the De Soto party knew the river to be navigable for at least a thousand miles, there is no account of any Spanish vessel having entered it to further trade between the mother country and the natives.   The maps of that time and for a hundred years after show but an insignificant stream, called the Rio del Espiritu Santo (River of the Holy Ghost).   Thus no permanent good resulted from the discovery, while those exploring the river a century later made accurate maps and left journals filled with accounts of their travels.

Nevertheless, both De Soto and the Frenchmen, Marquette and Joliet, are given credit for the discovery, as in the rotunda of the Capitol Building at Washington is the famous picture by Powell, of "The Discovery of the Mississippi by De Soto in 1539," and in Statuary Hall is the figure of Marquette, in white marble. the base of which bears the words, "Jacques Marquette, Who with Louis Joliet Discovered the Mississippi in 1673."

LOUIS JOLIET

JACQUES MARQUETTE

intrepid Joliet, first American-born explorer; both close and intelligent observers, Evanston's first white visitors, two and a half centuries ago.

The missionaries, sent out by their various orders that the "red men might not sit in darkness," accounted it a better death to die in doing their duty, whether death came by starvation, fever or the scalping knife, than to die in bed.

The explorers, sent out by their government intent on acquiring more territory to extend its power, or to find a more direct route for trade with China and Japan, faced danger and death on every side, traveling thousands of miles by water, now and then stopping with Calumet (peace-pipe) held high, placating the ire of a savage tribe of Indians, whose chiefs would then invite them on land, there to feast them unceasingly for hours, in order to prove their friendship toward the white men.

Strong characters, those explorers!

Men of high and noble purpose, those missionaries!

Small wonder, with such praiseworthy examples of unselfishness and self-sacrifice set before them that Evanston's founders should build, not for today, but for tomorrow!

Small wonder, with the memory of those invincible men, whose motto was so evidently "Nil desperandum," that Chicago should adopt the motto that evolved itself "I will!"

Although Hernando De Soto had seen and crossed the Mississippi River in the sixteenth century, the discovery was never made use of and was almost forgotten. De Soto died in the wilderness and was buried there. His men, fearing the Indians would desecrate his grave, took up his body at midnight and buried it beneath the waters of the great river.

A century later, men began to awaken to the fact that a great river, called by the Indians, Miche Sepi, existed. The prevailing idea was that this great river flowed into the Vermilion Sea (Gulf of California). If so, it would afford fine opportunities for direct trading by western passage with China and Japan.

At this time the reigning monarch of France was Louis XIV, the man who had the distinction, at his death in 1715, of having been king seventy-two years. Talon was intendant of Canada, and Frontenac was governor of New France. New France consisted of two cities — Montreal (sometimes called Mont Royall), and Quebec — and the far-scattered forts along the Great Lakes. In the early part of the seventeenth century the French had discovered the Upper Country, otherwise known as the Northwest, the region of the Great Lakes and the northeastern part of the Mississippi Valley; the first of these French explorers was Samuel de Champlain, called the "Father of New France," who discovered the Great Lakes and planted the flag of France on the shore of Lake Huron. Wherever a fort was established, soon there would be a mission station, and vice versa. The mission stations were all quite similar; each consisted of a chapel, and a few houses with store-house, which were usually made of logs, or of birch bark, this group of buildings being fenced in by palisades, making a stockade fort, and the whole surrounded by cultivated fields.

Louis XIV was not very much interested in his colonies in the new country, but Intendant Talon was ambitious for his government and decided to send an exploring party to the great river, hoping to add the vast territory east of the river to the French domain. The English occupied the sea-coast, where he decided they should be kept; as to the possessions of the Spaniards in the south, it was likely these would soon be wrested from them by the French.   In 1672, he chose Joliet, with Marquette to accompany him, for the expedition to the great river—two men born on opposite sides of the ocean and from different walks in life, but each fired with the same ambition, to explore.

Louis Joliet, son of a poor wagon-maker, was born in Lower Town, Quebec.   Lower Town was the part of Quebec where the humble folk lived and toiled contentedly on, while the society folk of Upper Town (Quebec) reproduced all the brilliancy and gaiety of the drawing rooms of Old France, each part of the town ignoring alike the ever impending menace of an Indian uprising. Louis Joliet[2] grew into a sturdy boy, with an aptitude for mathematics[3] and the languages.   He also possessed a talent for music.   All through his young life he had listened to tales of adventure from the missionaries and fur-traders, who came and went around Quebec, "along the mighty waters of the great St. Lawrence," and at twenty-one he renounced the clerical vocation, for which he had studied, and decided to become fur-trader and explorer.   His command of several Indian languages was no mean asset on a journey of this kind.

(2)   "Juillet" is the French spelling of the name.
(3)   At a very tender age, it is claimed, Joliet showed mature observation and, in his maps, accurate execution.   A map of the Island of Anticosti and of the Gulf of St. Lawrence, made when he was thirteen, holds a place in the Department of Marine at Paris.   This island was later presented to Joliet by the government for services rendered.

Jacques Marquette was born in Laon, France, of an old and honorable family. He joined the order of Jesuits at seventeen. Twelve years later he was sent to the missions in Canada, where he soon arrived at the conviction that the conversion of the red man was his real mission in life. With that end in view, he set himself to learning the Indian languages, of which he mastered no less than six in a few years. He was, of a gentle, noble nature, with a religious zeal far out of proportion to his health and strength.

These two were to be companions on a journey, the "duration of which they could not foretell, nor the end foresee."

Joliet, upon receiving the orders from the government for the expedition, began his long and tedious journey to St. Ignace, Michilimakinac, on the north shore of the strait, where Marquette was stationed. Traveling had become difficult by the eighth of December; ice-floes had formed in the straits and he found it no easy task to steer his canoe through the water, or pull it over the ice. Almost exhausted from the tiresome journey, he at last reached his destination. Marquette, hurrying out to welcome the weary wayfarer, found to his great joy that he was an old friend, and was delighted to receive the orders "to accomplish the discovery," and considered it a direct answer to his prayer that he found himself "in the blessed necessity" of exposing his life for the salvation of the red men.

All during the winter months the two men worked over plans for the trip, going carefully over the information they had in regard to the course of the great river, information so accurate that it might have been gathered by a white man who had traveled the river's entire length, instead of coming from the Indians.

Spring came. The sun's rays began to warm the earth; birds began to arrive from the south, hunting nesting places and vying with each other in song. The time was ripe for the beginning of the great journey. Marquette says, in his journal: "We were not long in preparing our equipment, although we were about to begin a journey, the duration of which we could not see. Indian corn, with some smoked meat, constituted all our provisions; with these we embarked, Monsieur Jolliet and myself, with five men in two canoes, fully resolved to do and suffer everything for so glorious an undertaking. Accordingly, on the 17th of May, 1673, we started from the mission house at St. Ignace, at Michilimakinac, where I then was."

It must have been a picturesque sight that May day, Marquette and Joliet and their five men, stepping into the two canoes, which had been previously equipped with their meager baggage — Marquette, frail and slight of physique, in his long black cassock and shovel hat; Joliet of sturdier build, in his fringed buckskin coat and trousers, and broad brimmed hat. With what joy they plied their paddles on the waters of Lake Huron, the Lake of Illinois (Michigan) and Green Bay, beginning their journey.

The first tribe of Indians they visited was the Menominee[4] on the Menominee River, who urged them to discontinue their journey, pointing out that there were unfriendly nations who would break their heads without

---

(4) The Menominee was an important tribe of the Algonquin family, living in Wisconsin; they derived their name from wild rice, plentiful in their habitat, which was their standard article of food.

provocation; that there were monsters who would devour
men and canoes together; a demon who swallowed all
who approached him; and lastly, as a convincing argument, that the heat further south was so excessive that
it would cause their deaths. In the face of all this, the
brave men pushed on, after thanking the Indians for
their kind and well-meant advice.

From the bay the travelers entered a beautiful river,
later known as the Fox River, on account of the Fox
Indians settling on its banks. This river was full of
bustards, ducks, teal and other birds, attracted by the
wild oats. Marquette says, "the birds rose in clouds
from the river, as we approached." On the Fox River
they came to the village of the Miami, the Maskoutens
(Fire Nation) and the Kickapoo. This was the limit of
the recorded discoveries that the French had made up to
that time. The Miami, they found, were of good disposition, civil, gentle and desirous of learning, and far in
advance of the other two nations.

As the river was winding and full of wild oats, it
was difficult to find the channel, and the travelers asked
for guides to take them up the Fox River and across the
portage to the Meskousing (Wisconsin)[5] River. Two
Miami guides accompanied them and left them after they
had crossed the portage of 2,700 paces[6] (one and one-
half miles) to the Wisconsin River. Thus they left the
waters that flowed into the great St. Lawrence and
embarked on waters that flowed — they knew not where!
Proceeding down the Wisconsin, they entered the Mis-

---

(5)   Wisconsin from Indian name, Meskousing, meaning the gathering place
of waters.

(6)   A pace is an ordinary step — 30 inches.

sissippi on the seventeenth of June, 1673, "with a joy I cannot express"—so writes Marquette.

What a trip for two men in the prime of life—Joliet, twenty-eight, and Marquette, thirty-seven—men keenly alive to all the beauty that Dame Nature, at her best in the month of June, spread before their eyes! The grandeur, as well as the glory of it all, must have caused them to gaze with awe on the wonderful scenes on either side of the river, these men—Joliet "who played the organ between voyages," fully capable of appreciating all that came within his vision; Marquette, whose eye for the beautiful missed nothing along the way, but noted with admiration the fertile lands, the woods and the hills, where oak and walnut and basswood trees abounded; he noted, too, the deer and large numbers of wild cattle (American buffalo). The latter interested him greatly, and, after giving a good description of them, he says, "If a person fire at them from a distance with bow or gun, he must immediately hide himself in the grass, as, if they perceive him, they will run after and attack him." The buffalo would kill men by trampling them under foot. The travelers saw many of them and Marquette counted four hundred in a single herd. A catfish that grows to immense size in the western waters struck their canoe with such violence that they thought it was a tree about to break their canoe to pieces. They caught sturgeon in their nets and a very rare Mississippi fish, called by the French le spatule. This fish frequently falls backward into the water when it leaps on account of the disk-shaped bone on its nose.

For eight days, after entering the Mississippi, the men saw no trace of human habitation—eight days of

solitude broken only by the songs of birds, the sound of
the wind through the trees, or the rhythmic ply of the
paddles, as the voyagers made their way down the great
river, building only a small fire toward evening to cook
their meals, passing the nights in their canoes that were
anchored some distance from shore in the river, always
posting a sentinel to prevent a surprise; eight days, in
which they covered sixty leagues, one hundred eighty
miles. Then on the twenty-fifth day of June, near the
water's edge, on the west bank, they saw tracks of men.
Following the tracks two leagues up the river (later
named Des Moines), Marquette and Joliet came to a village of the Illinois, the Peoria,[7] and saw two other villages on a hill some distance away. The Indians treated
them with great kindness, feasting[8] them and showering
them with presents.

After visiting with the kindly Indians, the travelers
embarked within sight of the whole village, when the
friendly natives expressed great joy at their visit.

Again on the broad bosom of the Mississippi, they
plied their paddles, while pleasant memories remained
with them of their visit and the gracious reception they
had been given by the old man in charge of the ceremony,
whose complimentary words to the lonely strangers will
live for all time: "Frenchmen, how beautiful the sun
shines when you come to visit us. All our village awaits
you, and you shall enter all our cabins in peace." The

(7)   Supposed to be derived from the word "Pimiteoui," meaning a place
where there is an abundance of fat beasts.

(8)   This feast consisted of four courses, the first being Indian meal boiled
with grease, which the master of ceremonies "fed to the guests in turn, like infants
from a spoon." The second, a platter of fish; the master of ceremonies removed
the bones with his fingers, blew upon the morsels to cool them and placed them in
the mouths of the two Frenchmen. The third course was a large dog roasted,
which the guests declined. The fourth was fat buffalo meat.

chief[9] (Marquette calls him the great captain) gave them his son, a little lad of ten, for a slave, saying, "Here is my son, whom I give thee to show thee my heart." He also made them a present of a calumet, which seemed to be the "god of war and of peace, the arbiter of life and of death," which the Indians valued higher than they did a slave. This calumet was the means of saving the travelers' lives on more than one occasion, as they made their way down the Mississippi, on, whose banks lived various savage tribes. Such was the attitude of the Illinois toward the white man; the Illinois, who held such a big place in the loving heart of Marquette, the nation that was forever being warred upon by savage Iroquois tribes, and a band of which was so cruelly destroyed by the Potawatomi at Starved Rock.

Other tribes, more or less friendly, the travelers passed and visited and were feasted by them, each tribe urging them to discontinue their journey and turn back.

They saw the "Ruined Castles" on the east side of the river, at the mouth of the Illinois, rocks given fantastic shapes by the elements; they gazed with sorrow on the "Piasa," a horrible painting of two Indian gods, on the flat surface of a high rock, north of the present site of Alton. This painting was still visible in 1848. Later a large advertisement for some kind of bitters was painted on the face of this rock, where the Piasa had been. The rock has now been quarried down.

The turbulent waters of the Missouri (Pekitanoui, meaning muddy) at its confluence with the Mississippi,

---

(9)   The chief is the Hiawatha of Longfellow's immortal poem, and Marquette's words are paraphrased by the poet.
8

tossed their canoes about like dry leaves before a wind, and carried logs, branches and uprooted trees.

They passed the mouth of the Ohio, the place where the roar of the waters was so great that the Indians thought a demon lay in wait for venturesome travelers. The Ohio had been given the very fitting name of "Beautiful River" by the Iroquois Indians.

Further on, the air was suddenly filled with angry yells and on all sides appeared savages. These were the Michigamea[10] Indians, also a branch of the Illinois, temporarily estranged from them. Just as the young men were about to pierce the travelers with their arrows, the old men on the bank beheld the calumet which Marquette held high in the air, "the arbiter of life and of death," and checked the ardor of the young men.

The voyagers reached the next village in the early part of July. This was the village of the Arkansas Indians (Akemsia, of Siouan stock), which was situated near the site where De Soto died in 1541. (A few years after Marquette visited them, the village was moved to the west side of the river.)

News of the coming of the strangers had preceded them, and they were met by some of the Akemsia Indians in a canoe, with calumet raised high, making friendly overtures. They were feasted all day without respite, according to the merciless Indian rule of hospitality. Alas! at night, some of their entertainers wished to break their heads and rob them, but the plan was defeated by the chief, who, after doing the calumet dance, presented them with the calumet, to reassure them.

---

(10)   This tribe formerly dwelt near Rohi, Michigan.   The lake and the state of Michigan take their names from the tribe.

They were informed that the mouth of the great river was about seven hundred miles further south, or a ten days' journey, and upon the advice of these Indians, they decided to turn back, as they were now convinced that the Mississippi flowed into the Gulf of Mexico and not into the Vermilion Sea (Gulf of California), nor into the Sea of Virginia (Atlantic Ocean). Moreover, the travelers were in no condition to resist the savage nations further south, who fought with European weapons; nor — which was of more importance — did they wish to lose the results of their journey by being taken captives by the Spaniards.

Accordingly, on the seventeenth of July, they started to retrace their course and found that breasting the currents of the Mississippi was a very difficult proceeding. By advice, they chose a shorter route back, one by the way of the Illinois River (nameless then). On this river, they first stopped at Peoria Lake for three days, when Father Marquette, at the request of the parents, baptized a dying Indian child. They next stopped at a village of the Illinois, containing seventy-four cabins, at what is now Utica, in LaSalle County. Their chief, with his young men, escorted them up the Illinois and Des Plaines, across the portage to the South Branch of the Chicago River, and through it to the Lake of the Illinois (Michigan).

Never getting far from land, but hugging the shore of this lake with their canoes, the travelers, no doubt, gazed with admiration on the lofty oaks, tamaracks and other varieties of trees that dotted the length of Evanston's holdings of today, the leaves in September just beginning to show the beautiful colorings of early autumn; and, as the men swung their canoes around the point where the lighthouse stands, the artist soul of Joliet and Marquette's keen eye must have delighted in the beauty of that point, a point so beautiful that it gained the name from sailors in a later day of "Beauty's Eyebrow."

And so they went on, the first white men that coasted Evanston's shores—Marquette back to the mission house at St. Ignace, there to resume his duties, and Joliet on to Montreal, to carry the report of the journey to the governor, only to lose his papers on the way, as well as the little Indian lad who had been given him as a slave by a chief of the first Illinois villages visited, and nearly losing his own life, when his boat capsized, almost within sight of his destination, after he had escaped the peril of Indians and passed safely forty-two rapids.

In the autumn of 1674, Marquette received the longed-for permission to establish a mission among his beloved Illinois Indians, and in November, he with two faithful companions, five canoes of Potawatomi, and four canoes of Illinois—ten canoes in all—coasted the western shore of Lake Michigan. On account of the storms, the cold and the rough lake, the journey took more than a month. On November 5th, Marquette, grieved at the sight of the Illinois Indians making a feast to a wolf skin, seized the opportunity of instructing them in religion.

On the third of December they were compelled to "make a point," on account of floating masses of ice. Here on "Beauty's Eyebrow," the only point within a day's journey of Chicago, they drew up their canoes and prepared to withstand the cold, and camp overnight.

The next day they reached the mouth of the Chicago[11] River, and Marquette says of the land bordering on the lake: "One can land anywhere, unless one persist in going where the waves are high and the wind is strong. The land bordering on the lake is of no value, except on the prairies." Ah, gentle Marquette, come back and gaze on that land today! He also says, "Deer hunting is very good, as one goes away from the Pottawatomies." During their stay at the entrance of the Chicago River, his men killed three cattle (buffalo) and four deer, one of which ran some distance with its heart split in two. Turkeys were abundant, many coming around their cabin because they were almost dying of hunger. The Indians were very eager for French tobacco and threw bear skins at the travelers' feet in order to receive pieces of it.

On account of Marquette's illness, brought on by exposure on his previous trip, they made camp and stayed over winter two leagues up the river (Chicago), where Illinois Indians from a nearby encampment and other Indians visited them frequently, bringing them game and Indian corn.

In the spring, they went on to the Illinois village at Kaskaskia, on the Illinois River, where Marquette was "received like an angel from Heaven." Here he gathered around him five hundred chiefs and elders, and fifteen hundred young men, besides women and children, and instructed them in religion. He was destined never

---

(11) Wm. Barry, first president of the Chicago Historical Society, says the Indians applied the term Chicago, spelled in various ways, to Mississippi, thunder or the Great Manitou, and the term signified strong, powerful or mighty. The name was given to great Indian chiefs of all tribes. Chicago was named after the grand chief of the Illinois Indians, in the opinion of Joseph Thompson, editor of the *Illinois Catholic History Review*.

again to see his mission station at St. Ignace, as his death occurred in May, 1675, in a wretched cabin of bark on the eastern shore of Lake Michigan, near a small stream, Marquette, which name was afterward given to a larger stream near it.

Claude Allouez was the next to visit our shore. In the winter of 1676 and 1677, on his way to the Illinois mission, to take the place of Marquette, he with his two companions, suffered untold hardships, traveling many weary miles over snow and ice. He passed our shores in an ice-boat, fitted up with sails, which was the first ice sail-boat on Lake Michigan. Allouez had spent seven years in learning the Algonquian language. During his twenty-four years of service, he instructed 100,000 western savages and baptized 10,000. Many times he went supperless to bed "on a rock, or on the ground." In one of his travels, he froze his nose, and had a fainting spell. His companions had gone on ahead. In his cloak, he found a single clove, which seemed to give him strength enough to proceed. Extremity of hunger often forced the missionaries to eat a certain moss or lichen, which had to be scraped with shells or sharp stones from the rocks, where it grew. It was a shell-shaped leaf covered with caterpillars and spiders. When boiled, it made an insipid soup, dark, clammy and viscous, like black starch, unpalatable. It was cooked with whole little fish and was said to ward off death, rather than to impart life.

Two years later came the great explorer and colonizer, Robert Cavelier de LaSalle, LaSalle being the name of the estate owned by the Caveliers. He, with Hennepin and fourteen Frenchmen, traveled from Green

HENRY DE TONTI

Courtesy of Chicago Historical Society

ROBERT DE LaSALLE

Bay, south on Green Bay Trail and along the western shore of Lake Michigan, on around the head of the lake to St. Joseph, then called Miami, camping on the banks en route. They met both friendly and hostile Indians, and, like Marquette, found game more abundant as they approached the head of the lake. Every night the canoes were shouldered through the breakers and dragged up the steep banks. The men paddled all day with only a handful of Indian corn for food. Tonti writes of La Salle that he was one of the greatest men of the age, a man of admirable spirit and capable of undertaking all kinds of adventures.

He traveled thousands of miles through swamp and forest, over snow and ice, and by water, baffled and disappointed, but pressing on with indomitable courage for the furtherment of civilization, as well as in the interests of France. His "Griffin," called Floating Fort by the Indians, was the first boat with sails to ply the waters of Lake Erie, 1679. It was lost, with crew and cargo in 1680, having set sail for Niagara from Lake Michigan at the entrance of Green Bay, in September, 1679.

La Salle was assassinated by one of his own men in 1687, on the west side of the Mississippi River, 240 miles from its mouth.

A year later, La Salle's faithful friend and lieutenant, Henry de Tonti,[12] and two companions, without food, sick and wounded, fleeing for their lives from the

---

(12)   Tonti, called the Iron Arm (he had lost his right hand in war, and wore an iron hand covered with a glove), was faithful to LaSalle, carrying out his plans, even after the latter's death. For twenty years he traveled back and forth between Chicago and Mackinac, passing here either on land or by water many times. He died September, 1704, near Mobile, Alabama. He was regarded by the Indians as a superman, on account of the great blow he could give with his iron hand. Tonti finished his signature with a flourish which gave rise to the idea that the last letter was "y" instead of "i."

Iroquois, began their long northward journey on foot from Chicago to the Potawatomi village at Green Bay. The cold was intense, and they lived on wild garlic, which they dug from the frozen ground. At a deserted village of the Potawatomi, they found "hardly as much as two handfuls of corn a day and some frozen gourds." Their shoes had given out, and, having no leather, they were compelled to make shoes from the cloak of Father Gabriel Ribourde, who had been murdered by the Kickapoo Indians. One of the men became ill from having eaten a piece of an Indian shield made of rawhide. A party of Ottawa Indians came along and kindly carried them in their canoes to a Potawatomi village, where they remained all winter, and where, after thirty-four days of starvation, their "famine turned to abundance."

The Northwest, which included this region, was twice declared to be under French rule. First, in 1671, St. Lusson took possession in the name of the French king, Louis XIV, of "all the territory around the Great Lakes, all countries, lakes and rivers, discovered and undiscovered, bounded by northern and western seas, including all its length and breadth." Again, in 1682, La Salle, at a place a short distance above the mouth of the Mississippi River, declared all territory "from the Alleghanies to the Rockies and from the Rio Grande and Gulf of Mexico to the farthest springs of the Missouri and the heads of streams flowing into Lake Michigan" to be under French sovereignty. To this vast territory he gave the name of Louisiana, honoring the French king.

As we read of the hardships and trials these early visitors to our shores endured, learn how they fought with cold and hunger, know how they must have grieved over the untimely deaths of loved companions, we feel a deep and everlasting gratitude toward those fearless men, who blazed the trail for civilization.

> Ah, shall I selfishly complain,
> When neither cold nor wind nor rain
> Affects me, who am housed and dry,
> When they went out "to do or die,"
> And suffered hunger, pain and cold
> To bring the red man to the fold,
> And blazed the trail from lake to sea,
> Where flies the Flag of Liberty!

CHAPTER VII

GROSSE POINTE

IN the latter part of the seventeenth century, when none but red men roamed these grounds, nearly one hundred and fifty years before Chicago had come into existence as a settlement, the name Grosse Pointe—from the French meaning great point—was given by early French traders to the great point or high bluff jutting far out into the lake.

It must have been a welcome sight, this great bluff, that told the weary travelers, patiently plying their paddles, that they were within a few miles of the mouth of the Chicago River.

Another name, too, was given this great point by later sailors, some of whom must have been imbued with a keen appreciation of beauty to have chosen a name at once so poetic and appropriate as "Beauty's Eyebrow." The very name makes us see the place as those early visitors saw it—a high bluff rising straight from the water's edge, curved as only the eyebrow of a beauty could be curved, and from its high prominence great oak and white trunked birch trees rising, the whole making a picture of unusual beauty.

As the years went on, all the territory extending north of the site of Graceland cemetery, indefinitely, came to be known as Grosse Pointe, and on the county records it is referred to as Grosse Pointe Voting District, or Precinct.

After the massacre[1] at Fort Dearborn, August 15, 1812, the fort was abandoned as a military post, and Antoine Ouilmette, one of the pioneer settlers of Grosse Pointe, a French Canadian, was the only white man who remained. He and a half-breed, Alexander Robinson (later made a Potawatomi chief), cultivated the garden outside the fort. Ouilmette and his family were instrumental in saving some of the white people at the time of the massacre.

The nearest postoffice to Chicago, previous to 1831, was Little Fort — later named Waukegan — fifty miles distant. Lincoln Avenue in Chicago was called Little Fort Road. The road from Chicago to Green Bay dates its beginning from an act of Congress approved June 15, 1832, for the establishment of a road between these two points. This road runs parallel to the west shore of Lake Michigan almost its entire length, being at no place further away than six miles. This was called in the beginning Green Bay Indian Trail, and over this trail had fled the heroic, but wounded, Tonti and his faithful followers from the blood-thirsty Iroquois. This trail follows the line of Clark Street in Chicago (called in the early days of Chicago the Old Sand Road) to a place north of Rose Hill cemetery, at which place the trail divides, one part taking the route over Ridge Road and the other over Chicago Avenue in Evanston, the two joining about four miles north at Ridge Avenue at a point just north of the site of the Evanston lighthouse (Hurd). Both trails through Evanston were used, but preference was probably given the Ridge Road Trail. Early pioneers told of the path along Ridge Road having

(1)   Mrs. Kinzie's *Wau-bun* makes interesting reading about those days.

been worn down more than a foot by centuries of constant Indian travel.

Over this Green Bay road traveled the early mail carriers, in 1816, between Chicago and Green Bay in the winter seasons. In the summer, the mail was carried by sailing vessels. The winter journey was hazardous on account of the hardships of wilderness travel. The mail carrier had to be a man of strong constitution and iron nerve, one capable of carrying a heavy mail-bag and a musket for hours at a time, lying down beside his camp-fire when too weary to go further, wrapped in his blanket to snatch a few hours' sleep, often with wolves howling and prowling around him. He had to wade through water and slush, pushing his way through underbrush, where no pony could have made its way; sometimes traveling when snow was so deep that he could have made no progress without his snowshoes. More than one man met his death at the hands of an Indian while traveling this trail. These carriers were the only white men to travel through this region for many years.

John H. Fonda, who "ran the mail" between Fort Howard (located at the mouth of the Fox River, Wisconsin) and Fort Dearborn in the winter of 1826, gives an interesting description of his dress as follows: a smoked-tanned buckskin hunting shirt, trimmed leggings of the same material, a wolf skin chapeau with the animal's tail still attached, and moccasins of elk hide. He carried a heavy mountaineer's rifle with a shortened barrel and a strap so attached that the rifle could be thrown over his back. A powder horn hung by a strap from his shoulder, while a belt around his waist held a sheath knife and a pair of pistols, in addition to a short handled ax. Attached to his belt, also, was a pouch of mink skin, in which to carry rifle bullets.

His companion, Boiseley, a Canadian, was similarly dressed, but carried a long gun and in his belt a large knife, pistol and hatchet. In addition, like most voyagers, being superstitious, he had several charms on sinew thongs, which were supposed to "possess mysterious power to preserve the wearer from harm."

The round trip of nearly five hundred miles consumed a month, and the men depended upon the game they shot along the way to sustain life, always carrying with them, however, a bag of parched corn, to be used in an emergency only.

Fonda tells of seeing tracks of a bear on an oak tree and on investigation finding within the tree's hollow a store of wild honey, which had evidently been the attraction for animals. The men helped themselves to a kettleful and during the evening ate so much of it that Fonda could never again endure the taste of honey.

In 1832, a Canadian half-breed froze his feet while carrying the mail between Green Bay and Chicago and one foot and a portion of the other had to be amputated. The work was done without the aid of anesthetics and with rusty instruments. This was the first capital surgical operation performed in Chicago.

The United States Post Office department usually opened the way for the stage coach lines of the west. This was a great financial help to newly settled regions. The first stage coach service along Green Bay Road between Chicago and Milwaukee was, according to the best records, about the spring of 1836, the proprietor

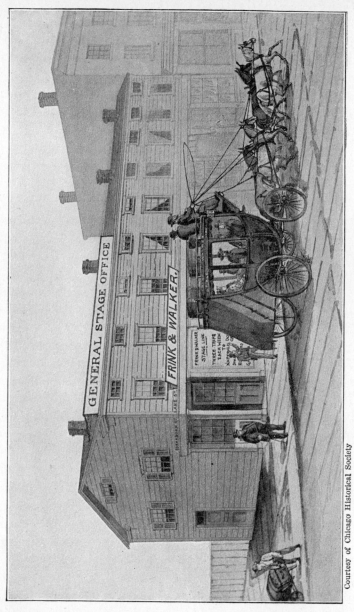

STAGE-COACH AND CHICAGO OFFICE BUILDING

of the line being one Lathrop Johnson, who used an open
lumber wagon—with four horses to give dignity to his
service—for transporting the mail and "such passengers as might choose to entrust themselves to his oversight." Later, Frink and Walker got the contract for
carrying the mail, and the coaches were scheduled to
run daily in winter and tri-weekly in summer, making
the journey in one and one-half days, stopping at
Kenosha over night. The stage coach made fewer trips
in summer, as the sailing vessels were preferred by
travelers. A story is related of Frink and Walker, which
shows the caliber of the men and proves that Frink and
Walker would brook no interference in their work. In
the middle forties an Ohio man captured the contract
for carrying the mail from Chicago east, and great
rivalry between the two firms began. When one firm cut
fares, the other made lower rates. Finally meals were
thrown in and traveling was practically free. While
this merry war went on, the public could travel more
cheaply than live at home. The Ohio man finally agreed
to buy the rival's property at an extravagant valuation,
giving notes which he was unable to meet. He fled to
Texas and his stage line went to ruin. The mail remained
uncarried for weeks and the contract was finally given
to the old firm.

Grosse Pointe's pioneers came mostly from the east
and from the nearer states of Ohio and Indiana. Those
from New England states were called Yankees and those
from any other state were called Hoosiers. It was
claimed that as soon as a wagon was sighted bringing
in a family, it could be told whether the occupants were
Yankees or Hoosiers by the make of the wagon, the New

Englanders' wagons being compactly built and orderly; all the others were great lumbering affairs with wide rims to the wheels and not so well put together.

In March, 1831, Congress voted $25,000 for a harbor at Chicago, and a channel was cut through the sandbar giving the river direct outlet to the lake. The channel, completed in 1834, was deep enough to permit the entrance of the heaviest vessels, affording for the first time safe anchorage at the south end of the lake. The rising of the Des Plaines River in the spring of 1834 completed the work done by the engineers, as its flood waters rushed down the Chicago River with such a force as to dredge the channel to its required depth.

Some of the pioneers came by water; others preferred to come by ox-cart, a slow but sure, if rather rough mode of travel.

According to Quaife, in the year 1834, 80,000 western emigrants embarked from the port of Buffalo, and, according to one observer, 250 covered wagons went through one village in a single day. In 1836 a line of wagons almost continuous passed through the village of Jonesville, Michigan, daily; and of these emigrants, Grosse Pointe and Chicago received a goodly number. Those traveling by water were advised to start in the spring. The route was by lakes to Chicago.[2] Those coming by land were told the time to start was in September, as autumn was the time of fat cattle and an abundance of fruit. It is said the travelers, when stopping for the night, looked for an inn, where the corral was well-trodden and a fat dog belonged. These were

---

(2) In 1842 the fare from Buffalo to Chicago was $20. By 1850 the fare had been reduced, by competition, to $10.

9

sure signs of a comfortable stopping place, with plentiful food. The land route was the Genesee Turnpike, which had been the old Iroquois trail from New York to Buffalo, being almost parallel to the Erie canal, then running along the south shore of Lake Erie, across southern Michigan, northern Indiana and on to Chicago. All roads finally converged into the Chicago road, the great highway between Detroit and Chicago, which dates so far back that no one knows whether it was originally made by the red men or the buffalo.

In 1826, Stephen J. Scott, a sea-faring man, embarked at Buffalo on the schooner Shelden, with his wife, Hadassah, their children and their household goods. En route, an altercation of a financial nature arose between him and the captain of the schooner, whereupon, being within sight of Grosse Pointe, the captain steered his vessel toward shore and deposited Scott, his family and his household goods at this point. The sturdy Scott, Grosse Pointe's first white settler, looked around and saw the Arcadian grove of native forest trees, at their best in the month of August, and probably recognized the natural fertility of the soil that furnished nutriment for such a healthy growth and decided to remain. He immediately began the erection of a cabin, with the help of his two sons. Their first cabin was called a "post and pole cabin", as the frame work was constructed of poles and upon these were hung blankets and pieces of bark. Having put up this structure for temporary use, Scott and his sons immediately set about building a cabin of logs, in which the pioneer family not only weathered the following winter, but remained in this rude habitation for five successive winters, twelve miles from Chicago, with swamp and forests between, and wolves their only neighbors. At this time Chicago was still in the fur-trading business, with a population of only about one hundred.

The only white man who roamed these parts, excepting those traveling on Green Bay Road, was John Kinzie Clark, nephew of John Kinzie and half-brother of Archibald Clybourne, two of Chicago's pioneers. Clark, born in Ohio and brought up by the Indians, had acquired many of the Indian ways and was therefore often called Indian Clark. He owned a ranch at Northfield on the North Branch of the Chicago River, where he raised ponies, and B. F. Hill tells of having seen him many times traveling through Grosse Pointe and the region further north with a string of ponies tied together Indian fashion, or tandem; that is, the bridle of one tied to the tail of the one preceding, and game — four or five deer — flung over their backs, Clark riding the foremost pony.

John Kinzie Clark was a widower. His first wife was Madeline Mirandeau, daughter of Jean Mirandeau and an Ottawa Indian squaw, the father being a sojourner in Chicago in 1811. Clark had obtained government land about where the north side rolling mills were later situated, and there the young couple set up housekeeping. After the Scotts came to Grosse Pointe, Clark turned his eye in their direction. His visits to Scott's cabin became frequent and regular and it was soon apparent that there was a romance in the air, Miss Parmelia, Scott's only daughter, being the lodestone that drew him. This romance terminated in a wedding July 21, 1829. In fact, it was a double wedding on that day, Miss Scott's brother and his bride being the other couple.

Clark and Parmelia commenced housekeeping in a log cabin about where the Wilmette sewers empty into the lake. Later they settled on a ranch on the North Branch of the Chicago River, where many of their descendants are still residing.

The family of Scott left Grosse Pointe and settled in Des Plaines, taking charge of a tavern, as the land on which their cabin stood was part of the two sections ceded by the government to Antoine Ouilmette's wife and children, in 1829, by Treaty Prairie du Chien. Mrs. Kinzie tells of calling on the Scotts in their new home and speaks of their having such things as carpets, a warm stove, and other luxuries not common in those days. Scott lost his life by drowning on a return trip from the gold fields in 1856.

In 1832 came the Black Hawk war. During this war the Potawatomi Indians remained true to the whites.

Asiatic cholera had been introduced into Chicago, when General Scott brought several hundred soldiers from the east, and most of Chicago's population had immediately left. In a few months both the cholera scare and the Indian war were passed, and the settlers returned to Chicago.

In August, 1833, Chicago was incorporated as a town.

In September, 1833, the treaty of Chicago was drawn up and signed, providing for the removal of the Indians to their western reservation; the removal, however, did not take place until the years 1835 and 1836.

By the treaty of Prairie du Chien in 1829, Archange Ouilmette, Potawatomi wife of Antoine Ouilmette, was ceded two sections of land for herself and her children.

This land, afterwards known as the Ouilmette Reservation, covered six hundred forty acres in Evanston and most of the village of Wilmette. The first cabin Ouilmette built was a substantial one of hewn logs on the shore of the lake, a little north of Lake Avenue in Wilmette. Ouilmette's cabin was in a line with Orrington Avenue on the lake bluff. It was a landmark for years after it was vacated. Ouilmette had a private graveyard. A severe storm caused it to dislodge its dead, "which came forth upon the sands of the lake shore." Its site is now gone, having been long ago washed away by the lake, as was also the site of Scott's cabin. The name, Wilmette, originates from the phonetic spelling of Ouilmette.

Ouilmette was born near Montreal, Canada, in 1760. He came to Chicago in the interests of the American Fur Company in 1790, and is claimed by some to have been the first white resident in Chicago. His was one of the four cabins that composed the settlement of Chicago in 1803.

Ouilmette was instrumental in saving at least two white persons during the massacre at Fort Dearborn. For four years after the massacre, he was the only white resident in Chicago. Later he was in the employ of John Kinzie.

In 1825, he was one of the principal taxpayers, paying four dollars on property valued at $400. Alexander McDaniel told of having stopped at the Ouilmette cabin and partaking of a sumptuous dinner prepared by Ouilmette's comely daughters. He said Ouilmette owned cows, horses, sheep, wagons and farm implements and lived comfortably in a house fit for a congressman to

HOME OF ANTOINE OUILMETTE (1828-1844)
From water color drawing by Charles P. Westerfield

HOME OF JOHN DOYLE, WHERE THE FIRST NORTH SHORE
WEDDING TOOK PLACE

live in. Mrs. Galloway, mother of Mrs. Archibald Clybourne, purchased wool from Ouilmette, from which she spun yarn and knitted stockings for the soldiers at Fort Dearborn.

Benjamin Hill described Ouilmette as a very old man in 1840, wearing a turban cap, dressed much like an Indian, and acting like one. Hill said he could not be told from one. The boys called him Owlmette, because they had heard him called that. He had a beautiful pair of ponies, which he would hitch up, one to the other's tail, and would go galloping off home or away hunting, returning from a hunt sometimes with a deer thrown over the second pony's back. Ouilmette's wife was just like any other Indian squaw. The Ouilmettes did not live in wigwams, as the Indians did further west. Antoine Ouilmette was married to Archange, daughter of a Potawatomi woman and a Frenchman named Chevalier, in 1796, on land (now Wilmette) occupied by a band of Potawatomi Indians. This was the first North Shore wedding of which there is any record.

As the Ouilmette Reservation could not be sold without the consent of the government, seven of the Ouilmette children joined in a petition to the government. This petition, dated February 22, 1844, was sent to the President of the United States and signed by the seven children, who were living with the Potawatomi tribe at Council Bluffs, Iowa. They asked that the government either buy back the Ouilmette Reservation at $1.25 per acre, or allow it to be sold, or leased. Henry W. Clarke was then appointed Special Agent to take care of this business, and the land was sold to real estate speculators, during the years of 1844 and 1845.

All of the Ouilmette Reservation, included in Evanston, 640 acres, was sold for $1,000 — a little over $1.50 per acre. The north section (in Wilmette) was sold in separate parcels, bringing in a larger sum. One brother, Joseph, sold his shares separately.

After the Treaty of Chicago was concluded, ceding the land to the white man and providing for the removal of the Indians, white settlers began to straggle in and put up cabins. A large proportion of these were lake captains who wished to retire. These settlers were mostly from the east and said to be of high character and great energy, drawn to Grosse Pointe by the glowing accounts of the fertility of the soil and the general desirableness of the place for settlement, this information having been carried back east by the soldiers who had fought in the Black Hawk war.

In 1834 came a settler who was a different type from the settlers that came later — one Abraham Hathaway by name and counterfeiter by trade, a rough and altogether undesirable citizen, who built a log cabin on ground for which he had obtained no title, at the northeast corner of what is now Raymond Park. Here Hathaway kept a tavern and, like most of the tavernkeepers of the day, had whiskey for sale. This cabin became known as a counterfeiters' den, and there were even worse rumors afloat. It is related that a peddler with a horse and wagon stopped at his cabin one day, and while the horse and wagon remained, which Hathaway claimed he had bought, the man was never seen again. A few days later Hathaway was seen filling up a good well. When asked his reason for doing so, he replied the water was not good. Some of his neighbors, doubting this statement, became suspicious that the peddler's body had been thrown in the well and began digging, but ceased shortly, fearful of what they should find, and so the mystery was never solved. A few years later Hathaway left the neighborhood where he was not wanted and went to parts unknown, but it seems he returned later for a short period of time.

When wreckers in 1895 were tearing down a cabin built by Abraham Snyder just south of the old Hathaway cabin, they were showered with what looked like bona-fide silver dollars. The surprised wreckers examined the "dollars" and found to their disappointment that they were imitations of Mexican dollars.

Along Green Bay Trail — later Ridge Avenue — most of the pioneers settled, although the ridge to the east, Chicago Avenue, also lured the early settler.

From the Ridge to the lake was a great swamp, broken only by the low ridge, Chicago Avenue, and the few cabins were great distances apart. This "Dismal Swamp," as it was called, was caused by the low land receiving the drainage from the ridges, whose great forest trees held the moisture in the mass of leaves around their bases, the water seeping out onto the low ground during the whole of the mild seasons. The ridge of Chicago Avenue itself was not always free from water.

Many pioneers traveling in their prairie schooners stopped in the little town of Chicago no longer than they were compelled to, their opinions of the low, swampy land concurring with that of gentle Marquette expressed more than one hundred fifty years previously, "the land bordering on the lake is of no value, except on the prairies.'' As these pioneers gathered their families together and cracked their whips at the patient oxen, to travel on and locate in the valley of the Des Plaines or further west, they laughed at those who were foolish enough to end their journey at such an uninviting place and termed it a one-horse, mud town. However, there were those who, appreciating the value of Chicago's location, divined that one day Chicago would become the metropolis of the west. Among these was Edward H. Mulford.

To the ''far west'' came Mr. Mulford, in 1833. He was a native of New York, major in the war of 1812, and at one time he formed part of an escort to General LaFayette. He had come to Chicago to engage in the jewelry business with his sons, who owned the first store of its kind in Chicago. In 1836, he preëmpted two sections of government land, 160 acres in Grosse Pointe, opposite the site Calvary cemetery occupies, paying $1.25 per acre, and, in order to perfect his title to the land, built a rough board cabin. This cabin, situated on the west side of the Ridge, was fourteen by sixteen feet in size, and its boards were placed upright. Mr. Mulford did not occupy his cabin until a year later. In October of 1836, he met on the street in Chicago an old war acquaintance, Arunah Hill, who had served as captain under General Winfield Scott, in the war of 1812. Hill had brought his wife and seven children on the Schooner Dolphin from Cleveland, Ohio—a trip that had taken three weeks to make. On arriving in Chicago, he heard of Mulford's unoccupied cabin and began to look about for Major Mulford, who was delighted at again meeting his old friend, and arrangements were soon made for

Hill to move into the cabin. Accordingly, Hill hired an ox-team and wagon, and, loading his family and household goods, started late in the afternoon of the next day, stopping overnight at Britten's, about where Graceland cemetery is now located. He arrived[3] the following day about noon at his destination, having consumed twenty hours in making the ten mile trip, half of which time was spent, probably, in actual traveling—and today we speed over the same route in seventeen minutes.

In those days it was customary for the pioneer to bring his own window sash and doors. In this roughly made cabin, Hill[4] fitted his two one-pane windows and door. There, was no opening for a chimney and the stove-pipe had to be passed through a window opening and changed from one window to the other, according to the direction of the wind. A member of the family, Benjamin F. Hill, then six years old, years afterwards said he remembered his mother often saying that it was the handiest house she had ever known, as all she had to do was to change the pipe from one side of the house to the other, through a hole, when the wind veered, to make the fire draw satisfactorily.

Where this cabin stood was, no doubt, a very attractive place in the day time, amidst the great forest trees, with wild flowers abloom and small fruit in abundance all around, but, as night came on, it took on a very different aspect. The great trees almost shut out the sight of the very stars, and the flickering light of the candles in the cabin showed the frightened children huddled together, as the howl of wolves and the screech

(3) He came over East Ridge and crossed with difficulty to the West Ridge (Ridge Avenue) through water.

(4) Arunah Hill was a cooper by trade.

of lynx or wildcat pierced their ears, and to these were added the eerie hootings of the owls in the nearby trees.

In time, the family grew accustomed to these sounds and even lost its fear of the prairie wolves, which would not harm humans, but were destructive to small animals and chickens.

Deer were so plentiful in the region at this time that one could hardly pass from one ridge to the other without starting up a drove, and it is said it was dangerous to climb the Winnetka hill further north, for fear of being charged by bucks. As most of the guns possessed by the pioneers were incapable of shooting further than six or eight rods, few deer were killed, and venison was a real luxury.

Late one afternoon, little Frank Hill, at this time seven years old, started out to find the family cow, which had wandered away. Turning into the Big Woods — west of Ridge Road — young Hill lost his way and tramped around from six in the evening until three the next morning, when he saw a cabin and knocked for admission. Mr. Doyle, the owner of the cabin, which stood within the limits of what is now Kenilworth, satisfying himself that it was no intoxicated person or rough character wanting to come in, admitted the boy, who was worn out from his long hours of tramping. From the extreme south end of Evanston to Kenilworth would have been quite a tramp for a little boy, but he had evidently covered many more miles in wandering through the woods.

The Hill family occupied Mulford's cabin a year, and then built a very comfortable log house on what was later known as "Hill's Ridge," where the present village of Gross Point is located, and moved into this new home. However, the various younger members of the Hill household later moved to Evanston and were very useful citizens, holding honored places in the community. Benjamin Franklin Hill, the six-year-old member previously mentioned, lived many years in Evanston and presented to the Evanston Historical Society a number of valuable Indian relics, most of which were found on the Ouilmette Reservation. He was a man of excellent memory, with a great fund of information of Evanston's early days, which caused him to be referred to as the John Wentworth of Evanston.

After the Hills vacated the cabin in 1837, Major Mulford decided to take up his residence there. When he arrived he found that a squatter had very comfortably settled himself therein.

The township System of Survey did not exist until 1850, twenty or more years after the Treaty of Prairie du Chien had been concluded, which gave government title to the land in this territory. The settlers obtained ownership of land under a system of patents, which in due time became valid titles. Settlers taking possession of land without obtaining the right were called squatters. Abraham Hathaway was a squatter, as was Major Mulford's new tenant. This tenant refused to vacate, thinking probably to prove the old maxim, "Possession is nine points of the law," but at the sight of the major's gun, whose muzzle pointed straight at him, he decided that "Might was Right" and moved on.

Major Mulford, a philanthropist and a deacon in the First Baptist church, which he founded, is described as a "gentleman pioneer, a tall and handsome man, re-

DESK MADE AND USED IN MULFORD'S TAVERN BY
FIRST POSTMASTER, GEORGE M. HUNTOON

MULFORD'S TAVERN

spected by all who knew him.'' He began to clear the land, and planted a garden, selling the garden truck in Chicago, where he found a ready market. Wood, too, he carted to the city and sold. As other settlers came into the neighborhood, his home became a center for social gatherings, and he gave it the name of Ridgeville, which he changed after a few years to the poetic one of Oakton.

Across the road from his cabin on Ridge Avenue, Major Mulford built a log house, quite a roomy affair, it being thirty feet wide by forty feet long. Into this he moved his family and kept a tavern, which was known as the ''Ten-Mile House,'' being ten miles from the Chicago courthouse. Timbers from the original tavern were re-employed in the building that forms part of St. Francis Hospital.

One of the first frame houses in Grosse Pointe was built a few years later by O. F. Gibbs for Major Mulford.

In regard to Mulford's tavern, it was said his accommodations were exceedingly good, but his rates were high. He never allowed wine to be served at his table, not even on holidays, Christmas or New Year.

Mulford had the distinction of being the first Justice of the Peace appointed, and he held the first court in Cook County in his thirty by forty log house. Sometimes the house was not large enough to accommodate the jury and others present. On these occasions court would be held in the open air.

He was a man greatly given to prophecies, and one of these was that Chicago would become the Queen City of the West. Another was that a railroad would be built on the ridge, on which Calvary station now stands. He would take visitors to the back door of his home and, pointing toward the low ridge to the east, exclaim, "Some day, my friends, you will see the Iron Horse speeding along its path of steel right out there." As the cabins were few and far between, this seemed most unlikely, but he proved to be a true prophet, and in less than twenty years the "Iron Horse," a brave, little, ten-ton engine, with its one lone coach, puffed and snorted its way over a single track railroad, through the growing town of Evanston. He not only had the pleasure of seeing his prophecies fulfilled, but saw many other wonderful improvements, as he lived to the ripe old age of eighty-six, passing away in 1876. Mulford Street is named in his honor and Oakton Street and Oakton School no doubt derive their names from the name of his home place.

The four-horse stage coach ran through his land twice a week between Chicago and Milwaukee and changed horses at his place, the Ten-Mile House. The next stop was on the Ridge at the place where Noyes Street now is. Between these two stops the settlers in general took up land and built their homes and began farming.

Chicago's charter of incorporation as a city was issued in 1837. Chicago had a population of 4,179, and was a town of shanties and frame buildings, with wooden side-walks and muddy streets along the water front. Fort Dearborn was a cluster of hewn log buildings, covered with clapboards, surrounded by palisades. The structure stood until 1852.

Philip Rogers came to Grosse Pointe in 1836 and settled on the southern part of Sections 31 and 32, now Rogers Park. He built a log house and made a living by

Daniel Pope Cook, After Whom Cook County
Was Named

burning charcoal, which he carried to Chicago by ox-team and sold.

In 1837 Sam Rohrer settled at Rose Hill. It is said he had considerable live stock. Deciding to go further north, he burned his shanty, in which he had lived, in accordance with a superstition, to insure good luck. Arriving in Glencoe,[5] he saw lake on one side, the Skokie on the other, bluffs and gullies before him, so he turned back and located in Evanston, on southeast quarter section 25, moving in 1847 to Niles.

The County of Cook, within whose boundaries Grosse Pointe, later Evanston, was situated, was named in honor of Daniel Pope Cook, a man who had never stepped foot within its territory and who died four years before the county's organization, which took place March 8, 1831; but Daniel Pope Cook was held in such high esteem by his fellow countrymen, that his name was chosen from among a great number proposed.

Daniel Cook was born in Kentucky in 1795 and died in 1827, at the age of thirty-two years. He had received a good education in his native state, and on his arrival in Illinois in 1815 began the practice of law at Kaskaskia. In a short time, he became editor and part owner of the "Intelligencer," the only paper at that time in the Territory. In 1816, he was appointed auditor of public accounts. In 1817, he was sent by President Monroe as bearer of dispatches to John Quincy Adams, then United States Minister to England, and was elected circuit judge on his return. He was elected to Congress two years after Illinois was admitted to the Union, and was

---

(5)   Glencoe was called by the Germans Ewige Qual (Everlasting Punishment).

re-elected several times. Although he was born and reared in a southern state, he was strong in his opposition to the attempt to make Illinois a slave state.

He married the daughter of Governor Edwards. His son was colonel of the first regiment organized in this state, after the first call for troops by President Lincoln. This was the Seventh Regiment of Illinois Volunteers.

Cook County embraced originally Du Page, Will, Lake and McHenry Counties. In 1926, of the six cities and sixty-two villages in Cook County, Evanston stood second in size.

Nathaniel Pope, uncle of Daniel Pope Cook, wrote the amendment to the bill admitting Illinois into the Union. When the "Enabling Act," as this bill was called, was first introduced, the north boundary line proposed for Illinois was to be from a point at the extreme southern end of the lake and run due west. Nathaniel Pope, a delegate in congress from Illinois Territory, after long consideration, foresaw the advantages to be gained to the state by having a coast line on the lake, connecting it in this way with points east, and he moved to amend the "Enabling Act," this amendment to place the northern boundary line further north. The bill was passed with "Pope's Amendment," and the northern boundary line was moved 61 miles north of the proposed boundary line named in the bill. This amendment also added about 9,000 square miles to the state, or nearly one-sixth of its territory, and—Evanstonians may write Illinois after their city's name, instead of Wisconsin.

"LOOK FORWARD"

Back silently the years I traveled,
  Back seven decades—yea—and more,
To stop before a lonely cabin
  And lightly step within its door;
Then trod I softly 'mongst the shadows,
  Away from firelight's fitful glow,
And sat me down, full eager, curious,
  A pioneer to watch and know.

    Loud rang the room with happy laughter,
      Of sturdy children playing 'round;
    The housewife busy, crooning softly,
      Each moment to her duty bound.

Long the shadows grew and lengthened;
  Low sank the sun—'twas eventide;
The word of God—mine host was reading—
  Came low to me, "with me abide."
Words they were that gave him courage,
  Helped him to "look forward" too,
And on his face I saw plain-written,
  "I'll not despair." My wonder grew.

    I lightly touched his arm and whispered,
      "Despair ye not when clouds hang low;
    When cold winds blast and hot suns wither,
      And ye reap naught, tho' much ye sow?"

"Daughter," ah, his eye was kindly,
  But his words rang like a dare,
"Know ye, we are sons of fathers,
  Who knew it *not*, the word *despair*."

CHAPTER VIII

PIONEERS OF GROSSE POINTE

THE settlers came mostly straight from comfortable homes in the old cities, villages and towns, and, without going through any intermediate stage, took up their abode in comfortless cabins, with the primeval forest not a hundred feet away, the women uncomplainingly taking up the pioneer work, sharing the perils and privations with the husbands and fathers. If the American women of the east merited credit for their housekeeping skill, how much more is credit due to the women of the west, real heroines, who attempted similar duties under so many disadvantages and amid such great deprivations!

In their trip to the unknown region, the pioneers brought mostly such articles as were absolutely necessary. A valued piece of furniture from the old home, or dear reminders of other days sometimes reached the end of the journey, but more often these would be found to be "excess baggage" and were left along the route. The doors and window sash had to be transported to the new home, as in some localities these were not easily procured. Trunks and carpet bags, with lock and key, carried the family's wardrobe. Nearly every family possessed a "hair trunk," a trunk covered with cowhide. Bonnet boxes were made of light-weight wood and had lock and key. A linen-lined silk traveling bag carried toilet articles for the fastidious ones.

Indispensable to the new home were the woolen coverlets (sometimes called coverlids) of bright colors, which had been woven by the women. The cotton filled comforters came into use about 1842, and directions given at that time for making them call for a covering three yards square and four pounds of cotton bats.

The kitchen furnishings that were deemed necessary were usually as follows: a nest of iron pots; long iron fork; an iron hook; a small gridiron with grooved bars and a trench to catch the grease; a Dutch oven or bake-pan; two skillets; a spider; ladles; skimmer; iron skewers; two tea-kettles; two brass kettles for soap boiling; portable furnace of iron or clay for summer washing, ironing and preserving; box and mill for spice, pepper and coffee; iron cleaver and board; apple-parer; sugar nippers; a dozen iron spoons; six or eight flat-irons; a ruffle-iron; crimping iron; lamp-filler; broad bottomed candle sticks; scoops; egg-boiler; a beetle for mashing potatoes; coffee stick; mush stick; a meat beetle to pound tough steak; bosom board; skirt board; large ironing board; linen pudding or dumpling bags; roller towels; a jelly bag (spelled gelly).

The keen eye of the early settler saw and appreciated the great possibilities of the new locality for successful farming. The thick growth of timber along the Ridge proved the soil to be of great producing capabilities, with strength and durability; a black sandy loam favorable to farming, easily and with little expense brought under cultivation. Long before, the Indian had taught the white man how to girdle the trees that cultivation might be carried on before the forest trees were felled, the ring of bark burned around the tree preventing the sap rising, thus killing the tree before the spring season had fairly begun.

The light, sandy soil of the oak openings was also highly prized for gardening purposes, as it was not easily affected by dry weather, and seldom suffered from excessive rains.

A great inducement, also, to the settlers was the fact that the government offered the land to homesteaders at $1.25 per acre, on condition that they make certain improvements and cultivate a certain portion of it for a period of three years. The time extended to a United States soldier who had seen service was shortened to fourteen months.

Under the United States system of surveying, lands are laid out in townships six miles square. Each township is divided into 36 sections, each one mile square, 640 acres. Sections are divided into quarter sections of 160 acres. Certain parallels of latitude are used as base lines; meridians of longitude are used as principal meridians. Townships are described as Nos. 1, 2 or 3 north or south of base lines, in Range 1, 2, 3, etc., east or west of principal meridian. Every 24 miles Guide Parallels and Guide Meridians are surveyed. Across Guide Parallels jogs allow for the curvature of the earth.

All territory from the site of Graceland Cemetery extending north indefinitely and west as far as the North Branch of the Chicago river was called Grosse Pointe.

As swamp covered most of the region from the Ridge or Green Bay Road to the lake, with the exception of the low ridge along what is now Chicago Avenue — which, too, was at times under water — it is easy to see why the pioneers began to settle along the Ridge.

SIMON V. KLINE
BENJAMIN F. HILL

OZRO CRAIN
SAMUEL REED

MRS. JUDITH BURROUGHS
MAJOR E. H. MULFORD
MRS. MARY FOSTER

Benjamin Hill says there were white and black ash trees in the early days where the business district grew later. The trees were noticeably larger on the Ridge. There were dark and white oaks on both the east and west ridges. Here and there were hickory trees. In the swamps were elm, ash and basswood, but not many of the latter. Further north there were hard maple trees. Maple orchards were called sugar bush. Hill's Ridge was on the site of the Catholic Church, in the present Gross Point, which is the only community that retained the original name of Gross Point.[1] Hill's Ridge was named after B. F. Hill's father, Arunah Hill. Below this place was a splendid sugar orchard of 1000 maple trees owned by Arunah Hill. He had paid five hundred dollars for one hundred sixty acres of land.

During the decade between 1837 and 1847 came the Carneys, the Pratts, the Huntoons, Benjamin Emmerson, the Reeds, Alexander McDaniel, the Burroughs, the Gaffields, the Fosters, the Crains and the Murphys, each family settling down and taking a part in the making of the new settlement in true pioneer fashion.

The Carneys, James and John and John's wife, Mary Lindsay, came from County Mayo, Ireland, in 1837, coming to the *Far West* and settling in the village twelve miles north of Chicago on a tract of land bounded by what is now Church and Dempster streets, and Asbury and Chicago avenues. This was bought by James Carney in 1840 from the government — 160 acres at $1.25 per acre, making a total of $200. They were typical pioneers, held in high esteem by their neighbors through their long lives, John Carney reaching the age of ninety-

---

(1)   The final e's were dropped from the name in 1846.

seven and his wife ninety-two. Their son John served twenty-three years as head of the Police Department and was often referred to as "the Police force of Evanston." His brother William was also on the police force.

Benjamin Emmerson came from his New England home, first settling in Chicago. He ran the first milk business in Chicago and was evidently successful in this work, as he was able to buy land in Grosse Pointe in a few years, 1839, and start farming. Emerson Street in the north end of town perpetuates his memory.[2]

The same year Paul Pratt and his wife, Caroline Adams Pratt, took up 140 acres of land with the boundary of what is now Church and Simpson streets and Maple and Asbury avenues, and became neighbors of Emmerson. Paul Pratt's father was one of the historical Minute Men, and Mrs. Pratt was descended from the famous Adams family that furnished two presidents. The Pratts built a cabin on Green Bay Road, near what is now Emerson street. Pratt hewed timber and floated logs, made into rafts, down the lake to Chicago. Some of these logs were used in making the first government pier at Chicago. His brother, George, lost his life on one of the rafts. Paul Pratt's daughter, Susan, born 1840, was the first white child born in Grosse Pointe. She died at the age of eighty-four in Wilmette in 1924. Pratt Court commemorates the family of Pratt.

Edward Murphy settled about one mile south-east of the Mulfords, at Indian Boundary line and the lake. His son, John, was the first white male child born in Grosse Pointe, 1841. Edward Murphy was born in 1805, a native of Kenmore, County Kerry, Ireland. He was a

(2)   The street is spelled with one m.

teacher and mathematician by profession, and was Government teacher in London, Canada, before coming to the United States. He taught in the public schools of Chicago and was generally interested in educational affairs. He was elected Deputy Sheriff, and later elected Coroner of Cook County, being re-elected at the expiration of his term of office. He was the first Supervisor of Ridgeville, being elected in 1850.

George Washington Huntoon came to Grosse Pointe by boat from Cleveland, Ohio, to visit in 1839. He was captivated by the place, and immediately decided to locate in it. Accordingly he arranged for the building of a house on Ridge Avenue between Crain and Mulford streets (middle section 19), while he went back to Cleveland for his family. The return trip to Grosse Pointe was made in an ox-cart, with his family and household goods, a slow, tedious and tiresome trip, but preferred by many as being safer than by water. When the Huntoon family arrived, the frame house on Ridge Avenue, corner of Main street, which had the distinction of being the first frame house in Grosse Pointe, was not yet completed, as it lacked doors and windows. Nothing daunted, the family moved in, used sheets and blankets in lieu of doors and windows, and settled down in regular pioneer fashion. Removing the blanket from one of the windows the following morning, the family beheld a deer in front of the house calmly chewing the bark from a maple tree.

Alexander McDaniel,[3] a Scotchman, arrived in 1842,

(3) McDaniel first settled on a claim of 160 acres of government land in Winnetka, in 1837, on which he built a house and kept bachelor's hall for five years. In 1853, he bought land and built a log cabin in Wilmette on the lake shore at Maple Avenue and Sheridan Road. He laid out the Village of Wilmette, in connection with H. A. Dingee of New York. McDaniel was the first postmaster of Wilmette, serving from 1870 to 1889.

and began the usual business of farming and wood cutting. Ten years later, 1850, he married Emmiline Huntoon. Squire Mulford performed the ceremony, the second in his capacity as justice of the peace, and he ever afterward called her, "My Emmy."

The McDaniel family purchased a cow from "Old Rose," a hermit who lived in a dugout, where the main vault in Rose Hill Cemetery is now situated. No one seemed to know much about him or his antecedents. This cow was christened Rose, in memory of Old Rose. (It might be mentioned here that the locality and the first railroad station at Rose Hill were called Chittenden.) Some time later a meeting was held, and Mr. McDaniel told the story of Old Rose the hermit living on, perhaps it would be better to say in the ground, since he lived in a dugout, and the name of Chittenden was dropped and the name Rose Hill bestowed upon the place.

McDaniel Street was named in honor of Alexander McDaniel.

The same year, 1840, which seemed to be an auspicious year for new arrivals, Charles Crain, a lad of eighteen, native of Stockton, New York, came from Hamilton, Steuben County, Indiana, to Dutchman's Point, now Niles, and worked a year for his cousin, John Miller, whose wife was a daughter of Elon Crain, Charles Crain's uncle. He had very little capital, but he had what was far better — a brave heart, a strong body, and willing hands. He immediately went to work chopping wood at sixteen dollars per month and his board. In the fall of 1841 with his savings of seventy dollars he went back to Indiana, but returned two years later with his brother Ozro.

CHARLES CRAIN

MRS. SARAH BURROUGHS
CRAIN

OZRO CRAIN HOME. LOG HOUSE CLAPBOARD-COVERED

Another important person in the building of Grosse Pointe was Samuel Reed, an Englishman, who came in 1840. He was public spirited, and seeing the needs of the little village, sought to lessen them. Frances Willard, in her *Classic Town* calls him "the almost immemorial pathfinder or roadmaster of this region." He took up Government land on the Ridge, near what is now Main Street, and built a log house. His cabin was surrounded by water nearly the whole year around and he often waded in water up to his knees looking for his cattle. Indeed, it was no uncommon thing for the cows to get mired and have to be pulled out by ropes or pried out by rails.

Mr. Reed's young sons used an old-fashioned baby cradle for a boat in which to go duck hunting. Mrs. Reed caught prairie chickens in a trap, sprung by a rope from her kitchen window, catching at one time twenty-one. This trap was a greater convenience than the telephone and delivery wagon of today. However, there were things to offset this good fortune. A wolf one day got into her barnyard and carried away a squealing porker, which was probably worth more than the twenty-one prairie chickens.

The Reed log cabin was a typical one of the pioneer days — loose board floor and roughly chinked crevices, through which the wind crept to make the housewife hasten to throw yet another log on the fire. Winter mornings, Mrs. Reed, after climbing the ladder to the loft where the children slept, often brushed the snow from their faces before waking them. An apple tree which this thrifty housewife planted bore its "thirty bushel quota" of choice fruit for over forty years.

The Burroughs family,[4] connected later with the Crains by marriage, was drawn to Grosse Pointe through a chain of interesting circumstances. The very interesting and absorbing tale goes as follows: Captain Sylvester Beckwith, married to Miss Lucinda Burroughs, could proudly boast that he had sailed the lake for fourteen years and had never had an accident. In the fall of 1841, while commanding the Brig Winslow, which carried lumber from Chicago to Milwaukee, he went ashore north of Winnetka, where lumber had been unloaded, to make final arrangements in regard to the cargo. In his absence, his first mate, Nelson Naper,[5] for reasons known only to himself, set sail without the captain. Captain Beckwith, discovering the ship gone, hired a team and started for Chicago. Meanwhile a severe storm had driven the ship ashore, opposite Hubbard's Hill. On reaching Hubbard's Hill, the Captain drove his team to the tavern of a Mrs. Patterson and stopped for the night. Here, to his surprise, he found his run-away crew, minus the first mate Naper, safe and sound, holding high carnival and merrily drinking the health of the absent captain. The captain, finding the ship undamaged, again started for Chicago, stopping for dinner at the home of George W. Huntoon on Green Bay Road; and so pleased was he with the surrounding country that he decided to give up sea-faring life and settle down as a farmer. He located on the North Branch of the Chicago River at a place called Dutchman's point, later called Niles. The following spring, 1842, his wife and her brother, Alonzo Burroughs, and sister, Sarah, came from Ashtabula, Ohio.

(4)   Mr. and Mrs. Sylvester Beckwith, Mr. and Mrs. David Warner Burroughs, and Mr. and Mrs. Alonzo Burroughs all lived to celebrate their fiftieth wedding anniversaries.
(5)   Naperville was named after Nelson Naper.

Mrs. Beckwith and her sister, Sarah, painted such a charming picture of the new country in their letters to their parents that their parents decided to come. They came the following year, 1843, with three younger children, from Ashtabula, by ox-team and cart, taking three weeks to make the trip.

The elder Burroughs, David Norton Burroughs, and family came first to Dutchman's Point, then later to Grosse Pointe where Mr. Burroughs rented a cabin on Green Bay Road on the southwest corner of Ridge Avenue and Greenleaf Street, near the present Crain Street. This cabin was occupied at the time by Eli Gaffield, whose house on land adjoining at the south was not quite completed.

The Burroughs family moved in with the Gaffields and the two families spent the winter together. There were fourteen in the cabin that winter, and a merry time they had. The cabin had three large rooms downstairs, but only one large unpartitioned room above, so improvised bed-rooms were made by stretching clotheslines, with bed blankets thrown over them for partitions.

The year 1843 saw Charles Crain returning. This time he had induced his brother Ozro to accompany him. The two brothers started from Hamilton, Steubin County, Indiana, on foot along a wagon trail and reached Dutchman's Point, south of Glenview, after four weary weeks of travel. Charles Crain soon came to Grosse Pointe where he learned the cooperage business of William Foster. Ozro hired out to Arunah Hill to learn the cooperage trade. After he returned from California in 1850 he took up farming.

There was no "Micawber" among these early settlers, "waiting for something to turn up." Samuel Reed,
ever with an eye to possibilities for betterment, did not
believe in the region suffering a want that could be supplied, and decided that a corduroy road was needed to
connect the east and the west ridges across the "dismal
swamp." Accordingly, he, with the assistance of the
Crain brothers, George W. Huntoon, and other early
settlers, built the first road over the low ground at Rose
Hill which crossed diagonally southeast from the west
ridge to the east ridge. These determined pathfinders
hauled logs, mostly whole trees roughly trimmed, and
made a "corduroy road" of them laid closely together.
At times even this log-way was under water. The next
crossing was four miles north of this, where the two old
Indian trails joined on the Ouilmette Reservation, north
of the site of Evanston lighthouse.

In the early days, those living on the two ridges in
Grosse Pointe might as well have been living miles apart
instead of only a few hundred feet, for the swamp between made it impossible to go from one ridge to the
other at certain times of the year. The people received
their mail at Dutchman's Point or at Chicago. Signals
were exchanged between the ridges, when a settler intended going to Chicago for mail or supplies. This man
usually went on horseback. On receiving such a signal,
some one from the other ridge would mount a horse and
meet the other man at Rose Hill, exchange the news of
the day, give such orders for supplies as his ridge people
needed, and return; while the other proceeded to Chicago to fulfill the orders and get the mail for both ridges,
to be met again on his return trip by a man at Rose

11

Hill, who received the mail and supplies for the other ridge.

Green Bay Road, in the early days was, at best, a difficult road to travel. It was made by cutting out trees to the width of two rods, and driving down stakes. The route led over many unfordable streams and over these, rough puncheon and logs were laid to complete the road.

HOME OF ELI GAFFIELD, THE BEST PIGEON-FISHER
IN TOWN

Eli Gaffield's home, which was under construction at the time the Burroughs moved to Grosse Pointe, was on land which lay west of Asbury Avenue and north of Greenleaf Street, where wild pigeons were numerous. Grosse Pointe lay in what might be called the pigeon belt,[6] or in the line of the passenger or wild pigeon's

(6)   The passenger or wild pigeons, so numerous over this region in the spring and fall, and extinct since 1878, migrated not in hundreds, but in thousands, as far south as South America and as far north as the Arctic Circle, and South Evanston lay along, or more probably at the edge of their route of flight.   John James Audubon says in his works that their favorite nesting places were in great forests, where there was not much underbrush.   Along the Green River in Kentucky

migration. Pigeon fishing was a popular sport, and Mr. Gaffield was called the best "pigeon fisher" in town, and

Courtesy of American Field

PASSENGER PIGEON

Natural size 15 inches. Color slate blue and black, with iridescent neck feathers

one nesting place was forty miles long and more than three miles wide, and here people would gather from over a hundred miles distant, awaiting the arrival of the pigeons, having driven their hogs to fatten on the birds. Audubon arrived one year two hours before sunset, the day the pigeons were expected to put in appearance, and long before a bird was in sight, the sun was entirely obscured. Finally they were sighted and there was great excitement. To quote him: "As the birds arrived and passed over me, I felt a current of air that surprised me. Thousands of birds were knocked down by the pole men (men standing on high ground switching back and forth long poles stuck in the ground, having sharp knives attached). The birds began to pour in, arriving by the thousands. They alighted everywhere, one above another until solid masses as large as hogsheads were formed. Here and there the perches gave way with a crash and falling to the ground destroyed hundreds of birds beneath, forcing down the dense groups with which every stick was loaded. It was a scene of uproar and confusion."

Alexander Wilson, another ornithologist, says the noise was so great as to terrify the horses, and it was difficult for one person to hear another speak unless he bawled in his ear. The extinction of these pigeons may have been due to the wholesale slaughter that went on. Wilson, in speaking of their flight, says: "They were flying with great steadfastness, close together, several strata deep and as far on right and left as eye could see. This was at one o'clock in the afternoon, and at four o'clock the living torrent seemed as numerous and extensive as ever." It is estimated they flew about a mile a minute.

it was claimed he never lost a bird. He used a net, three sides of which were fastened to the ground leaving space enough for the birds to run under. Grains of corn thrown under the net would attract the pigeons, and in two minutes the ground would be covered with them. A quick pull of the rope attached to the fourth side would imprison all under the net. T. C. Goudie of north Evanston could supply food for all of his town (six families) with one shot from his gun.

In 1843 John O'Leary and Edward Davlin located on the North East Quarter of Section 30, now the site of Calvary.

From 1844 to 1847 David Hood, John Beck, Peter Rinn, Peter Bletch, Henry Fortmann, Jacob Klein, Frank Schmidt, and Peter Monroe, settled along the Ridge. Other settlers were John Tillman, Henry Reinberg and Michael Breit.

The land west of the Ridge and as far south as Rose Hill was heavily timbered. This land was called the Big Woods. Further south of Rose Hill was prairie and the road running through there was often called Prairie Road. The logs cut from the trees of the Big Woods had to be made ready for hauling when the ground became frozen, as it was impossible to haul the logs over the marshy ground during other seasons. These logs were made into rafts, hauled to the lake, and navigated down to the mouth of the Chicago river by a tow line fastened to a yoke of oxen. Oak wood sold for seventy-five cents a cord.

After the land was cleared of the oak trees, the stumps were put in piles ten or fifteen feet high, covered with light stuff, hay or straw, then a top covering of dirt, with holes through to make a draft; fire was then set to the stumps. A pile would be two or three weeks burning. This was quite an industry in itself, as money was made from the selling of charcoal obtained in this way. The charcoal sold for five cents a bushel.

A man could pay his road tax by pulling up stumps at twenty-five cents per stump, be the stump large or small. One wonders whether any man sacrificed his early morning's sleep that he might pull out his allotted number of stumps among the small ones. This was true of other localities.

Wheat was scattered by hand and dragged in by harrow or bushy tree. The passenger pigeon would follow and pick up the grain as fast as deposited, and the men had to resort to shot guns to save their seed. They had boys go along to pick up and carry the pigeons away as fast as they were shot. The following lines were familiar, when the passenger pigeons were plentiful:

> When I can shoot my rifle clear
>   To pigeons in the sky,
> I'll bid farewell to pork and beans
>   And live on pigeon pie.

The Ozro Crain homestead, a log house covered with clap-boards, was built by Isaac Burroughs in 1845, on the west side of the Ridge and a little north of Greenleaf Street, where Crain owned eight acres between Maple and Asbury Avenues. The Crain brothers now carried on a cooperage business of their own, manufacturing barrels and casks in a log house on the Ridge, selling them in Chicago to Gage and Haynes, flour dealers, where they found a steady market. Ozro Crain later built on the northeast corner of Ridge Avenue and Crain Street.

The settlement was still sparsely settled, when it was decided that the children must no longer be without a place of learning, the true index to civilization, for many of the families were "from the rugged hills and rocky mountains of New England, where the chief agricultural productions were schoolhouses and men," and from the nearer states of Ohio and Indiana, which already had several decades of good schools to their credit.

About 1842, the log house used as the first school house in the south end of town was built. It was situated on the west side of Green Bay Road or Ridge Avenue, where Greenleaf Street crosses, on a lot which Henry Clarke deeded to the township for school and cemetery purposes, or, as he specified very quaintly, "for the quick and the dead." The school house was on the corner, and the burial ground to the west and north of it, between the present Greenleaf and Lee Streets. The sale of the burial lots paid for the ground, $150. Greenleaf was then a thirty-three foot lane, and later thirty-three feet more were taken from the cemetery to widen the street.

Pupils along Chicago Avenue and Hinman Avenue reached the school by horseback or by means of boats or rafts during the wet season.

The little log house served not only as a schoolhouse, but also as a meeting-house, where the circuit rider, as the visiting preacher was called, preached to the faithful ones, who faced storm and cold, or the summer's hottest rays to go to meeting. One time the services were enlivened and probably nearly broken up, when an Indian stalked boldly into the church in his dignified Indian manner, followed by two softly stepping squaws, and stretching himself on the floor before the open fireplace, calmly went to sleep.

At what better place could the young folk — yes, and the older ones, too — meet, than under the roof of this lowly log schoolhouse? It was here they met of winter evenings for spelling bees and singing school, when the very rafters rang with the sound of their lusty, young voices, and swains entered into friendly rivalry for the good graces of the most popular belle.

Mainly for the convenience of the children from the east ridge (Chicago Avenue) to get to school, a narrow bridge was built at Calvary on crotched sticks, from one ridge to the other, and over this precarious footpath went not only the children, but the older residents from both ridges, thankful that they did not have to pull their feet, one after the other, through the mud of the Dismal Swamp.

William Foster, a native of Ireland, built a log house on Ridge Avenue, near Grant Street, in 1846. He was a true son of Erin, with his genial disposition and love of fun. Uncle Billy Foster, as he was fondly called, was the life of many occasions, especially "raisings," as the building of cabins was called, which were turned into times of merry-making. The settler wishing to put up a cabin got together all the material needed — poles, logs, etc. — at a chosen site, and then would request the assistance of his neighbors, who gladly acceded to his request, having memories of other raisings, when Uncle Billy cracked his jokes and gales of laughter followed his witticisms, and all the while Uncle Billy was surreptitiously keeping an eye on each worker, to see that the work did not lag, in consequence of which Uncle Billy was very much in demand at every raising. There was the keeper of the demijohn, who did no other work than hand over the demijohn to the workers, that each one might take a long pull after every fourth log was put in place, a custom very much in practice in those days.

No less in importance to the building of the cabin was the digging of the well, but before the digging could be done, an expert must be secured to locate the place where the water could be found. The expert would walk over the ground with a forked branch from a peach tree held loosely in his hands, the prongs pointing upward. When he came over the place where water was nearest the surface the prongs of the branch would suddenly turn downward, and point to the ground. Here the settler would dig his well.

Though evening clothes, waxed floors and many pieced orchestras were missing, their lack was no drawback to the good times. Major Mulford's home was the scene of many a social gathering, and the Pratts threw open their doors with true pioneer hospitality, while the Burroughs' cabin held many a merry-making party, when youth and maid tripped the light fantastic toe to the merry strains of Dad Shippy's fiddle, which was sometimes accompanied by discordant howls of the wolves outside; and older members of the party "do-si-doed" and "balanced to their partners" or joined in the old-time waltz, "round and round and round," that would make the present day jazz dancers dizzy.

Many a romance had its birth in these gatherings. Sarah Burroughs, quick of wit and ready of tongue, just blooming into womanhood, attracted the notice of young

Charles Crain, and in 1846 he and his bride, the afore-
said Sarah, began housekeeping in the cabin her father
had rented when he arrived at Grosse Pointe. Charles
Crain, by assiduous work and honest labor, had prospered, and now the cabin at the present Crain Street and
Green Bay Road, with forty-four acres of land around
it, belonged to him, a typical pioneer, upright, generous
and kindly, esteemed by all who knew him. Ozro Crain
had already claimed for his bride, Olivia Hill, a daughter
of one of the first settlers, Arunah Hill, and had settled
on the west side of the ridge.

The first post office was established in 1846 in Major
Mulford's home, George M. Huntoon, son of George
Washington Huntoon, being appointed postmaster and
serving for two and a half years. The post office, during
the early years, was usually kept at the home of the postmaster, and thus several houses on Green Bay Road held
the post office at one time or another. At this time the
final e's were dropped from Grosse Pointe, making the
name Gross Point. The region hitherto known as Grosse
Pointe, recorded as Grosse Pointe Voting Precinct, had
its first post office established in 1846, which was given
the name of Gross Point Post Office. The Evanston Historical Society has in its possession a case with eighteen
pigeon holes, which was made and used by Postmaster
Huntoon. Each patron was allotted a box or pigeon hole,
which was numbered, in which was placed his mail, awaiting his call.

Isaac Burroughs, son of David Norton Burroughs,
was a carpenter and joiner, building many of the houses
on Green Bay Road. In 1848 he built a house for his
brother Warner, who in 1849 moved in, and gave the

BUCK-EYE HOTEL

SNYDER FARM-HOUSE

place the name of Buck-Eye Hotel, as several families as well as his own claimed Ohio for their native state. Isaac Burroughs built a house for himself across the street from the hotel. The original crescent-shaped sign, which hung from the old tavern, may be seen at the Evanston Historical rooms. Buck-Eye Tavern or Hotel was situated on the east side of Ridge Avenue, a well built frame building, two stories high, the rooms of which, though small, were well planned. Later its number on the Avenue was 2241. The building was moved to 1204 Noyes Street in 1916 and transformed into a modern house, and the occupant said the timber was still in such fine condition that the bark was too hard to allow a nail to be driven through it.

The post office was moved to Buck-Eye Tavern in 1848, and David Burroughs was appointed postmaster. He brought mail once a week from Chicago on horseback. In 1855, after the railroad went through, there were so many newcomers that mail service was increased to twice a week.

The next tavern to the north was Wigglesworth Tavern, at the southern limits of Ouilmette's Reservation. Coming from the south, the stage coach stopped at Brittons, where Graceland cemetery now is; the Seven Mile House, Baer's Tavern, at Rose Hill; the Ten Mile House of Mulford, where St. Francis Hospital stands; the Buck-Eye Tavern, belonging to Warner Burroughs; then further north at Wigglesworth's Tavern. These early taverns consisted usually of four rooms — one large room, which was the bar-room and dining room, two bedrooms for guests, and one bedroom for mine host and his family. If there were more guests than the two bedrooms could accommodate, the men were expected to sleep on the floor in the bar-room. Buck-Eye Tavern was frequented by a rough set — sailors, wood-choppers, hunters and Indians — all of whom were good customers for the "wet goods," great libations of red-eye and tangle foot decoctions which the tavern carried.

Up to this time there was no particular business district, but the houses between the taverns carried a stock of groceries needed by the settlers in the neighborhood, as well as a supply of "wet goods," for which there was a lively demand by those traveling to and from the north along Ridge Road. In reading of the sale of "wet goods" one must remember this place was Gross Point and not yet Evanston. In the winter, freezing to death was the common end to many who imbibed too freely and died from exposure while intoxicated.

Charles Wilson, Warner Burroughs' brother-in-law, an actor from Chicago, kept a notion and grocery store in a small building south of the Buck-Eye Hotel, but business was probably not very brisk for he stayed but a short time, selling out to Warner Burroughs and returning to the theater. Later, the building he occupied was moved to the rear of the Buck-Eye Hotel.

Many Indians, growing homesick for their old home, returned and wandered around, and holding their blankets over their heads to exclude the light, they would peer into the windows of the cabins, much to the discomfort of the housewife and terror of the children; or they would stalk into the cabins, without the ceremony of knocking, and squat before the fire place, waiting for refreshments to be given them. They were peaceable and would go away without trouble as soon as they received food. They were fond of chickens, and many young fries gladdened the stomachs of the red men, as the housewife was very careful to refuse them nothing they desired, even though her family went without on some occasions.

The flare from the burning logs in the open fire place usually furnished the necessary light in the evening. If that light were not sufficient, oil or grease was put in a dish or saucer, with a strip of cloth leading into it, and the lighted free end drew up the oil and gave out a yellowish, flickering light.

Candles were used and candle making was one of the various tasks of the housewife. The best candles were made in molds. The candle wicks were first soaked in lime water and salt petre, dried, and hung in the mold; and over them was poured suet or mutton tallow, which had been previously melted with white wax, alum and camphor. After the candles had been left overnight to harden, the molds were slightly heated to loosen the candles, which were then taken out and packed in a box.

Dipped candles were made by throwing the wicks over rods and twisting them, the wicks having first been dipped in lime water and vinegar and dried. The tallow, with the proper proportion of wax and alum, was melted in a kettle and kept flush with the top of the kettle by the addition of hot water as fast as the mixture was used. The sticks were dipped again and again, until the proper thickness of the candle was reached.

Cheap lights were made by dipping rushes in tallow. The children were told they might stay up until the candle burned to a certain mark. Candle screens, as well as fire screens, were used.

Matches had been invented not a great while before this period and were still very much of a luxury, and very sparingly used, folded paper or rolled tapers being used to economize on them.

There were no starch factories in those days and the women manufactured their own starch by soaking unground wheat in soft water for several days, then rubbing off the husks with the hands, allowing the soft part to settle, and changing the water every day. If the water was clear, after the mixture was stirred and the wheat allowed to settle, it could be poured off and the starch left in the bottom of the kettle, dried, and put away for use.

Calicoes were dipped in beef's gall to keep the colors bright, and were stiffened with glue, instead of starch. Beef's gall was used also in washing of woolens.

Though the pioneer woman might have help, these homely duties were taken care of under her eye.

The wells and cisterns were in the yards. The cisterns were large receptacles, like immense wooden tubs. They received their supply of water through pipes leading from troughs on the roofs, which caught the rain water falling on the house.

The pumps were carefully wrapped in blankets during freezing weather, and the handles lifted. To start the water flowing, it was sometimes necessary to prime the pump — pour water in the top of it and work the pump-handle.

Shoes were rubbed with India rubber melted in oil, to render them waterproof, or rubbed with grease.

The making of lye (written ley), soft and white soap, were also duties of the housewife.

With all her numerous tasks the housewife found time to cultivate flowers, and the yards, without exception, were gay with such flowers as sweet alyssum, candytuft, ice-plant, verbena, heart's-ease (pansy), love-in-a-mist, primrose, phlox, coxcomb, larkspur,· aster, petunia, marigold, zinnia, morning glory, columbine, bleeding-heart, sweet william, prince's feather, fox-glove, mignonette, pinks and the much prized tuberose. The pioneers were early risers, and the sun would not be very high in the heavens, before the housewife donned her sun-bonnet, collected her garden implements and started for her flower garden. Four cents would buy a bag of flower seeds sufficient to supply many families.[7]

Kitchen walls, cellars and fences were frequently whitewashed.

Study gowns were used by men of studious habits in the evening. These were long straight robes, similar to the lounging robes of today.

Blocks of wood and carpet-covered bricks were used behind doors to preserve the wall from being injured. Stools and ottomans were covered with carpet to match that of the room, in which they were used. Catherine E. Beecher (Henry Ward Beecher's sister), in her domestic economy book, gives this advice: "Sweep the carpets as seldom as possible, as it wears them out. Shaking is good economy."

Mattresses of hair were expensive and those made of husks dried and drawn into shreds were commonly used; others were made of alternate layers of cotton and moss.

Feather-beds were much in favor, but were laid aside during the mild weather and straw ticks substituted.

(7)   The half cent was still in use, its coinage being discontinued in 1857.

Where the bedroom space was limited, the children slept in trundle or truckle beds, which could be shoved under the big beds when not in use.

Instead of springs, the beds had slats placed crosswise, about four inches apart. Previous to the time of this custom, woven rope was used to support the mattress. The rope was placed around pegs, which ran all around the inside of the bed frame. When the rope began to sag, as rope will, it was a real trick to tighten it. A man walked back and forth on the rope, pulling the rope that his weight had loosened and drawing it tight at the final row. It is said many a bumped shin and skinned nose was the result of this necessary rope walking. All "bedsteads" were made of wood.

The wishbone of a fowl was called the "merry thought" or "merry bone."

Sewing machines were a luxury in the late forties, not being invented until 1846, and but few women were fortunate enough to possess one. The sewing was done by hand on material spun at home and woven on a hand loom by the persevering pioneer woman. Some of Mrs. Judith Burroughs' work may be seen at the Evanston Historical rooms.

The dense woods at the present site of Calvary Cemetery attracted great flocks of wild pigeons in their flight in spring and fall. Raccoons were fond of the ripening corn on the stalk, feasting on it until a dog would discover them, and drive them into the trees, where they would be brought down by the shot gun. In the fall, wild ducks infested the swamp and were bagged in great numbers. The weasel and mink burrowed under the chicken houses, sometimes killing whole flocks in a

night. Now and then a fox was caught in a trap intended
for other game. The skunk went on his way in his deliberate and self-possessed manner. Once an eagle was
winged while he was flying low over a barnyard. The
chicken hawks were numerous, each flying round in his
ever lowering circle, then swooping down on his unsuspecting victim to carry it screeching away in his claws
into the woods to devour at his leisure. The snipe was
a familiar sight flying along the shore of the lake. The
woods, swamps, sand ridges and hills along the lake
proved a real "Mecca" for the early settler with sporting instincts. Muskrats frequented the route along Judson Avenue, where many were trapped by Leander Crain.
Yellow perch were plentiful in the lake, and Ozro Crain
was a familiar figure going home with his catch.

To the east of the Ridge the swamp blossomed with
water lilies in the proper season, and a little later in the
year the cat-tails and reed grew thick. The bull frogs
broke the quiet of the early spring and summer nights
with incessant croaking, almost drowning the hoot of
the owl or the call of the whippoorwill, and causing the
low land west of the Ridge to be given the name of Frog-
town.

The early settlers planted fruit trees, peach trees
predominating, which flourished and bore rich harvests
until the forests, extending to the North Branch of the
Chicago river, were destroyed. This brought climatic
changes which spelled the doom of the peach harvests,
and made it almost impossible to grow peach trees on
the west side of Lake Michigan.

Hazel brush and red raspberries were very plentiful
between the ridges, and west of the Ridge there was an

abundance of blue berries and huckleberries, which drew wagon-loads of people from Chicago to gather them. There were nearly always gypsy camps in the woods and in University grove. Mrs. Crain said she would as soon meet an Indian as a gypsy. The Indians were peaceful and quiet and usually went about their own business.

The first blacksmith shop was on the corner of Ridge Avenue and Noyes Street, owned by a Mr. Fox, who sold out in the fifties to a Mr. John Anderson.

Mrs. Charles Crain's memoirs are a source of both interesting and fruitful information. Many of the incidents she tells are worth repeating.

The usual picnic place was the site of the present University Grove, a beautiful spot. After a picnic dinner, the men played ball or pitched quoits. The ladies played "Grace Hoop." In this game, each lady must toss, with two sticks, a hoop, which is about a foot in diameter, to another lady, who in turn tosses it on to the next, and so on. The object is not to touch the hoop with the hands, nor let it drop to the ground.

Leander Crain, captain of a schooner that sailed the lake, was a great and interesting story-teller, and after each trip his friends and acquaintances gathered around him to hear the latest tale that was sure to prove interesting. On one of his return trips, Joe Butterfield, a sailor, who lived in Gross Point, was swept overboard by a sudden sweep of the boom, which had escaped control of the man at the rudder, who was also handling the halyards. The schooner at the time was rushing through waters at a race-horse speed in pitch darkness during a terrific storm. The captain, knowing it would be impossible to find the man in the raging waters, threw a number of planks overboard in the hope that he would be fortunate enough to grasp one. However, he felt that Butterfield's situation was hopeless, and when the schooner landed, the unfortunate man's effects were auctioned off to the sailors, according to custom, and the loss of a man was reported. What was the captain's surprise several days later to meet Butterfield in Chicago on the street! The accident happened five or six miles from shore, and by good fortune, Butterfield got hold of one of the planks and drifted toward land, holding on till daylight, when some Indians caught sight of him and went out in their birchbark canoe and brought him to shore.

The North Branch of the Chicago river was deep enough to float saw-logs down from a short distance further north to a saw-mill owned by John Miller and his father-in-law, Elon Crain, and situated a mile south of the present site of the Glen View Golf grounds. The river held many fish, which were caught by spear, instead of hook and line. The men fished at night, their lantern light attracting the fish, which were then easily caught. The old saw-mill was torn down about 1850.

On the east side of the river, through the woods, were large mounds in the shape of graves, differing only in that the ends were round instead of square; the centers were about three feet high, and trenches were dug around them. These mounds were thought to be Indian graves, but no one had the temerity to investigate.

The only dentist in the country in the early forties was a Mr. Munn, who used to pull teeth with what were called "cant hooks." Mrs. Crain says, "It was enough to scare you to death to look at the instruments. I was there once and that was enough for me." One obliging dentist in Chicago who had a barber shop, pulled teeth, one for fifteen cents, two for twenty-five cents, and talked of weather instead of giving gas.

Warner Burroughs, brother of Mrs. Crain, for two years ran a general store in the wing of the Buck-Eye Tavern building, which was probably the first store in the neighborhood. After these two years' experience as a merchant, he laughingly told his sister Elmina that if he could find anyone with twenty-five cents, that person could have the store. She immediately produced the quarter and took possession of the store. She gave up the store at the end of a year when she was married to Dr. Palmer. Lorenzo Burroughs was the first man ever called from Evanston, or rather Gross Point, to serve on a Chicago jury.

Mrs. Crain's mother, Mrs. David Burroughs, was an expert wool weaver, and specimens of her work may be seen at the Evanston Historical rooms.

In April, 1850, Ridgeville Township was organized and the name of the post office changed to Ridgeville.

The year of 1849 was one of the most important in the history of the 19th century. The newspapers all over the country were aglow with accounts of men seeking their fortunes in the new Eldorado—California. Ozro Crain was one of those smitten with the gold fever and began the journey across the plains that took two and one-half months.

He returned to Gross Point with such enthusiastic reports that the following year a party of thirty men, his neighbors and friends, decided to make the trip, and their wagon train was called "Lightening Express" as it passed almost everything on the way, although it took over four months to make the journey. The party started from Buck-Eye Tavern on the morning of April 8, 1850, and there was a wagon to each four men and a horse to each man. Their wives were called California widows, after the departure of the men, and as some of the men were claimed by death, a few became real widows. The women carried on the work of the farm, cheered by letters from the absent ones. Some of the men accumulated fortunes, while others lost everything they had, either through misfortune or by theft.

Keen was the disappointment of Ozro Crain, who, on returning to the gold fields, found his claim "jumped" and that it was proving rich. Benjamin Emmerson saw the result of his three years' labor in California to the amount of $3,000 taken by thieves on his way home. He immediately turned back and at the end of one year he had accumulated $2,000, which he was able to bring home without mishap.

So many rough characters were attracted to the gold fields that a Vigilance Committee was organized, and after this wise move there was "a semblance of law and order." McDaniel, writing to his wife under date of June 6, 1851, from Greenhorn Canyon, said that people conducted themselves more like heathens and brutes than like civilized people from the States. He had laid in his winter supply and gave a few prices prevailing at the time:

Flour	$28.00 per 100 lbs.
Molasses	4.00 per gal.
Pork	54.00 per bbl.
Coffee	.75 per lb.

Potatoes . . . .   .25 per lb.
Tea . . . .   3.00 per lb.
Beans . . . .   .42 per lb.
Fresh beef . . . .   .25 per lb. (when they could get it)
Sugar . . . .   .32 per lb.
Butter . . . .   1.00 per lb.

McDaniel was fairly successful in his adventure, and was able to clear up some indebtedness on his farm and buy more land on his return. His gold amounted to about $2,700. He worked a claim which he called Gross Point Gulch. He was very methodical and kept a diary, giving interesting details of life in the "Golden West," as well as an account of his journey thither over the plains.

This is his report for one week:

"Monday I took out $6.25.

Tuesday, wet and rainy, did nothing.

Wednesday, helped hunt all day for a young man from Milwaukee, who was sick and had strayed from his cabin in the night. Did not find him.

Thursday, I made $49.00.

Friday, $17.00.

Saturday, I sunk a hole 12 feet deep and took out the whole sum of fifty cents."

McDaniel said he was as hearty and tough as a grizzly bear, and had not been sick one minute. A copy of this diary is preserved at the historical department in Evanston.

Crain made a third trip, in which he was quite successful in his labors. Ozro and Charles Crain were with McDaniel at Gross Point Gulch. The population of

Gross Point Gulch was about two hundred inhabitants, consisting of gamblers, blacklegs, thieves, preachers, and miners, the gamblers being the most numerous. Thousand of men who went to the gold fields did not make enough to pay their board.

Of the thirty men who started from Gross Point to California in 1850, Mrs. Crain remembered the following: four Crain brothers, Ervin Crain, from Indiana, Leander Crain, Ozro Crain, Charles Crain, Orson Crain, a cousin, Alonzo Burroughs, Sylvester Beckwith, Alexander McDaniel, Andrew Robinson, Eli Gaffield, John O'Leary, Henry Hazzard, Fox, Gillison, Wm. Foster, John Foster, his son, Bowman, Fluent, Sawyer, Miller, Benjamin Hill, Benjamin Emmerson. Hartwell Pratt, son of George, was also one of the party.

Charles Crain was the first of the party to return home. He arrived with $1,600, quite a fortune in those days. He, with fourteen others, left San Francisco for home the first part of February and reached home about seven weeks later, March 20, 1851.

"LOOK FORWARD"

Later there came men of vision
    Along the Ridge—'twas then Green Bay—
Evans, Lunt and Brown and others;
    A place they sought—a site where they
Might erect a place of learning
    For the youth. Off toward the west
High the forest's great trees towered—
    A fitting place to end their quest.

Lunt, gazing through a vista eastward,
    Saw the waters shining bright;
Nearby, stately oak trees swaying,
    Bending, beckoning from their height—
Inviting his consideration.
    'Twas an answer to his prayer!
He cried, "Eureka! I have found it!"
    No other site could be so fair!

They built not themselves to profit,
    They who gave and gave again.
Their motto was, "Look forward" always,
    And homage great is due these men.

Ah, rich the heritage they've left us,
    To look for light past clouds, through tears;
In clarion tones has come their message,
    Theirs, *theirs*—"Look forward" through the years.

CHAPTER IX

THE BIRTH OF NORTHWESTERN UNIVERSITY [1]

THE year of 1850 saw the dawn of a new era. A portion of the Township of Ridgeville, already sparsely settled, became the chrysalis from which Evanston developed and in time spread its beautiful wings to the north and west and south, one of the finest cities educationally and one of the best by government on the map, the pride of its citizens and the admiration of its neighbors. The idea of a great university, the nucleus of a great city, a university with its university environment, was conceived and fostered in the minds of a few men.

The idea realized would prove of value not only to the community, but to the whole of the Northwest Territory, the territory at that time being Iowa, Wisconsin, Illinois, Michigan and Northern Indiana. These men felt that a place was needed where the youth could be taught something of the sciences and humanities, get a higher education than was possible within a reasonable distance. There was nothing of the kind near Chicago, which, with a population of 28,000 could boast of nothing more than common schools, no high school, as yet, having been established. John Evans, Orrington Lunt and Grant Goodrich, at the head of a small group of men, visualized a great university, around which would spring a community of desirable citizens; a university in what they

---

(1)   The corporation was known as "Trustees of the Northwestern University" until 1866, when it was changed to its present name Northwestern University.

ORRINGTON LUNT

considered "the center of influence in the Northwest," one under the patronage and government of the Methodist Episcopal Church. Their plan was to have not a number of higher institutions of learning, but a single place, where the Methodist people could concentrate their efforts.

To gain this end a meeting was held May 31, 1850, in the office of Grant Goodrich, a young lawyer. His office was situated in the very heart of the business district of Chicago, on Lake Street between Clark and Dearborn Streets, over the hardware store of Jabez K. Botsford. In 1850, there were but three Methodist churches in Chicago, and these three churches were represented at the meeting by their respective pastors, namely, the Reverend Richard Haney, Clark Street church, the foremost preacher in Rock River Conference, a man of commanding presence and great persuasive powers; the Reverend R. K. Blanchard of Canal Street church, and the Reverend Zadok Hall of Indiana Street church. Besides these men, there were present Grant Goodrich, keen, combative, persistent; John Evans, a dreamer of great dreams, with ability and force of character to make them come true; Orrington Lunt, he of sweet and sunny temper, quaint humor and tender heart, but with a quick, strong mind and fearless mien, that made him an ideal public spirited and patriotic citizen; Andrew J. Brown, who had been elected Probate Judge before his twenty-first birthday; Jabez K. Botsford, quiet, unassuming, but one who knew his own mind and always voted the right way; Henry W. Clark, shrewd attorney, with an appraising eye to the future. They were a goodly lot—these men—three ministers, three attorneys, one physician and two merchants, not one of whom had reached the forty year mark, but were, nevertheless, well qualified to bring to a successful issue the great plan proposed; men with faith in their undertaking and faith in the future, men who built not for to-day, but for tomorrow. None of these was a college graduate, excepting Dr. Evans, who had graduated from the medical department of Cincinnati College.

Orrington Lunt called the meeting to order. A prayer was offered by the Reverend Zadok Hall, asking for guidance in this great venture. Grant Goodrich was made chairman and Andrew J. Brown secretary. Mr. Goodrich had drawn up a set of resolutions, and after the purpose of the meeting was explained, these resolutions were offered and unanimously adopted.

The resolutions read as follows:

"WHEREAS, The interests of sanctified learning require the immediate establishment of a university in the Northwest, under the patronage of the Methodist Episcopal Church:

"RESOLVED, That a committee of five be appointed to prepare a draft of a charter to incorporate a literary university, to be located at Chicago, to be under the control and patronage of the Methodist Episcopal Church, to be submitted to the next General Assembly of the State of Illinois.

"RESOLVED, That said committee memorialize the Rock River, Wisconsin, Michigan and North Indiana conferences of the Methodist Episcopal Church, to mutually take part in the government and patronage of said university.

"RESOLVED, That a committee of three be appointed

to ascertain what amount can be obtained for the erection and endowment of said institution.''

Dr. Evans then took the floor and spoke with the force and conviction of a great orator. He saw a great future in the undertaking, visioned the inevitable growth of Chicago and the increase in land values. The gist of his speech was, let men sacrifice something now, and the coming peoples would pay tribute to their devotion and sagacity.

Two committees were appointed, the committee on the charter being John Evans, Andrew J. Brown, E. G. Meek, A. S. Sherman and Grant Goodrich. The other committee was to work for the co-operation of the Northwest conferences and its members were Reverend R. Haney, Reverend R. H. Blatchford and Dr. John Evans. These committees were to report two weeks from that day. Promptly at three o'clock on that day, the men gathered at the appointed place, the rear of the parsonage of the First Church on Clark Street, and Dr. Evans reported for his committee, the draft of the charter, drawn up by Grant Goodrich, which for completeness of detail and comprehensiveness of meaning could scarcely be surpassed.

The Trustees of the university named in the charter were as follows: A. S. Sherman, Grant Goodrich, Andrew J. Brown, John Evans, Orrington Lunt, J. K. Botsford, Joseph Kettlestrings, George F. Foster, Eri Reynolds, John M. Arnold, Absalom Funk and E. B. Kingsley.

Representatives from the various Methodist Episcopal conferences of the Northwest named in the charter were Richard Haney, Philo Judson, S. E. Keyes, A. E. Phelps, Henry Summers, Elihu Springer, David Brooks,

Elmore Yocum, W. H. Reed, I. I. Stewart, E. M. Smith, George M. Teas. The Michigan, Northern Indiana and Illinois conferences were named, but no names of their representatives given.

The term of office of the Trustees was to be four years. However, the length of the first term of each member of the Board was to be fixed by lot at the first meeting. Thereafter, by this arrangement, the terms of different groups, three members to the group, expired annually, giving the Board perpetual succession.

Each conference had the right to appoint annually two suitable persons, members of its own body, to visit the university and to attend the examinations of students. These persons were entitled to participate in the deliberations of the Board of Trustees, and to enjoy all the privileges of members of the Board, but they were not to have the right to vote.

The university was to be situated in or near Chicago. A student of any religious faith could be admitted.

The corporation was not to hold land to exceed 2,000 acres at any one time, unless it was a gift, grant or devise, in which case the corporation was to sell, or dispose of the same within ten years. Upon failure to do so, such lands over and above 2,000 acres were to revert to the original donor, grantor, devisor or their heirs.

Sections 6 and 7 deal with the appointment of president or principal and the necessary instructors, and the establishing of departments for the study of any and all the learned and liberal professions, and the conferring of degrees.

Section 8 covers the examinations of applicants for degrees.

The charter became a law by Act of Legislature January 28, 1851, chiefly through the efforts of Grant Goodrich. The Act was signed by Sidney Breese, Speaker of the House, and Lieutenant-Governor Wm. McMurtry, President of the Senate, and it received the approval of Governor C. A. French.

The instructors were to be appointed for their qualifications and not with regard to their religious views.

One of the charter members, Eri Reynolds, having died, Dr. N. S. Davis was elected in his place at the next meeting, January 14, 1851. At this meeting, a Preparatory School was contemplated and a Committee on Site was appointed, which, at the meeting of August 4, 1852, recommended the purchase of property with eighty foot frontage on Washington Street in Chicago, for this school. Although a bid of $4,800 was made on the property, it was not accepted and Dr. Evans and Mr. Lunt were appointed to look further. (About six years later, this property was bought by Mr. Lunt and Dr. Evans for $32,000.)

Another desirable piece of property, which belonged to P. F. W. Peck, was purchased. This lot was about 200 feet square and was situated at the corner of La Salle and Jackson Streets in Chicago. The price was $8,000, $1,000 down. Here the Trustees showed their loyalty to the good cause by subscribing among them the $1,000. This proved a good investment, as the property in a little over fifty years brought an annual rental of $79,000.

At the meeting in September, 1852, the erection of a building on the lot for the Preparatory School was authorized; the school was to be spacious enough to take

care of 300 pupils. A committee was appointed to recom-
mend a site for a collegiate department. S. P. Keyes,
N. S. Davis and Orrington Lunt comprised the committee.
Although a site along the lake was desired by the executive committee, several locations came under consideration. The only lake shore site available not too far from
the city was at Winnetka but the price was prohibitive.
Rose Hill was recommended by Hon. W. B. Ogden. This
place was just north of the site of what is now Rose Hill
Cemetery and was known as Rose's Ridge. The same
objection as to price was found in regard to this place.

A farm near Jefferson was considered, and the day
was approaching to vote for the college site. Orrington
Lunt could not give up the idea of a lake shore site, but
he could not conscientiously vote against the Jefferson
site, as the lake shore property was held at a figure too
high to consider. One day he drove north with a friend,
and while the friend was engaged with his business, Mr.
Lunt wandered toward the lake, through the wet land,
over bogs[2] and planks. To the south he saw that the
land was wet and swampy, but looking north he saw
large oak trees, and the thought struck him that there
the high and dry land began. It was too near night to
make a closer inspection and he decided he would not
vote to accept the options for Jefferson until the committee should make another trip north. To quote him,
"I began to think this might be the place we were seeking. It continued in my dreams all night and I could not
rid myself of the fairy visions constantly pressing themselves upon my thoughts,—fanciful, beauteous pictures of

---

(2)   Bog is here used in the New England sense of the word.   Probably Mr.
Lunt always used this term, being a Maine man.   It is employed in several histories
in speaking of his walk that day.

the gentle, waving lake, its pebbly shore and its beautiful bluffs.'' On the following morning, a pleasant August day, the trustees in several vehicles drove over the old Sand Road, took lunch at Rose's Ridge Tavern, came along Ridge Road to the place Clark Street crosses, followed an old cow path in an easterly direction over the slough in the region of Davis Street and Sherman Avenue and drove into what is now the campus, whereon stood the fine oak grove skirting the lake shore, a place as beautiful then as now, and so delighted were the Trustees that some of them threw up their hats and shouted, ''This is the place!''

The owner of the tract of land, 379 acres, which the Trustees now decided to purchase, if possible, was Dr. J. H. Foster. They found he was not anxious, nor even desirous of selling. The land, according to the doctor's own statement, was not worth more than $15 or $20 per acre, and when pressed to make a price and terms, he set the price high, $25,000, about $70 per acre, probably thinking the high price would discourage the would-be purchasers, but they agreed to his price and terms, $1,000 down and the balance in ten years at 6%. Mr. Lunt said when he called on Dr. Foster to tell him of their acceptance of his terms, the doctor's face fell, showing he was not really pleased with the transaction.

It was then decided not to build a Preparatory School in the city of Chicago at that time. The ground purchased for this school became later the site of the Grand Pacific Hotel, and still later that of the Illinois Trust and Savings Bank, yielding a princely annual income.

The next step was to elect a president of the institution, whose duty it would be in the beginning to solicit subscriptions. A young man thirty-six years old, Dr. Clark Titus Hinman, of the Michigan Conference, a graduate of Wesleyan University, Connecticut, and former principal of Newbury Seminary in Vermont, was chosen.

CHAPTER X

THE NEW UNIVERSITY

MONEY was needed to carry through the enterprise undertaken. Dr. Clark Titus Hinman was elected first president, and his work, before the University opened, was to be the raising of subscriptions and the selling of scholarships.

The Trustees of the University voted to raise $200,-000 by the sale of scholarships. Dr. Hinman, in his enthu.iasm for the undertaking, mentally made the figure $500,000 and set his goal to that end. With this figure in view, he started zealously to work to sell scholarships for the new university, and so successful was he that within a year he had sold to the amount of $64,000 and others working under him had sold to the amount of $37,000.

Perpetual scholarships were issued, which sold for $100 each. These entitled the purchaser, or his heirs, to tuition forever, but in time these proved impractical, as the terms were too liberal.

Transferable scholarships sold for $100, entitling the holder to $500 in tuition.

Scholarships that sold for $50 entitled the holder to $250 in tuition.

One-half of the funds was to go toward tuition and the other half toward the purchase of lands, which were not to exceed 1,200 acres, for the site of the University and erection of buildings.

Dr. Hinman, ardent worker and eloquent speaker, went from place to place in his task of selling scholarships. At Janesville, Wisconsin, where his work had taken him, in such glowing terms did he speak of the future university and of the new town, that Frances Willard—then a young lady—and her father, who was with her in the audience, then and there decided to come to the university town to live.

In 1854, the year before the opening of the doors of the University, where he had been engaged to teach Moral and Intellectual Philosophy, Dr. Hinman died, and the office was not again filled by a regular president for nearly two years.

A piece of land, comprising 248 acres, lying just west of the Foster tract was bought by the Trustees of the University from Harvey B. Hurd and Andrew J. Brown. The ground owned by the Trustees was now laid out in lots and blocks and given the name of Evanston, after John Evans, one of the founders of the University. Margaret Evans, wife of John Evans and sister to Mrs. Orrington Lunt, suggested the final syllable, making the name Evanston, instead of Evansville or Evanstown.

Orrington Lunt, Vice-President of the Board of Trustees of the University, had been asked to allow his name to be given to the new town. He it was who had made the first donation toward the University. It was his tenacity in holding out for a site along the lake shore for the University that had resulted in the town's ideal location, and the honor was none too great to confer on him. However, he modestly declined. His home was pleasantly situated in Chicago, where he had settled in 1842. The lake he loved so well washed almost to his doorstep, and he preferred to make no change in his residence.

Dr. Evans, President of the Board of Trustees, wished the new town to carry Bishop Simpson's name. Dr. Evans had become interested in religion through Bishop Simpson and had been persuaded by him to come to Chicago, that being a broader field for his work. Bishop Simpson felt that the new town should have Dr. Evans' name and so urged it.

Dr. Evans had already given generously to the University, but with characteristic liberality he made further donations and decided to make his home in the new town. His home was located in the block between University Place and Clark Street, on Hinman Avenue.

The Trustees bought up yet more land—the Billings farm, comprising 28 acres. Land values were increasing, both in Evanston and in Chicago. The new town looked well on paper and was beginning to take shape in reality. Arrangements were made to beautify the place by six public parks. The University ground was to occupy the exact "latitudinal center" of the town.

The increase in the value of their holdings gave great encouragement to the Trustees. In two years the value of the Peck property in Chicago rose from $8,000, the purchase price, to $42,500; the Foster tract from $25,000, the purchase price, (its real value was about one-quarter of that amount at the time of purchase) to $102,000; the Billings farm from $3,000 to $4,200. The outlook was now favorable for the opening of the school.

In June, 1853, a small corps of professors was elected, Henry S. Noyes, instructor in Mathematics, W. D. Godman, instructor in Greek, and Abel Stevens,

DR. CLARK TITUS HINMAN

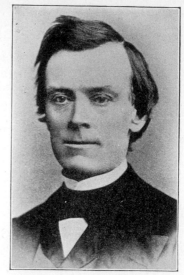

PROFESSOR HENRY S. NOYES

GRANT GOODRICH

THE REV. PHILO JUDSON

instructor in Literature. In such high regard did the
Trustees hold the merits of these men that they say, "To
speak of their qualifications is superfluous." However,
they did say of Abel Stevens that he "stands beside the
finest writers of the age." And it so happened that he
was the only one of the three that never taught in the
University!

Hurd and Brown donated the right of way for the
railroad and also ground for the station. In 1854, the
Chicago and Milwaukee Railroad began carrying passengers to and through the growing town, the little ten-
ton, wood-burning engine belching forth great volumes of
grey smoke. The streets were undergoing grading, being
put in usable condition. In the fall and winter months,
the residents whose business took them to the city, each
day carried their lanterns to and from the station, to
help them pick their way over the muddy streets and
across lots before daylight in the mornings and after
dark in the evenings, as there could be no choice of trains,
which were few and far between. The lanterns stood in
a row during the day on the station platform, and were
reclaimed at night.

Schooners and other vessels were discharging lumber, or taking their way past the college town to its larger
sister settlement, Chicago, now a full-fledged city.

At the meeting of June, 1855, the liberality of the
Board of Trustees showed itself in the donation of a
large lot for Evanston public schools.

That month saw, too, the laying of the corner stone
for the first building of the University.

The Trustees were happy in the knowledge that
their five years of hoping, praying, working were at last

bearing fruit. The idea conceived in their brains five years previous, in May, 1850, had its material beginning in the building that was erected on the southeast corner of Block 20, on Davis Street, near Hinman Avenue—Old College—the first on the campus, and, it follows, the first in the hearts of the alumni of those early years. This building, albeit a modest one in the eyes of later students,

OLD COLLEGE

was, no doubt, quite a pretentious one in the eyes of those most interested at the time. It was fifty feet by forty feet, three stories high, with an attic and a belfry. This first college building held a chapel, a museum, six class rooms, and halls for two literary societies. The Trustees hoped that aspiring students would wish to use the three rooms in the attic, exchanging their work of ringing the college bell for their lodging. Five years passed before a second building was erected on the University grounds.

Reverend Philo Judson was business agent of the University and did the laying out and platting of the lots. These lots were to be sold one-fifth down and the balance in five years.

The streets began to take on names familiar in sound, names of friends of the new town, friends who with labor and love and money gave the place an impetus toward big things and a big future: Sherman, Lunt, Hinman and Judson. Other names suggested the religious leaning, such as Asbury and Wesley. Nevertheless, it must be remembered that the professors for the University were chosen absolutely without regard to their denominational training and wholly with regard to their character and qualifications. Students were to be admitted under the same conditions.

No president had, as yet, been elected to fill the place of Dr. Hinman, nor did the Trustees elect another president until June following Dr. Hinman's death when Professor Noyes become "Acting President." He was not eligible to the office of president, as he was not a clergyman, a requirement in those days.

Henry S. Noyes was born in Landaff, New Hampshire. He graduated from Wesleyan University at Middletown, Connecticut. At the time Clark Hinman urged him to come west, he was principal of the Newbury (Vermont) Academy. Professor Noyes turned his back on the brilliant future the east evidently held for him and accepted a place in the young University as instructor of Mathematics.

Professor Noyes arrived several months before the date set for the University to open its doors and at once took up the task of collecting money due on the scholarships promised Dr. Hinman. Day after day he traveled around on horseback, or in an open buggy, over muddy country roads, in pursuance of his duties. How unpleasant his self-appointed task became is shown by the fact that when the faculty and friends of the University met for a joyful occasion, his speech consisted of half a page recited from Homer. It is not difficult to picture him sitting quietly among his associates, listening to tale after tale of happy, successful endings to tasks others had undertaken; keenly appreciative of all that went on; then, when called upon for a speech, rising almost reluctantly to respond.

Far be it from him to put a damper on the meeting; not for him was it to tell the whys and wherefores of non-payment of money due, or of disheartening postponements he had met—rather not speak of his work at all—and so he recited Homer, whose words he had at his tongue's end. But the words of Homer fell on deaf ears. Suddenly his associates knew—knew better than if he had told them in so many words, and their hearts went out to him in kindly understanding and loving sympathy.

Circulars were sent out, inviting the students to assemble November, 1855, as the building would be completed by that time. November 5, 1855, the University was opened without pomp or ceremony, beyond a single prayer, with the ever dependable Orrington Lunt and John Evans present. Only four students appeared. These, with the two professors, Noyes and Godman,

Philo Judson,[1] the business agent of the University, and a few townsmen completed the number in attendance.

Professor Noyes had hoped to have more time to devote to his favorite subject, mathematics, in the new University, than he had had at the Vermont Academy, but in this he was to be disappointed, as his days were filled with his various duties.

Professor Godman, too, gave much time to collecting money and selling scholarships, but he had the advantage over Professor Noyes in being a clergyman and therefore he could appear before the Methodist conferences.

There were ten students enrolled the first year, nine of whom were as follows: Thomas E. Annis, Winchester E. Clifford, Samuel L. Eastman, J. Marshall Godman, Horace A. Goodrich, C. F. Stafford, Hart L. Stewart, Albert Lamb, Elhanon Q. Searle, all from or near Evanston.

The requirements for entrance were to be the same as those for Harvard, Yale, Wesleyan and other similar first-class institutions of learning, but—to Northwestern's everlasting glory be it said—with the added requirement of United States History.

There were plans for fourteen professorships. Some young men whom the Trustees had in mind were to travel

(1) Philo Judson learned the trade of hatter in New York State. He followed this trade but a few years. After uniting with the Methodist Episcopal church and joining the Rock River Conference, he received the appointment of Savannah Mission, a circuit of 240 miles, over which he traveled horseback, and his study for the ministry was said to have been made upon his horse on the Western prairies. He was elected business agent for Northwestern University in 1852 to raise funds for the building of that institution and also for Garrett. In 1853 he came to Evanston to reside, at first being secretary, financial agent and treasurer for the University; later trustee and vice-president, filling the latter office up to the time of his death in 1876.

He surveyed the Northwestern grounds and platted the Village of Evanston.

and study a year or more in Europe before taking up their work, that they might increase their efficiency. Meanwhile the two professors comprised the faculty, and it was well that each had a broad general education, as the first years they had to instruct the students in Greek, Latin, Mathematics and Literature. The students profited by the classes being small, in that they received individual attention.

The rules were simple, but strict. If a student expected to be absent from town, he must secure a permit beforehand. Attendance at Sunday services was compulsory.

Tuition, where a scholarship was lacking, was $45 per year. Board was $2.50 to $3.50 per week in the homes of residents.

The college bell announced recitation hours and devotional services.

The students wore a uniform cap, and the professors wore the Prince Albert coat and tall silk hat.

Dr. Hinman, bright and shining light, had literally gone down under the duties he had assigned himself. In loving memory the students organized a literary society and named it for him. ''The Hinman Literary Society'' inherited his library, and held its meetings in the northeast corner of the third story of the college building.

The University was at last a reality, the dream of Evans, Lunt, Goodrich, Brown, Botsford, Clark and the three goodly churchmen, Hall, Blanchard and Haney, come true!—a great undertaking still in its swaddling-clothes, to be nurtured and watched over carefully, that its growth might be steady and its feet be kept on solid ground.

CHAPTER XI

SUCCEEDING YEARS OF THE UNIVERSITY

THE Anti-Liquor Limit was established February 14, 1855, by an amendment to the University's Charter, signed by the Speaker of the House and President of the Senate, and approved by Governor Joel A. Mattison. Its Section II created a prohibition district within the four-mile limit, protecting both the students and the citizens, and making Evanston a prohibition city.

In view of the fact that Northwestern University was an institution of public value, Section IV ordained, "That all property, of whatever kind or description, belonging to and owned by said corporation, shall be forever free from taxation for any and all purposes." The exemption from taxes has been the subject of controversy many times, but the question was legally settled by decision of the United States Supreme Court. The University pays all street improvements — sewers, water mains, and sidewalks.

One June day in 1856, the Trustees met in their own building, which had been recently completed. One can almost see that little group of men, with their self-congratulatory smiles, as they clasped hands in greeting. It had been a long and tedious climb, but they had trodden each step of the way with sure and steady feet, upward and onward toward their goal. More than one important milestone had been passed: the charter had been granted in 1851; the site for the University had been decided upon and bought, in 1853; the University had opened November, 1855; during the first year two professors had been teaching at salaries of $1,500 per annum; a business agent had been busy selling lots and scholarships; the Drainage Committee had been formed, (1855), and soon the land would be reclaimed and made habitable for the incoming citizens—the land that now held only swamp grasses and croaking frogs. Reason enough for the Trustees to be proud and happy, congratulating themselves on the success of their tremendous undertaking!

At this meeting Dr. Randolph S. Foster was elected second president. There was but one dissenting vote and this was cast in favor of Dr. E. Otis Haven. Dr. Foster's salary was to be $2,000 a year. Daniel Bonbright was elected to fill the chair of Latin Language and Literature, but was to be allowed a year's absence in Europe before taking up the work.

Dr. Foster was a diligent student, having the power to master any subject he attacked. Miss Willard says he not only took up the subject of geology at a time when it was considered antagonistic to Christianity, but he delivered many sermons and lectures on it from his pulpit—always to crowded houses. This was true also of astronomy and evolution. He was not, however, an evolutionist in the modern sense of the word. Dr. Foster was considered one of the greatest orators in the Methodist pulpit, and was described as "pre-eminently a preacher," "a natural leader," "a living flame," "a consuming fire." With his great gift of eloquence and power of persuasion, he was at the same time singularly simple-hearted, enjoying games with his children, even helping them compose verses for their valentines.

PROFESSOR
WILLIAM P. JONES

NORTHWESTERN FEMALE COLLEGE

According to Miss Willard, no teacher was more beloved. In 1873, Dr. Foster was elected bishop of the Methodist Episcopal Church.

At this time, 1856, it was decided to invite Rush Medical College, still in its infancy, and Garrett Biblical Institute to unite with Northwestern University. Rush Medical College preferred to continue as it was, and the charter of Garrett Biblical Institute and Mrs. Garrett's will prohibited that institute joining with another.

In 1854, Professor William P. Jones made plans to open the Northwestern Female College and Male Preparatory School, for which he had secured a charter, in buildings to be erected on the west side of Chicago Avenue, between Greenwood Boulevard and Lake Street. He asked the Trustees for space in their building, until such time as his would be ready for occupancy. In this he was refused, as the Trustees were not pleased with the idea of another school opening in their neighborhood.

There is probably no more interesting personage of those early days than zealous Professor Jones, a young man barely twenty-two, but far ahead of the times. At that time, 1854, it was the general opinion that seminaries and academies — finishing schools — answered all the requirements of young ladies, women not being considered capable of grasping the "intricacies of higher education."

In *The Story of Northwestern University*, Miss Ward tells us that on a trip through the east to study educational methods, William Jones and his brother met Matthew Vassar, who urged them to locate their school in the east, and drove them over ground where later were built the Vassar College buildings. They met Henry

Towle Durant, a wealthy young lawyer of Boston, who became attracted to the idea of a college for women as outlined by the Jones brothers, and later used his great wealth to found Wellesley College.

The young professor had the support of his family in his undertaking. One brother devoted all of his earnings in the gold fields to the project. His father and the four brothers dug the cellar and built the foundation walls of his building. Its corner stone was laid the same day the corner stone of Old College was laid, June 15, 1855, and Bishop Simpson conducted both services.

Professor Jones used a room over Colvin's store as a classroom, until his building was completed. His only assistant was Mary E. Hayes, a Mount Holyoke graduate, whom he married within a few years. His pupils numbered eighty-three. The preparatory department for boys became popular among the younger set of men preparing themselves for college. Tuition was low, which was a big item in the school's favor. Within a year, on one of the coldest days of a cold winter, the building burned and Professor Jones injured his health permanently in trying to save his property. Northwestern University, having overcome its ill feeling toward the young professor, generously threw open its doors and allowed his classes to use some of its rooms. There was no insurance on the building, but the Jones family again showed its loyalty, and rebuilt the college, having it ready for the opening term in the fall.

The Willard sisters, Frances and Mary, Mary Bannister—later Mrs. Oliver Willard—and Katheryn Kidder were among the early students of the Northwestern Female College—"The Nunnery of St. Jones," as it was

FRANCES AND MARY WILLARD

THE WILLARD HOME, NOW REST COTTAGE

called by Northwestern students. Professor Jones one morning found this name painted on crescent shaped boards over several entrances to the grounds.

The first printed sheet in Evanston was published by Professor Jones' students, *The Casket and Budget,* dated December, 1858.

The Northwestern Female College flourished for sixteen years. It was then merged into Evanston College for Ladies, with Frances E. Willard president.

In July, 1856, Dr. Foster urged the Trustees to consider erecting appropriate permanent buildings for the University, but the matter of permanent buildings rested for ten years; then subscriptions were raised for University Hall, which was completed in 1870.

The Northwestern University catalogue of 1856 speaks of its Museum of Natural History as being, perhaps, the best in the west, the specimens having been labeled by a scientist under the auspices of the Smithsonian Institution, and exchanges were made with that institution. The collection for the museum was begun by Robert Kennicott, and was housed in the fourth story of University Hall.

In a circular issued during the summer of 1857 three classes were promised by the University for the following year and a fourth class, if students applied who were far enough advanced.

In 1857, Dr. Bonbright was given permission to remain a second year in Europe and Dr. W. S. Blaney was added to the teaching force for Natural Science.

The University started educationally on the very highest plane, but the building of its home site began with pioneer work, as its record of expenses shows such

OLIVER MARCY.

DANIEL BONBRIGHT.

JULIUS F. KELLOGG.

JOSEPH CUMMINGS.

HENRY S. CARHART.

HERBERT F. FISK.

JANE M. BANCROFT.

ROBERT L. CUMNOCK.

CHARLES W. PEARSON.

ROBERT BAIRD.

DANIEL BONBRIGHT   OLIVER MARCY   JULIUS F. KELLOGG
HENRY S. CARHART   JOSEPH CUMMINGS   HERBERT F. FISK
ROBERT L. CUMNOCK   JANE M. BANCROFT   CHARLES W. PEARSON
                    ROBERT BAIRD

items as ditching, chopping, fencing, surveying, grading, platting, clearing streets, bridging, draining, grubbing, and building breakwaters.

Eighty-five home sites were sold at prices from five dollars to ten dollars per foot during the year of 1857, most of them adjoining the University grounds.

A preparatory school was established this year, occupying part of the University building. The preparatory students and the University students continued to use the same building until 1873, when the University students moved into other quarters. For nine years the two departments were under the same faculty, when a change was made. However, Professor Kistler, who had charge of the preparatory department, continued teaching in the University for the next two years, at which time the preparatory work was turned over to Acting President, Dr. D. H. Wheeler. In 1891, there were nearly seven hundred pupils in the preparatory department, in Old College building.

In 1857, the University assets exceeded its liabilities by more than $315,000, and its financial agent, Philo Judson, was jubilant over this condition.

The first graduating class made ready to leave its Alma Mater in June, 1859. The University now had twenty-nine students in attendance. Those who proudly delivered their graduating orations and received their various degrees were Thomas E. Annis, Winchester E. Clifford, Samuel L. Eastman and Elhanon Q. Searles, receiving the degree of Bachelor of Arts, and Henry M. Kidder, the degree of Bachelor of Philosophy.

Philo Judson, who had done such good work as the University's financial agent, now resigned, and the

beloved and overworked, but willing Professor Noyes
who was appointed business agent to succeed Judson,
cheerfully added this work to his other duties. He had
been taking care of the financial affairs of the University,
which were connected with college expenses, tuition, etc.,
and he now assumed the property management and other
business of the institution, not sparing himself in any
service he could render to the object of his affections.

In 1860, Dr. Foster resigned and Dr. E. O. Haven
was elected to fill the chair, but refused it to go elsewhere.
Professor Noyes was elected vice-president and served
for nine years as Acting President. Dr. Godman, instructor in Greek, resigned, and Professor Noyes offered his
tired shoulders for yet another burden. Professor Noyes
was at this time Professor of Mathematics, Acting President, Secretary of the Board of Trustees, and Financial
Agent, so it was voted to give him $600 more per year
than the other professors, in consideration of his extra
work in teaching Greek.

The students had but few occasions to use spending
money, so the parents were asked "to place funds to be
used for pocket money in the hands of the faculty," thus
avoiding temptations that might come the students' way.

When the war broke out in 1861, the ranks of both
professors and students were reduced. Dr. J. V. Z.
Blaney resigned the Chair of Natural Science to enlist,
and many students followed his example, among them
Plympton, McCasky, Spencer, Haney, H. A. Pearsons,
O. C. Foster, Charles F. Smith and M. C. Springer.
There were but two left in the senior class, and very
soon there was but one remaining. The recruiting officer
had an easy task in Evanston, after a rallying meeting

in the white frame Methodist Episcopal Church that stood on the ground of the present library.

Doctors Dempster and Bannister were called upon to help fill out the teaching force. In 1862, Oliver Marcy was elected Professor of Natural Science, to take Dr. Blaney's place.

The first experiment in the way of a dormitory was a building erected on Orrington Avenue, near Clark Street, which accommodated about twenty students.

In 1863, the mortgagee, Dr. Foster, from whom the 379 acres of land were bought in 1853 for the site of the University, received the final payment on this property.

Chicago's liquor league was determined to break down the four-mile limit and many suits were brought and fines inflicted. Finally it was decided to take a case to the Supreme Court. In this case James Mulligan took the side of the liquor league against John L. Beveridge, who represented the University. After these men went to war, Harvey B. Hurd argued the case in the Supreme Court. His antagonist was so intoxicated that Mr. Hurd had to present both sides of the case to the Court. The Court's decision was in favor of the University. However, the question was to come up again.

The Reverend Louis Kistler was made principal of the Preparatory Department in 1865, and occupied temporarily the Chair of Greek, which was later filled by Robert Baird.

In 1865, Orrington Lunt donated a tract of land adjoining Wilmette for library endowment. The University valiantly set out to meet certain obligations that this endowment entailed. The Trustees turned their attention to more buildings on the campus, and went about making

UNIVERSITY HALL

plans to raise subscriptions to accomplish the building
of University Hall, which was to be the first permanent
building of the group. The subscriptions to this building amounted to $48,000 in 1866. The Trustees were
doubtful, however, as to the wisdom of completing the
building until there were sufficient funds in hand. Harvey
B. Hurd proposed that the building be completed before
halting the work, and his proposition carried. This was
a wise plan, as the report of Professor Noyes proved.
In this report, he says that the erection of the building
greatly inspired public confidence and had a marked
influence in raising the price of the University property.
University Hall, completed in 1870, is of Athens stone.
It was designed by G. P. Randall, one of Chicago's
leading architects. Mr. Randall claimed to be the first
architect to use the dished floors and semicircular
arrangement of seats in churches. The University of
Chicago adopted a style of architecture similar to that
of University Hall. Evanstonians sometimes referred to
this building as a Poem in Stone. The clock in the tower
was the gift of the class of 1879; the bell, the gift of the
class of 1880.

In 1866, a stimulus was given to the college work
by various prizes offered—the Lunt Prize in Philology;
Haskin Prize in Mathematics; Hurd Prize in Physical
Science; Kedzie Prize in Declamation; Hamilton Prize
in Composition and Reading.

This year, 1866, the corporate name of the University
was changed from *Trustees of the Northwestern University* to *Northwestern University.*

The Snyder farm, south of Dempster Street and
running from Chicago Avenue to the lake, was bought

and subdivided into lots. The sales and leases on this property, made by that indefagitable worker and keen business agent, Professor Noyes, earned a profit of more than $15,000 over the original investment in less than two years, and there were still lots unsold which were valued at more than $74,000. This property proved itself to be one of the choicest that the University owned.

Professor Noyes at last succumbed to the weight of his many tasks. He had dropped part of his work in 1869, and resigned the secretaryship in 1870. He had been Acting President for many years, and was succeeded at his death, in 1872, by Professor D. H. Wheeler, as Acting President. We, who have never known him, cannot but feel a bit of a heartache in reading of his passing. We span the intervening half century or more, and see him sitting behind his sorrel horse, driving through muddy roads and over unpaved streets, at all hours and in all weathers, trying to collect money due on scholarships; we hear him recite a bit of Homer, in order to spare his colleagues a tale of distress and disappointment; we see him take on his frail shoulders burden after burden that others have laid down. Ah, the name of Noyes Street is not his only memorial! The great University, in its wholesome wholeness of today stands a glorious monument to him, as well as to other blazers of the way for the University, during the latter half of the nineteenth century!

About 1868, the Chicago Medical College, at Prairie Avenue and 26th Street, became a part of the University.

In 1870, Dr. Erastus O. Haven, President for six years of the University of Michigan, was elected President of Northwestern University at a salary of $4,500.

He was a graduate of Wesleyan University. He had been Principal of Amenia Seminary, New York; Professor of Latin at Michigan University and later of English Language, Literature and History, a member of Massachusetts State Senate, and Overseer of Harvard University.

The accumulated volumes of twenty years at last found a home in the north end of the third floor of University Hall, and twenty thousand books were added to these from the Greenleaf Library, donated by Luther L. Greenleaf, a friend of the University, and one of its trustees.

Dr. Haven held the presidency for two years, then resigned, to answer a call of the General Conference, and Dr. C. H. Fowler, a graduate of Garrett, succeeded him in 1872.

Professor Robert McLean Cumnock, A.M., L.H.D., became connected with Northwestern University in 1868 as Doctor of the School of Oratory. He was born in Ayr, Scotland, and graduated from Wesleyan University at Middletown, Connecticut, in 1868. Frances Willard says she was a pupil of this accomplished artist in 1872, "when to help our Women's College, he taught its president as a free-will offering on the shrine of improved English and ameliorated manner."

The Evanston College for Ladies had its beginning September 24, 1868, at the home of Mrs. Mary F. Haskin, where a number of women met who believed in higher education for women. These women formed the Women's Educational Association, with fifteen members on the board of managers. Mrs. Haskin was elected president; Mrs. J. K. Huse, vice president; Mrs. Elizabeth M.

Greenleaf, treasurer; Mrs. Harriet N. Noyes, recording secretary; Miss Cornelia Lunt, corresponding secretary. The board was organized under a charter the following April (1869). The Village Board of Trustees donated a tract of land. Until the building for the college was ready for occupation, the board leased the old North-western Female College building. The alumnae of the Northwestern Female College were made the senior alumnae of the new institution. Professor Jones sur-rendered his charter to the President of the Board, Mrs. Haskin. Frances E. Willard was made President of the Faculty. Ground was broken for the building June 3, 1871. This was a gala occasion, with religious and Masonic ceremonies. The corner stone of the new build-ing, Woman's Hall, was laid July 4, 1871. Ten thousand people came to University Grove from nearby towns and the surrounding country. Excursion boats ran out from Chicago. This day was probably the first field day in Evanston. There were such athletic sports as jumps, ball-throwing, tub races, boat races on the lake, and the baseball game between Northwestern University and the Evanston College for Ladies, which resulted in a score of 57 to 4 in favor of Northwestern. Baseball, the national game, began to be indulged in about this time. On this day $10,000 was raised for the University and of this amount Governor Evans of Colorado Territory gave $2,500.

There was no catalogue issued 1871-1872. In 1873, the Evanston College for Ladies was merged into North-western University, remaining the Evanston College for Ladies. Miss Willard was made Dean of the new organi-zation. The following is quoted from Northwestern University catalogue of 1873: "The Evanston College for Ladies is recommended to young women who wish to avail themselves of the advantages of the University. The students are provided with comfortable rooms and boarding in the college."

Courtesy of National Woman's Christian Temperance Union

FRANCES E. WILLARD
Dean of Woman's College,
Northwestern University

Dr. Haven had accepted the presidency of Northwestern University only on condition that women should be admitted to the University on equal footing with the men.

The name *Fem Sem* was bestowed on Woman's Hall by Northwestern students, and the name was not frowned down by the girl students. For many years this name clung to the building, much to the disgust of various members of the faculty. In 1895, the editors of the Syllabus were asked to refrain from using the objectionable term in the book that year, to which they agreed, but a jingle "A-HEM," written by Walter Dill Scott of the class of 1895, and published in the Syllabus, shows how close they came to the danger line.

The name of Woman's Hall was changed to *Willard Hall* in 1900, in honor of Frances Willard, and the name *Fem Sem* became only a memory on the campus.

Dr. Fowler in starting new movements, especially the merging of the Evanston College for Ladies with the University, had brought new financial burdens. The budget of 1878 showed a discouraging outlook, but the next year, with a new Ways and Means Committee, there was a better showing.

Then came another menace. From the first, there had been more or less ill feeling in regard to the University's tax exemption. In Chamberlain's *Chicago and Its Suburbs,* published in 1874, is the following: "The question of their exemption will probably soon be decided. On the instance of Mr. James Root, County Attorney, the property was assessed this year. Legal measures are, if necessary, to be resorted to, to enforce the assessment." Two years later the climax was reached when the assessor listed the property for taxation. Backed by their chartered rights, the Trustees stood firm for tax exemption, and the case went to court. The University lost in both the Lower Court of the State, and the State Supreme Court. The case was carried to Washington with Grant Goodrich, Wirt Dexter, and Senator M. H.

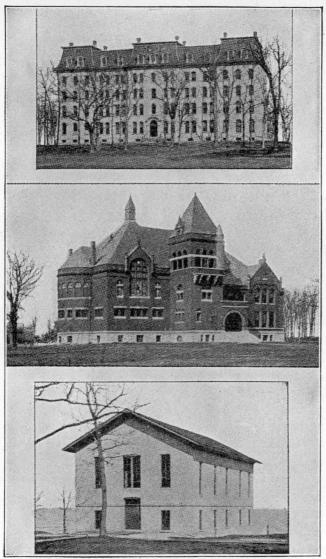

HECK HALL   MEMORIAL HALL

FIRST GYMNASIUM BUILDING

Carpenter as attorneys for the University, and the decision was made in favor of the University, which meant exemption from taxation forever.

The second dormitory for men was built on Cook Street, the result of Dr. Robert Hatfield's labors. This dormitory housed thirty men.

There was an early attempt at gymnasium work on the campus. Melville C. Spaulding, of the class of 1860, solicited ten cents each from the students, and with the six dollars collected created the first gymnasium. This consisted of uprights, parallels, bars, etc., in the northwestern corner of the college lot, the site now occupied by the Orrington Lunt Library.

In 1876, a stock company of students built a much-needed gymnasium, forty feet by eighty feet, with a bowling alley in the basement, and a room above for exercises. This gymnasium building was the result of efforts of two undergraduates, Frank M. Elliott and W. G. Evans, son of John Evans. Most of the stock in the building was bought by undergraduates in shares of ten dollars each. By 1878, the building was greatly in need of repairs and it was decided to transfer the majority of the stock to the Trustees. In 1881, under Dr. Cummings, the newly elected president, the place was put in good repair, the outside of the building receiving a veneer of brick. The woodwork on the interior casing was done by students and faculty members, including the good president himself, Dr. Cummings. The *College Journal* in 1883 said, ''We now have one of the finest and most complete gymnasiums in the West.'' Prizes were offered for various gymnastic efforts. On October 15, 1892, a movement was started by George Muir, who owned a bookstore on Davis Street, to raise a building fund. The $2,500 grandstand on the new athletic field north of the site of the Patten gymnasium was the result. Dr. Sheppard furnished lumber for an enclosing fence and the undergraduates did the work under the supervision of a boss carpenter. The field was named Sheppard Field, in honor of this very generous friend of athletic sports.

The old Rugby game of football began to be played on the campus in the fall of 1878.

In 1865 the name of Nicholas Cawthorne is mentioned in the catalogue of the Northwestern Female College as being in charge of the music. He was succeeded by Oscar Mayo, a professor highly recommended, coming from the Ohio Wesleyan Female College. Professor Mayo's assistant was Count Laurent de Fosso, who taught not only music but French, Spanish and Italian. There were from sixty to seventy students of music.

Mr. Mayo continued in charge of the music department when the Northwestern Female College became the Evanston College for Ladies, in 1871. The third story of Woman's Hall was devoted entirely to art and music, with Professor Mayo still at the head of the music department. The first mention of Professor Mayo in Northwestern University catalogue is in 1873.

In 1876, Professor Oren E. Locke succeeded Professor Mayo, continuing in charge eight years. At the end of Professor Locke's first year, there were enrolled two hundred thirty-one students. In 1891, Professor Locke resigned. At this time, the school had such poor attendance that discontinuing the Conservatory of Music

15

was seriously considered. By advice of Miss Cornelia (Nina) Lunt, it was decided to continue the classes in music in the University, and at her suggestion, Peter Christian Lutkin was placed in charge. Eighty-nine pupils attended during Mr. Lutkin's first year, and the name was changed from Conservatory of Music to Department of Music. The second year saw an increase in the number of students to one hundred twenty-eight. In 1896, the official title of the school was again changed, this time to School of Music.

Professor Lutkin was appointed Dean, and the other members of the faculty ranked as instructors.

The Department of Music occupied three rooms of Woman's Hall on the main floor and six rooms in the basement.

Ground was broken for Music Hall in 1896. The building was finished and dedicated April, 1897.

Dr. Marcy, who had been elected Acting President June 22, 1876, resigned from the University in 1881, after clearing off $200,000 of the school's indebtedness, Governor John Evans helping, and William Deering, that ever faithful friend of the University, bearing the lion's share. Others agreed to help lighten the burden, under the persuasive powers of Dr. Cummings and Dr. Hatfield.

The Illinois School of Pharmacy became the property of the University, and thereafter was known as the Northwestern School of Pharmacy.

Dr. Joseph Cummings succeeded Dr. Marcy as president, and filled the chair for almost ten years. At his death in 1890, Dr. Henry Wade Rogers was elected president.

In 1892, the American College of Dental Surgery was combined with the Northwestern Dental School. The Women's Medical College, on Lincoln Street in Chicago, was also purchased.

The Orrington Lunt Library was erected and named in honor of its principal benefactor. This is one of the finest buildings on the campus, and is pure classic in style of architecture.

The Annie May Swift Hall was chiefly the gift of Gustavus F. Swift, in honor of his daughter who died during her college career. The building is devoted to elocution and oratory, and dramatic arts in general.

Science Hall grew out of a pressing need for proper facilities for laboratory work in chemistry and physics. A liberal friend made a donation of $45,000 to the University for this purpose and the building was begun in 1886. Each of the two departments was equipped with a lecture room, apparatus room and professor's room, a laboratory for physics and two for chemistry, besides workshop and storeroom and smaller rooms for special work. In a few years each of the departments had outgrown its quarters.

A bequest of $100,000 came to the University from Daniel Fayerweather, a leather merchant of Brooklyn, N. Y., who had made benefactions to many colleges. This bequest was brought about through the efforts of Dr. Robert Hatfield.

Fisk Hall was built by William Deering, and named for Dr. Herbert Franklin Fisk, President of Northwestern University Academy.

Many improvements were made on the campus by William Deering, such as fencing in the campus, building gateways, and enlarging Woman's Hall. He also made a donation of $200,000 worth of securities and later $50,000 for charity work in the Methodist Church, and donated property worth $100,000 for future endowment. Other donations came from this generous man—$5,000 at one time and $25,000 at another.

In 1889, the new observatory on the north campus of the University received the telescope and other astronomical apparatus. When the University of Chicago met with loss by foreclosure of its mortgage, the Astronomical Society moved the telescope to Evanston and remounted it in the new building, which was a gift from the University and from Honorable James B. Hobbs. Professor George W. Hough became Director of Dearborn Observatory. The building was constructed under his supervision.

In 1899, Dr. Rogers resigned and Dr. Bonbright, who had been connected with the University since 1858, became Acting President. Dr. Bonbright at his death in 1912 had been connected with the University over fifty-four years.

The splendid buildings on the McKinlock campus had not been thought of, when the new century was ushered in.

CHAPTER XII

GARRETT BIBLICAL INSTITUTE

GARRETT Biblical Institute had its beginning in
1854. The idea of such an institution had its inception in the minds of the same men who founded Northwestern University. These men were going forward with plans for a school of theology, when Eliza Garrett by her will provided for the endowment of one. At that time, of the fifty-four institutions of like character, there were but two west of the State of Ohio.

Eliza Clark was born near Newburg, N. Y., in 1805. She was married to Augustus Garrett in 1825. In 1834 Mr. and Mrs. Garrett came to Chicago to reside. At that time Chicago held but 400 inhabitants. Augustus Garrett was an auctioneer, with rooms at the corner of Dearborn and South Water Streets. He was said to be "a musical man, full of wit and curious pranks." His auctioneering business netted him a good income and in time he became fairly well off, one of the prominent men of Chicago and one of its early mayors (1843-1846).

At a great religious revival in 1839, both Mr. and Mrs. Garrett were converted and received into the First Methodist Church of Chicago. Eliza Garrett, a devout and earnest Christian, decided after the death of her husband in 1848, to use her fortune, $150,000, for religious purposes, and upon consulting Grant Goodrich, one of the founders of Northwestern University, she was advised that her money could be put to no better use than the founding of a School of Theology. In December, 1853, she made her will, bequeathing the larger part of her property—real estate in the business section of Chicago—to found the school that later received the name of Garrett Biblical Institute. Mrs. Garrett arranged that her will was to be put into execution at once, so that the

MRS. ELIZA GARRETT

school could be started without awaiting her death. She reserved but a small sum, $400 per annum for herself. Less than two years after this date she passed away, on November 23, 1855.

The Reverend John Dempster,[1] son of a Scotch

(1)   Dr. Dempster was born in 1794, and died in 1863.

missionary who was sent to America by John Wesley, was invited by those who represented Mrs. Garrett to co-operate with them in carrying out her plans. Dr. Dempster had had experience in this line. In 1845 he began the work of the first theological seminary of the Methodist Episcopal Church at Newburg, Vermont, where Clark T. Hinman was one of the professors. This seminary was transferred in 1847 to Concord, New Hampshire, and ultimately became the School of Theology of Boston University. Dr. Dempster had been a circuit preacher in the wilds of Canada, a popular New York preacher, a pastor in several other important churches, a presiding elder and a missionary to Buenos Aires, before he came west to found a School of Theology and accepted the invitation to co-operate with Mrs. Garrett's representatives.

In February, 1854, the Trustees of Northwestern University offered a site at a nominal rent for the Garrett Biblical Institute. The offer of the site was accepted and the institution was established at the northern extremity of the ground platted for the campus, beyond the ditch called by students "The Rubicon."

The institute was organized with five directors, Grant Goodrich, Orrington Lunt, John Evans, John Clark and Philo Judson, who were to act as trustees until a charter for a permanent institution should be obtained.

In January, 1855, the first building, later known as Dempster Hall, was dedicated. Chicago friends drove out in sleighs and Mrs. Garrett herself was present. The date of the charter is February 15, 1855, and the incorporators were the same as the directors, with the

DEMPSTER HALL

THE REVEREND JOHN DEMPSTER

exception of Stephen P. Keyes, who was put in the place of John Clark.

The first term opened September 22, 1856, with an enrollment of four students and ended with sixteen. Among the first professors elected were the Reverends William Goodfellow and Wesley P. Wright.

At the first meeting of the board, June, 1855, Judge Grant Goodrich was elected president and Orrington Lunt secretary and treasurer. Judge Goodrich served thirty-five years and was succeeded at his death by William Deering. Orrington Lunt served until his death in 1897.

Dr. Dempster was made Professor of Systematic Theology; Daniel P. Kidder taught Practical Theology; Dr. Henry Bannister, Greek, Hebrew and Sacred Literature. Reverend John K. Johnson was principal of the Preparatory Department. Reverend Obadiah Huse was appointed House Governor of the school building.

Tuition was free and the students roomed in the attic of Dempster[2] Hall or exchanged labor for their keep with the townspeople, by whom each student was treated as one of the family and given the use of the library.

The College of Liberal Arts gave free tuition to the theological students.

Among the names of the trustees, besides those already given are many familiar ones: John V. Farwell, William Deering, the Reverends Charles Fowler, and Robert D. Sheppard; and among the faculty, the Reverends Francis D. Hemenway, Miner Raymond and William X. Ninde, who was president from 1879 to 1884,

---

(2)   Dempster Hall burned to the ground in 1876.

when he was succeeded by the Reverend Henry B. Ridgaway.

The property of Mrs. Garrett was mostly unproductive when it was turned over to the trustees, but their skill in handling it, putting as much as possible under rents, brought good results. In 1860 the Wigwam was erected where Lincoln was nominated, and rented for a nominal sum. This building was converted into business tenements. These were burned in 1867. The row of brick buildings that was later put up on this ground was swept away by the fire in 1871.

To help pay its share of the church's contribution to suffering Chicago, after the fire of 1871, the Institute erected, in 1872, a larger building for rental purposes. This did not prove a success as the panic of 1873 lowered the rents and made many of the lessees bankrupt, so the trustees, becoming alarmed at the financial condition of the Institute, decided to make an appeal to the church. The members of the faculty generously contributed one-fourth of their salaries, which helped a little. Dr. W. C. Dandy was chosen at the Rock River Conference to make an effort to arouse interest in the needs of the Institute. In this, he was very successful.

The gift of $30,000 for the endowment of the Chair of Practical Theology was received from Mrs. Cornelia A. Miller of Joliet, Illinois. Other gifts were received at this time. Dr. Dandy not only succeeded in bringing about financial relief, but awakened an interest "in the ministerial education in the church at large."

In the early nineties Garrett Biblical Institute announced to the church that all of its indebtedness had been paid. This was the result of Dr. Dandy's intelligent and persistent labors and the sale of some riparian rights.

In 1866, the centennial year of American Methodism, Heck Hall,[3] a commodious dormitory, was begun, being completed in 1867, at a cost of $60,000. It was named in honor of Barbara Heck, called the Mother of Methodism in America. Dr. James S. Smart was made financial agent, and he was ably assisted in raising money for the new building by the Ladies' Centenary Association, of which Mrs. Hamline (wife of Bishop Hamline) was president and Frances E. Willard was secretary.

The year the Methodist Episcopal Church saw its hundredth anniversary, in 1884, the idea of Memorial Hall originated. Three of the professors pledged themselves to the amount of $800. The Reverend E. H. Gammon generously pledged $5,000 and this pledge was followed by one by William Deering for a like amount. The trustees then promised $6,000 or one-fifth of the cost, provided the cost did not exceed $30,000. With these subscriptions pledged, the contract for the building was let. Drawings were submitted by Professor Charles F. Bradley and plans were worked out from them by W. W. Boynton, of Chicago. The ground was broken for the building by Judge Grant Goodrich, President of the Board of Trustees, May 13, 1885. The building, 60 feet by 115 feet, is of red pressed brick on grey limestone foundation, with trimmings of buff Bedford stone and red terra cotta. The entrance on the south is east of the base of a tall tower, in the open belfry of which is

---

(3)   Edgar O. Blake, in Hurd's *History of Evanston*, says: "The so-called Victorian Gothic style was now making its appearance, and examples may be seen in Heck Hall, built on the campus in 1867 and Willard Hall built in 1871, with their mansard roofs and other characteristic details."
Heck Hall was destroyed by fire in 1914.

space for a bell or chime of bells. Frances Willard says of its peculiar architecture that it might be called Romanesque.

Memorial Hall[4] contains large lecture rooms, a library, a reading room, a chapel, and offices for the president and professors. Rich memorial windows of exquisite coloring commemorate Dr. Dempster, Dr. Bannister, Dr. Hathaway, Bishop Simpson, Bishop Wiley, the Reverend Hooper Crews, the Reverend A. G. Button, the Reverend S. G. Lathrop, Judge Goodrich and Robert F. Queal. These windows were donated by the Alumni, the First Methodist Church of Evanston, the Cincinnati and Rock River Conference, Mrs. A. G. Button, H. N. Higinbotham, and William H. Craig.

From Chicago north as far as thirty-five miles and west twelve miles, there was no church with a regular minister and throughout these localities the students from Garrett trudged through mud and storms to preach to a congregated few. Many miles south of Chicago they went, too, according to a diary written by one of Chicago's pioneers, Mrs. Cynthia Shafer (born 1829, died 1926). She tells of ministers, who came to her house from Evanston to preach, in 1856. Her home was ten miles south of the court-house at the edge of the great Chicago marsh, in which the water was six feet deep for miles, and where, in winter the wolves played on the ice. There were but two American families near. A few families of foreigners, in huts on the prairie, lived by cutting wild hay or prairie grass. One day, one of Mrs. Shafer's maids answered the door and then reported, in great excitement, that a preacher was at the door—he had come

---

(4)   When the new Garrett Biblical Institute building was erected in 1923, Memorial Hall was taken over by Northwestern University.

to preach! Mrs. Shafer immediately gathered together a congregation of about twenty-five, her own help, some Catholic neighbors and some foreign squatters. A young theological student from Evanston preached that day. Later, other theological students came from Evanston and preached. The students were always welcome, but poor transportation made the trip too difficult for regular visits.

During the first thirty-seven years of the existence of Garrett Biblical Institute, over twelve hundred young men received instruction. Its Alumni have gone to many lands—a goodly number to foreign missionary fields. Up to 1900, at least six of its graduates had been elected bishops of the Methodist Episcopal Church. Dr. Vincent, the founder of the Chautauqua Literary and Scientific Circle, whose influence was felt all over the world, was one of the instructors at Garrett.

According to its charter, Garrett Biblical Institute can never be absorbed by another institution, but must always remain independent.

CHAPTER XIII

EARLY DAYS OF EVANSTON

ALL the government land had been taken up before the Trustees of Northwestern University came out in 1850 to decide on a site for the University, most of the land having been preëmpted during the preceding fifteen years.

By 1850 Ridge Road had been improved by the construction of Mulford's Ditch, and was much used in the hauling of wood and produce to Chicago. It was not unusual for one hundred ox-teams to pass over it in a day. Between 1850 and 1860 settlers began to appear, attracted by the University. They were not only neighbors, but friends, greeting each other with a pleasant How-do-you-do, or perhaps a Howdy. now and then.

Previous to the platting of the town, there were a number of settlers in the neighborhood of Ridge Avenue. George Kearney came in 1855 with his brother, who was contractor for the Chicago and Milwaukee Railroad. He built north of Emerson Street and west of the Ridge. Here he kept a general store. Eli Gaffield lived north of Foster Street and east of the Ridge. Mrs. Eliza Pratt, Gaffield's sister, resided in her new frame house south of Emerson Street and west of the Ridge. John Carney lived west of the Ridge, north of Dempster Street. The Crains, Ozro and Charles, lived south of Dempster Street on the Ridge. William Foster, "Uncle Billy," lived

HARVEY B. HURD

LYMAN J. GAGE

EDWARD EGGLESTON

ALEXANDER HESLER

south of Main Street and west of Ridge Avenue, a next
door neighbor to Charles Crain. The Foster house
became the home of S. V. Kline, but "Uncle Billy"
remained in the neighborhood. David Burroughs lived
south of Foster's place, on the west side of the Ridge.
Mrs. Jellerson, widow of O. Jellerson, was the next neighbor south; then came Paul Pratt, lately moved from his
log cabin at Leon Street and the Ridge. Mr. Kearney
shortly followed Neighbor Pratt and built just south of
his place. George W. Huntoon's log cabin was at the
northeast corner of Ridge Avenue and Main Street, the
latter street not named then. Alexander McDaniel lived
at the northwest corner of Ridge and Church Street. He
sold his property to Julius White. Charles Wilson's
general store was on Ridge Avenue, north of Noyes
Street. Anthony Haskamp lived east of the Ridge and
north of the present Central Street. Abraham Snyder's
house was on Chicago Avenue, south of Dempster Street.
S. S. Billings resided on the corner of Ridge Avenue and
Central Street. Andrew Robinson, John Spence and a
few others were also among the early settlers. David
Burroughs was postmaster at this time, 1854.

Others living within the limits of Evanston and
closely adjoining it were the following men with their
families: Dr. John Evans, Philo Judson, John L. Beveridge, Dr. Jacob Ludlam, Harvey B. Hurd, Andrew J.
Brown, Professor Henry Noyes, Dr. Daniel P. Kidder,
Dr. John Dempster, Dr. Francis D. Hemenway and
Edwin A. Clifford, practical pioneers, religious, friendly
and capable of performing many and varied tasks, from
sawing wood and currying horses, to leading prayer meetings and financing a town and two great institutions of

learning, as Miss Ward very ably puts it in her *Story of Northwestern University.*

A University student one time seeing Dr. Dempster hard at work sawing wood in his back yard, immediately asked him to saw some wood for him. Evidently Dr. Dempster allowed himself to be "engaged" to do the work, as it is recorded that the student wondered why the man he had hired never put in appearance.

The Webster, Pearsons, Dempster, Hinman and Noyes families all hailed from Newburg, Vermont. Before coming west, Mrs. John A. Pearsons had been bridesmaid to Miss Martha Morse, when the latter became the wife of Dr. Clark Titus Hinman.

Professor and Mrs. Noyes, and child with nurse, had landed in Evanston in a field near a small tank and found shelter a mile up on the other ridge (Chicago Avenue), and lived the following winter in a summer house, taking in members of the faculty, who would otherwise have had to live in Chicago. Among these was Dr. Kidder, with his family.

John A. Pearsons moved from his log cabin on Hinman Avenue to his new home on Chicago Avenue in 1854. The latter place was the first house built within the platted limits of Evanston. The Davis Street pier had not yet been built and the lumber for the house was unloaded directly on the shore. Mr. Pearsons used the old Hathaway cabin as a stable. Philo Judson had built his home before this, but it was outside the limits. Another man to build this year was Harvey B. Hurd. His home was at 1572 Ridge Avenue.

During the summer of 1854, Philo Judson negotiated for lumber to be used in the building of Dempster Hall.

16

A propeller and a schooner, both loaded with the lumber, arrived one Saturday morning, and had to be unloaded that day. Mr. Judson succeeded in getting together forty-five men, mostly farmers, to do the unloading. These men would have to be fed. There were no cafés or cafeterias or pantries or grills, where the men might get a hasty lunch and run; so that problem had to be solved by the women, and solve it they did! Neither was there a butcher shop near, but Mrs. Beveridge says they broiled and fried and cooked all the morning, so it is presumed many a young broiler lost its head that day to tickle the palates of the hungry men.

At noon the energetic women filled two or three clothes-baskets with food and dishes, put them in a farm wagon and drove to the place where the men were working. All of the men were barefoot, some were in water to their waists, others up to their shoulders. Plates and food were placed on the wet timber that had been unloaded and lay on the knoll. The hungry men came out of the water and soon showed their keen appreciation of the women's thoughtfulness and fine culinary ability.

The afternoon was spent by the women in preparing food for the evening meal and at six the hearts, and likewise the stomachs of the tired workers were gladdened by another bounteous spread. Mrs. Beveridge calls this Evanston's first picnic.

Thirty-six hours the men worked, stopping only long enough to eat. One of the main workers among the women was Mrs. John L. Beveridge, whose husband was later the Governor of the State of Illinois, and she the First Lady. Of such indomitable courage were the pioneers of Evanston made!

Davis Street was the center of the shopping district, even in those early days. James B. Colvin had his general store in Philo Judson's building at the northeast corner of Davis Street and Orrington Avenue, facing on Davis Street. Here one could buy almost anything. In those days yards of striped ticking, gaudy calicoes and bright red flannels were draped conspicuously around the entrance of the store, spread out on boxes on the sidewalk, and hung from the open windows. There was no mistaking what was for sale within!

Davis Street, at this time, was unpaved and nothing more than a wagon track—an unworked country road. The sidewalk was made of planks laid end to end, placed there by the business men and the residents. The Drainage Commission commenced work in 1855, but the streets were in a deplorable condition for a long time after that, and there were placards marked "No Bottom," where the mud was extra deep.

The ditch between the east and west ridges had but one crossing.

Quite a furor was created some years later when the first sidewalk was built, many citizens lamenting the fact that the rural simplicity of Evanston was gone forever. This sidewalk was built by Colonel Brainard, who had held various offices and was said to be a man of ability. He was the brother of Mrs. Lyman J. Gage.

There was a carpenter shop on the site that is now occupied by Chandler's book store, owned by a man named Williams. In this place, on a rude carpenter bench, was performed the first operation in Evanston. A man who had been hurt on the railroad was hurried into this shop and had his arm amputated by Dr. Bond, while a curious crowd peered in at the window.

James B. Colvin was called a power in the early days. He was the first store-keeper and the first town clerk, as well as one of the founders of the Methodist Episcopal Church, and postmaster during 1854, and again in 1856. It happens that he was also the first hotel proprietor, if one may designate those who preceded him as

AVENUE HOUSE

inn or tavern keepers. He built a one and a half story house on the site occupied at the present time by the North Shore Hotel. This early hotel was bought in 1857 by Albert Danks and became known as Danks' Hotel. A visitor in 1857 found every room in the hotel taken. Danks' son, H. P. Danks, composed the music of the famous song, *Silver Threads Among the Gold.*

George W. Reynolds built his house on Davis Street, near the corner of Chicago Avenue. He later bought the Danks' Hotel, and named it Reynolds House. One time when there was a neighborhood gathering at his home, the floor suddenly gave way and down went a struggling mass of humanity into the cellar, an episode that was anything but funny at the time and nothing but funny

"ROUND HOUSE" BUILT BY BIBLICAL STUDENTS IN 1856

ever afterward, if one were to judge by the tales related in after years about it. The same thing happened to a house belonging to George F. Foster on Chicago Avenue, near Church Street.

In 1863 Seth A. Mattison bought the Reynolds House and the name was changed to Mattison House.

In 1875 Mattison sold out to Charles H. Quinlan, when the place became known as the Avenue House. The Avenue House remained in the Quinlan family forty years. In Andreas' History, biographical section, is the following, "In 1875, he [Charles H. Quinlan] moved to Evanston and commenced building the Avenue House, completing it in 1882." Quinlan probably remodeled the original building. Banquets, political meetings and celebrations of all kinds were held in this hotel.

Dr. Dempster lived on the lake shore, north of Simpson Street.

Dr. Henry M. Bannister lived in one of Dr. Dempster's small apartments at the foot of Cook Street.

The Round House, so named on account of its shape, was built by Garrett Biblical Institute students in 1856, of lumber washed ashore from wrecked vessels. It was moved later to the east side of Orrington Avenue, half way between Davis and Grove Streets, and contained eight rooms, four above and four below. There were four entrances and four staircases. The last few years before it was demolished, it housed some of the colored population.

At the north end of the campus, a small stream ran in the ravine that cut through to the lake. When there was a heavy rain this stream swelled to considerable size. On one occasion, after a rain, it swept away a bridge that had been built across it. The University students called this stream or rivulet *The Rubicon*. After a few years the ravine became a dumping ground and finally disappeared.

The old oak and ash trees began to show the result of the draining of the land, and seeing that they could not survive the change, Philo Judson and William P. Kimball had elm saplings brought from the Big Woods and set out along the line of future streets. By the time the old trees were gone, the new line of elms had become stately trees. Mr. Kimball, when the young elms were set out along Hinman Avenue, charged the residents to water them, "not with one or two bucketfuls, but twenty or more, for each tree, every morning." The beautiful trees along Hinman Avenue are proof of the wisdom of his advice. It is said that the little trees at first resembled a long line of trolley poles, bare of branches, excepting green tufts at the tops.

The first fences in Evanston proper were made of three or four six-inch boards, running lengthwise around the lots. As new style houses began to appear, property owners decided the fences must be kept in keeping with the dwellings and picket fences came into vogue, made like those in eastern villages, from which a goodly proportion of the residents came.

The townspeople made and received calls, if not in the good old-fashioned way, at least in the best way they could. When Mrs. John L. Beveridge returned Mrs. John A. Pearsons' call, she went in a farm wagon, resting her feet on a board to keep them out of the water when crossing between the ridges.

When the good-looking frame houses began to be erected by the University people, the townspeople felt the University folk were putting on airs. However, the townspeople soon saw that the new residents were a friendly lot of people, who proved the fact, when they took self-supporting students into their homes and befriended them.

The Hand-book of Etiquet for Ladies, published in 1847 by Leavitt and Allen, tells many interesting rules of the day, and proves that good manners are never old-fashioned and only customs change. The whole book seems to be a treatise on the proper conduct of the ladies toward the gentlemen, as marriage was an envied state, and an unmarried lady, in the vernacular of the times, was an old maid or spinster. The following are excerpts from the book:

"Flattery is a powerful weapon in conversation; all are susceptible to it . . . . used skilfully, never direct.

"Laugh heartily, when amused, but avoid the horse-laugh.

"A lady's visiting card should be of small size, glazed, but not gilt, engraved in script letters, not in German text or Old English, nor printed.

"Never display visiting cards by placing them in the frame of your looking-glass.

"The most honorable place to offer a visitor is the corner of the fire-place.

"A lady's handkerchief should be as fine as a snowy cobweb, for a ball. She should have white gloves and shoes small and perfect fitting.

"Let your dancing be quiet and unobtrusive, your movements characterized by elegance and gracefulness, rather than by activity and complexity of steps.

"Silver forks are now met with in almost every respectable house. Steel forks are seldom placed upon the dinner table.

"Do not beat the Devil's tattoo.

"A hostess never confuses her guest by apologizing for the bad cheer, which she may offer.

"Women should never play cards, unless they can keep command of their temper. She who wishes to win a heart or retain one should never permit her admirers to behold her at cards, as the anxiety they produce is as destructive to beauty as it is to sentiment."

How times have changed! As this was a Methodist community for the most part, it is assumed the rules in regard to card playing and dancing were not needed by the Methodist adherents.

Ridgeville Township now had a population of 443. The name of the postoffice had been changed in 1850 to Ridgeville. Colvin was both postmaster and general store keeper. With both the postoffice and the general store at one place, the residents had the opportunity of frequent meetings and interchange of neighborly gossip and opinions on the big questions of the day, especially the slave question. Henry Clay's Omnibus Bill included the Fugitive Slave Law, which was stirring up considerable agitation and was bitterly resented in the northern states, quite the reverse of what Clay expected.

Henry Ward Beecher's eloquent sermons and lectures in the anti-slavery cause were topics of conversation the civilized world over, and Evanston's scattered citizens awaited with more or less impatience the mail that came but once a week to read the great man's words and get the general news on the momentous question of the day, as portrayed in the Chicago and eastern papers, the latter of which were hailed with joy by many Evanstonians, who, though loyal citizens, welcomed the sight of a home-town paper.

The little general store held many an impromptu public meeting, as the Uncle Tom Cabin serial revealed much that was hitherto unknown on the slavery question, and the northerners changed from a state of calm indifference to righteous indignation.

The Republican Party came into existence during this decade, at Jackson, Michigan. Its commemorating tablet reads, "Here under the Oaks, July 6, 1854, was born The Republican Party, destined in the throes of civil strife to abolish slavery, vindicate democracy and perpetuate the Union." Dr. Evans organized the Republican Party in Illinois, and several other Democrats changed their political views at this time, as their sympathies agreed with the platform of the Republican Party, in regard to the slavery question.

The residents walking along the streets in the fifties presented a far different appearance to the present day residents. There was no need for mad rush, and their gait was slower, more deliberate. The members of the faculty dressed much alike, long Prince Albert coats and high silk hats. Dr. Marcy and Dr. Davis, who came in the next decade, always wore the spike-tail coats or clawhammers, as they were called, and the side-board collars. A gentleman with a shawl thrown over his shoulders was a familiar sight. At home the gentleman of the house wore a study-gown.

A lady's attire consisted of a full skirt made up of many breadths of goods over several stiffly-starched petticoats. The tight fitting waist tapered to wasplike slenderness at the waist-line. The sleeves were close fitting. A little bonnet set well back on the head, with a drape of soft material, a capacious cape for cool weather and high cloth gaiters for the feet completed the outfit, with, of course, the proper gloves or lace mitts, the latter being

1853

1861

1872

1881

1891

1900

EARLY FASHIONS

made both with and without fingers. A tiny parasol was carried when walking or riding. The ladies were gentle and dignified and gracefully deliberate. Perhaps in the outfit of the day, one could be nought else, and how any young woman in such a garb could trip the light fantastic toe will ever remain a puzzle to the latter day maids.

The boys between the ages of ten and twelve wore box coats and long trousers, similar to the 1926 style.

The small girls wore dresses reaching half way between knee and ankle.

Candles were still used, but kerosene lamps began to replace them about 1857.[1] The ladies usually cared for their lamps, not wishing to trust the hired girl with anything as dangerous as a kerosene lamp was supposed to be, fearing an explosion.

Coal was beginning to replace wood in the stoves and a housewife accustomed to the clean wood, looked ruefully at her soot-begrimed hands, after replenishing the fire.

The lighting proposition for the village was a serious one, as the residents had bought large lots and built their houses well within their property lines, and lighting in a satisfactory manner would be too expensive, so only here and there could be placed a street lamp. These street lamps, flickering and smoky though they were, were real oases in a desert, welcome guides to the weary way-farer on his road home, which road was mostly ruts

---

(1)   Petroleum was valued by the Indians as early as the first part of the nineteenth century.   They collected it on the shores of Seneca Lake and sold it as a medicine, calling it Seneca Oil or Genesee.   Great ceremonies were held by them on the banks of Venango County Creek, at which time they fired the scum of oil on the surface of the water.   Dr. Hildreth speaks of this oil in his Journal of Science in 1826, as being used in lamps in workshops and producing a clear, bright light.   Previous to 1857, the oil was obtained by soaking blankets in it and wringing it from them.   In 1857, it was discovered oil could be obtained by boring, after which time it came into general use. The oil used in lamps sold for $1.50 per gallon.

and mud and mire, and the next street lamp was always so far away, that it looked not unlike a dim, distant star.

After the wreck of the Lady Elgin,[2] it was thought wise to establish a coast guard station in Evanston. This disaster occurred September 8, 1860, and caused the loss of nearly three hundred lives. About three o'clock

CAPTAIN LAWRENCE O. LAWSON (Inset)
COAST GUARD STATION

in the morning of that fatal day, the Lady Elgin, a side-wheeler steamer, and the largest and finest passenger vessel on the lake, while carrying an excursion party on a sight seeing trip for the day, suddenly collided with

(2) The ball from the forward flagstaff of the Lady Elgin may be seen at the Evanston Historical rooms. It was presented to the Historical Society by the sons and daughters of Mrs. McLean, who found it among the wreckage washed ashore. The plush hand-rail and ornament from the top of flagstaff are also in the Historical rooms.

the lumber schooner Augusta. On board were 393 persons, including the forty-five men belonging to the ship's crew. A hundred head of cattle had been taken on at Chicago to be delivered at points north. The captain of the Lady Elgin had felt no uneasiness in starting out in the face of a northeaster, on account of the staunchness of his craft. The young people engaged in dancing and games, and the band played its merriest tunes as the boat glided out of the harbor into the open lake. About three miles from the shore at Highland Park, the Augusta, driven before a strong wind, struck the Lady Elgin, her bowsprit penetrating the wooden hull of the steamer. Lady Elgin's captain, thinking no serious damage had been done to his boat, refused help from the schooner, but within half an hour the fires were out, and the captain and passengers realized their danger and began to look around for means to save their lives. The captain ordered all on board to go on the hurricane deck, in the hope that it would carry its human load to safety when it separated from the main part of the boat, but the deck was dashed to pieces the instant it reached the breakers and the unfortunate victims were left struggling in the raging sea. The cattle had been driven from the lower deck into the water, in order to lighten the cargo. In desperation many persons mounted the backs of the swimming cattle, hoping to reach shore in this manner. The strong wind had driven the boat south toward Evanston, where, before daylight came, hundreds of persons lined the shore, anxious to render any assistance possible. Several students taking an early morning walk were heroes of the day. Among these were Edward W. and William Spencer, two brothers who had learned the art of strong swimming in the Mississippi River, James O. Cramb, John B. Colvin, George Wilson, John O. Foster, Henry M. Kidder, W. B. Friggell, J. C. Garrison, W. T. Harrington, Charles H. Fowler, B. D. Alden and G. R. Van Horn. Fowler and Cramb were later bishops of the Methodist church. Again and again Edward W. Spencer dashed into the raging waters, bringing back another and yet another of the ill-fated boat's passengers. Seventeen times he braved the angry waves, and seventeen times he came back with his human load. Once he was seen throwing off the safety rope that impeded his progress. Then exhausted and giving up only when he could do no more, he accepted medical attention for himself. His health was that day wrecked, and he had to abandon the hope of the clerical vocation he had chosen. As a small token of their great appreciation of his noble work, the citizens of Evanston presented him with a gold watch. In the Patten Gymnasium a bronze tablet, given by the class of 1898, commemorates his noble work of that day.[3] Two weeks after the wreck a man was found lashed to a spar, and was revived.

As a result of the valuable assistance given by the students at the time of the Lady Elgin wreck, a volunteer life-saving crew of five men from the senior class of Liberal Arts was organized in October, 1872. In this first crew were George Lunt, George Bragdon and M. D. Kimball. A fine life-boat was presented to Dr. E. O. Haven by Commodore Murray, who was in charge of the United States life-saving service. This boat was to be committed to the care of the volunteer crew. In September, 1876, the students petitioned that the members of the crew be

[3]   Spencer died in California in February, 1919, never having fully regained his health.

selected for the best physical and moral qualifications, irrespective of classes. The petition was granted and an experienced seaman was engaged by the government to captain the crew. In April, 1877, E. J. Bickness, of the class of 1877, was appointed captain of the crew of students, who were to receive forty dollars a month each during the season, and three dollars for each trip at the time of a wreck. At first the life-boat was housed on the beach in a temporary building. In 1876, it was moved to the eastern part of the present structure, which occupied the site of Fisk Hall. It was moved to its present site on newly-made land near the water's edge previous to the building of Fisk Hall in 1899.

To the credit of the life-saving crew is the saving of over 400 lives, and property amounting to millions of dollars in value. Captain Lawrence O. Lawson, a native of Sweden, who came to Evanston in 1864, was appointed captain of the crew of 1880, and did noble work for twenty-three years. In the rescue of the Steamer Calumet, stranded 1,000 yards from shore, Captain Lawson and his crew displayed such fine bravery that the United States government awarded each man a gold medal. In Hurd's History Professor J. Scott Clark says of Captain Lawson, "In addition to his services in aiding to save nearly five hundred lives, Captain Lawson originated the system of righting the Beebe-McClellan surf-boat, which has since been adopted by the Government for use by all the crews of the service." On March 10, 1864, when the Steamer Storm was wrecked, J. C. Hartzell (later a bishop of the Methodist church) saved four exhausted sailors from drowning by swimming out to them with a rope around his waist.

Returning to every day life, we find a very important visitor came to Evanston and stayed overnight, one who, though already well-known, was soon to become a national figure, Abraham Lincoln. Mr. Lincoln was in Chicago attending a law trial, when Julius White, an old friend, invited him to be his guest. While in Chicago, Mr. Lincoln had been sitting for his bust. After receiving Mr. White's invitation, he told the sculptor that he would rather not accept, as he knew he would meet a lot of University professors. Mr. White, however, would not consent to his staying away. Harvey B. Hurd was given the honor of accompanying him out on the train and he describes him by quoting another man's words, "Not that he knew it all and that I knew little or nothing, but that he and I were two good fellows well met and that between us we knew lots." In the evening a great crowd gathered, carrying lighted torches, and serenaded the noted man with tin pans and horns. Mr. Lincoln came out and addressed the people assembled on the lawn. Mr. White then invited them all in to meet his guest, who gave each a friendly greeting and a cordial handshake. A quartette sang a group of songs which particularly pleased Mr. Lincoln, who laid his arm across the shoulders of C. G. Ayers, the leader, and said, "Young Man, I wish I could sing as well as you. Unfortunately, I know only two tunes. One is *Old Hundred* and the other isn't." Mr. Henry Pearsons remembered the cheerful speech and apt words of his address, the exceeding tallness of the man and the awkward way he had of turning one way or the other and bending his knees a little, when emphasizing a point, or coming to a climax. About this time, Alexander Hesler, who had a studio on Sherman Avenue,

17

took a number of photographs of Lincoln, which are among the best of the Lincoln pictures. Some of these are at the Evanston Historical rooms with the Hesler papers, and they show him without a beard. The story is told that a little girl sitting on Mr. Lincoln's lap said she would like to see how he would look with a beard. He said he would show her. This was in 1860 or 1861. He wore a beard only about five years, but his pictures with a beard seem to be the best known ones.

Watson Ludlam, son of one of the pioneers, Dr. Jacob Ludlam, was conceded to be the tallest man in Evanston. He and Lincoln were found to be exactly the same height, six feet, four inches. When President Lincoln was visiting an encampment of troops during the civil war, he saw and recognized Ludlam, and invited him to the White House to sing some of the songs he had heard him sing, and which he had so much enjoyed during his stay in Evanston.

Evanston, though refusing a city charter in 1869, had become a village of real importance, spreading out and gaining new inhabitants each year, with a university well attended. No longer was Evanston a home for wild animals, as the increasing number of residents interfered with the raising of their families in peace within the village limits. The old log school house no longer served its original purpose, but had been turned into a dwelling house, and was being occupied by Mancer Thompson, brother-in-law of Mrs. Alexander McDaniel. Among the marriages were those of Joel Stebbins and Ruth Colvin, George Monteath and Betsy Ann Snyder, George Kearney and the daughter of Uncle Billy Foster.

The State Fair that lured many from Evanston each fall raised its price of admission from twenty-five to thirty cents.

Bishop Simpson, the great emotional speaker, whose oratorical powers helped so vitally to lengthen the muster roll in 1861, made a trip to California, and on his return half the town turned out to meet the beloved preacher, headed by a group of young people carrying the old melodeon and singing, "Home again, Home again, From a foreign shore."

The University students continued to play their pranks. They thought the one they played on Dr. Weller, the first physician in Evanston, was as good as any. A group of jokers led a cow up the steps of the good old doctor's porch and tied her tail to the doorbell. A doorbell in those days was attached to a spring with a wire leading through the house to the front door. The constant jangling of the bell almost drove the doctor mad, before he could make himself presentable, but he immediately saw the humor of the situation when he opened the door.

One Simon Peter Douthit fell through the roof of the Methodist church, while trying to play a practical joke on the congregation. The records do not say whether he was of the Town or Gown group.

Of a more serious turn of mind was "Uncle" Mark DeCoudries, a devout Methodist, who at the age of ninety years, it is said, "shingled his home with his own hands" in order to contribute $100 to African Missions.

The postmasters who were appointed from the earliest days up to 1870 were as follows: George M. Huntoon, with postoffice at Mulford's Tavern, 1846; David W.

Burroughs, Buckeye Hotel, 1849; D. W. Burroughs, 1850; James B. Colvin, 1854, office at Orrington Avenue and Davis Street; Dr. Jacob Ludlam, 1855; James B. Colvin, 1855; Fayette M. Weller, 1857; Webster S. Steele, 1861; Edwin A. Clifford, 1865. According to a letter on file at the Evanston Historical rooms to J. Seymour Currey, from Blain W. Taylor, Postoffice Department, Washington, D. C., the postoffice at Gross Point was established December 28, 1846. The name was changed to Ridgeville, April 26, 1850. The name Ridgeville was changed to Evanston, April 27, 1855.

The village of Evanston was soon to see a change. The peaceful, little place was to see an influx of another element, and was to take on more citified ways because of it. The great Chicago fire of October 9, 1871, caused the citizens of Evanston to open their hearts and their homes to the homeless, and never again would theirs be the quiet, rural place of former days. There was to be a quickening of the pulse, and the beginning of civic activities that would continue through all the years to come.

In ten years the population of Evanston more than tripled itself, being 831 in 1860, and 3,062 in 1870, according to the Atlas of Illinois.

CHAPTER XIV

CHURCHES

TOLERANCE is and always has been the key-note of harmony in Evanston's religious life, and it began back in the thirties and the forties with the first pioneers, Edward Mulford, a deacon in the Baptist church; the Fosters, the Burroughs, the Pratts, also Baptists; the Murphys and the Carneys, Catholics; the Crains, the Wigglesworths and the Huntoons, of Methodist persuasion. The Baptists and Methodists and Presbyterians knelt side by side in the meeting-house and continued to do so until each denomination had its own home roof. Before the meeting-house, or to be more specific, the log school house on the Ridge, was built, the religiously inclined—and there were few who were not—met at the various homes on Sundays and held church services.

After the log school house was erected, which was about 1841, the services were conducted in it by circuit riders, as the visiting preachers were called, who came every two weeks, and sometimes not so frequently.

Mrs. John L. Beveridge speaks of attending services there one Sunday in 1854, at which time all the women were dressed in "primitive style," calico dresses, and large sun-bonnets on their heads, she and her mother, Mrs. Philo Judson, being the only ones wearing dress-bonnets such as ladies wore at the time. There were fourteen that day in the congregation. She says of the preacher, the Reverend John G. Johnson, "He was a tall, lank individual, dressed in dark blue cotton overalls, with large patches of new cloth on each knee, while the rest of the cloth had been washed until it was almost white. He always carried a big blue umbrella, bulged in the center.''

Long before the time set for the services to begin, farm wagons had arrived from up and down the Ridge and from the other Ridge (Chicago Avenue), across the slough, and their occupants had solemnly and reverently entered the House of Prayer. Not till a later day did late-comers interrupt the services by their tardy appearance. The settlers were early risers and always allowed themselves sufficient time to reach their destination early. At the front of the room, near the preacher was the ''Amen Corner,'' and here the patriarchs echoed their ''Amens'' again and again, as the preacher uttered some great truth or voiced an approved sentiment. There was wholesomeness and sincerity in the singing of the congregation, and none was too proud to bend his knee as well as bow his head during the long, and sometimes tedious, prayer. The sermons were of greater length than those of the latter days, but being infrequent, this was justifiable.

Then when the services were finished, came the kindly greetings with glad handclasps, friendly smiles, and the happy exchange of neighborly gossip. A few slowly turned their steps toward the little burying-ground to the rear of the church, to linger a moment over grassy mounds beneath which lay all that was mortal of loved ones.

Untying their horses from the fence, snapping the reins, and cheerily calling, ''Giddap,'' the members of the congregation drove away to their respective homes, there to partake of the usual sumptuous Sunday dinner, which in most cases, especially with the New Englanders, had been prepared the day before, that work might not desecrate the Holy Sabbath Day. The afternoon was spent in serious, though pleasant reading, music and visiting, and at candle-light, the Bible was opened and a chapter read therefrom by the head of the house, after which all knelt in prayer of gratitude and thanksgiving. Sunday was to them a real day of rest; a day wherein their souls were uplifted and their hearts lightened; a day that strengthened their courage and braced their shoulders for burdens sure to come; a day that brought a complete and needed change for both mind and body.

The first quarterly conference for Evanston was held July 13, 1854, in the little log school house on the Ridge. Those present were the Reverends Philo Judson and J. G. Johnson, traveling preachers, George W. Huntoon, class leader, James B. Colvin, John L. Beveridge and A. Danks, stewards, and Abraham Wigglesworth, Sunday School Superintendent.

The first Sunday School was started in the old Mulford house and afterward moved to the log school house. Mrs. Edward Mulford had brought a collection of fifty books with her from the east. These she presented to the Sunday School. Soon afterward the church maintained three Sunday Schools, one within the village plat, under John L. Beveridge, one in the old log school house in the Huntoon District, under A. Danks, and another on the North Ridge, Stebbins District, under A. Wigglesworth.

As the University drew more people to Evanston, there was need of a more central place of worship than the log school house, and the chapel of the first building of Garrett Biblical Institute—Dempster Hall—was used from January, 1855, to about May, 1855, when the services were held in a room over Colvin's store at the corner of Orrington Avenue and Davis Street. Philo Judson, who owned the building, had remodeled the room, furnished it to accommodate forty persons, and given it rent free to the church people. In November, 1855, the church services were transferred to the University building just completed and dedicated.

The Colvin store building, the one-time church home, was moved back of its original site and Garwood's drug store occupied the original site. On its new site the old building housed a barber shop, and was later moved to Ashland Avenue.

There is record of much moving of buildings in those days. There seemed to be a full appreciation of the labor spent in the erecting of a building, and instead of tearing one down that the site might be used to better advantage, it was moved to cheaper ground and sometimes utilized for a different purpose, the church buildings being the exception.

In September, 1855, the Reverend John Sinclair was appointed preacher in charge. Professor P. W. Wright of the Institute preached during the time the church services were held in the Institute Chapel.

The members of the young church now began to feel the need of having a roof-tree of their own. Accordingly, the first church building within the Evanston plat was erected at the northeast corner of Church Street and

OLD FIRST METHODIST EPISCOPAL CHURCH

FIRST METHODIST EPISCOPAL CHURCH COMPLETED IN 1872

Orrington Avenue in 1856, at a cost of $2,800. This was the first community church in Evanston, composed of all denominations, though under Methodist control. A bronze tablet on the Public Library grounds commemorates this modest little edifice—yea, more, the tablet marks the very site of the pulpit, where, at various times, stood some of the best known preachers as well as the finest orators of the Methodist Church, to expound the teachings of the Bible to an appreciative congregation. Among these preachers were A. L. Cooper, Charles P. Bragdon, J. R. Goodrich, O. H. Tiffany, D. D., Miner Raymond, W. C. Dandy, James Baume. In 1867, during the Reverend Mr. Dandy's pastorate, plans were discussed for a new church, and the location decided upon was the southwest corner of Hinman Avenue and Church Street.

The "straight and narrow path" of the early day Methodists was decidedly straight and exceedingly narrow. Cases of non-attendance at class meetings were reported and investigating committees were appointed "to labor with the delinquent." Questionable business dealings of certain members were looked into and the report fully set out. One gentleman and his wife were expelled from church for not attending a class meeting. A young man and a young lady were deemed disorderly, for having danced at a picnic. They were asked to acknowledge their fault and not repeat the offense.

In the old record books in the basement of the present Methodist Episcopal Church, many interesting things came to light in regard to the Sunday School. A line on the record sheet held the weather report of the day. There was a noticeable increase in attendance as Christmas approached, and a proportionate falling away afterward. At one time in 1857, Superintendent F. H. Benson felt so discouraged at the small attendance at Sunday School, that he announced his intention of resigning, but subsequent record sheets show he changed his mind.

The infant classes were given poetical names. Miss Mary Bannister on March 27, 1859, took over part of the infant class, which was called "The Casket of Jewels," and named her part of the class "Little Pilgrims." Mrs. Clough was teacher of "The Sparkling Gems" in 1860.

John L. Beveridge was class leader in 1859, and George Reynolds in 1872. Other class leaders were L. Clifford, John Fussy, P. Judson, A. C. Stewart, I. Smith, H. S. Noyes, William Triggs, A. Vane, F. H. Benson, S. Springer, and J. W. Clough.

The little white church with its green shutters, its papered walls and plain furnishings, served the Methodist congregation for sixteen years, after which time it lent its friendly shelter more than once to other denominations. It was removed in 1881 to Church Street and Sherman Avenue to become the Norwegian-Danish Methodist Episcopal Church. In 1900 it was torn down after an existence of nearly half a century.

The liberality of Northwestern University showed itself in donating sites for the churches of five denominations, beginning with a lot for the new Methodist church building. The Presbyterians, the Congregationalists, the Episcopalians, and the Baptists were equally favored.

While the Reverend M. C. Briggs was in charge, the new church was finished and dedicated, the cost of it being nearly $69,000. The organ cost $4,500.

In the history of every church the women's work stands out conspicuously. Festivals, harvest homes, concerts and even a restaurant in the University Grove one Fourth of July, conducted by the women of the church, helped pay off what was beginning to be looked upon as an everlasting debt. Mrs. Marcy (spoken of as Mrs. Dr. Marcy in the early histories), was chairman of the committee of women on the "church debt." Unceasingly and tirelessly did these women work, with the result that they paid off $10,000 of the church debt and the trustees paid off the balance, $18,000, and the church was saved from being sold under the hammer. Frances Willard pledged $100 toward the payment of the church debt when, she says, she had not one cent in her pocket, nor had she any idea where she would get any money. The following week, she received an invitation to give a lecture at Pittsburgh, Pennsylvania, for that very sum. Her fare was paid to and from Pittsburgh, and she was able to give her check for the amount pledged within ten days to the treasurer of the church.

Miss Willard presented the diplomas to the five "sweet girl graduates" at the only commencement the Evanston College for Ladies ever held, as this college was later merged in the University. These exercises were held in the basement of the unfinished church, June, 1872.

The first gathering in the church proper was a farewell to Dr. Kidder and his family in the lecture room, which was just finished, August, 1872.

In the auditorium of the church, the largest in Evanston for a number of years, such noted persons as Edward Eggleston, Wendell Phillips, Henry Ward Beecher, General Lew Wallace, James Whitcomb Riley, Henry M. Stanley, Edward Everett Hale, and Frances E. Willard have talked to crowded houses.

BISHOP MATTHEW SIMPSON

THE REVEREND E. D.
WHEADON

THE REVEREND GEORGE C.
NOYES

THE REVEREND ROBERT M.
HATFIELD

T. C. Hoag, banker and grocer in the village, became church treasurer in 1858, and continued in that capacity for nearly forty years.

In 1875 came the Reverend J. B. Wentworth, followed by the Reverend R. M. Hatfield, whose fame as a minister had preceded him. The Reverend Amos W. Patten served from 1880 to 1883, when the Reverend Lewis Curts took charge. Later pastors were Dr. H. B. Ridgaway, S. F. Jones, D.D., Charles J. Little, President of Garrett Biblical Institute, Acting Pastor, the Reverend Frank Bristol, D.D., who remained nearly five years, Charles Little again, and William Macafee, D.D. The new $12,500 organ was completed January, 1901.

The history of the DesPlaines Camp meeting has always been so closely connected with Evanston history as to be almost a part of it. The first camp meeting was held in August, 1860, on Squire Rand's farm, across the railroad from its present site, a thirty-five acre plot, three-quarters of a mile from the village of DesPlaines to which place it was moved after five years in its first location.

Camp meeting week was a time to be looked forward to with keen anticipation. Farmers drove to camp from a radius of a hundred miles, their wagons laden with household goods, while the members of the family perched themselves within wherever there was available space, arriving several days before the opening date, that the housekeeping wheels might be running smoothly before that time. Joyful occasions, those drives, with the hymn singing and general good cheer!

The cottages and tents surrounded the circle, enclosing the meeting-house, which was a rude board building with earth floor and no roof. The cottages were small one-room-and-porch shacks. There were also a number of tents on the grounds. Kerosene lamps furnished the illumination at night.

A lake captain living in Evanston whose name was Lindgren, used one of his sails to erect a tent on the grounds for the first Swedish Methodist services.

Elder Boring called the members to worship with a loud blast from his horn, which reached grove and riverside.

BAPTIST

The Baptists, after having worshiped with the Methodists for more than a decade, decided to launch their little craft. It had a hard pull and more than once it had to drop anchor and stop awhile, but there were pilots with great faith and strength of purpose; so the stops were of short duration and at last it was out in clear waters and its sailing had become smooth.

The first meeting to form a Baptist Church was held in the chapel of Northwestern University April 24, 1858. E. H. Mulford was elected moderator and Moses Danby, clerk. The church was to have the name of "The Evanston Baptist Church." The constituent members numbered but six, E. H. Mulford, Rebecca Mulford, Francis M. Iglehart, Judith W. Burroughs, Rebecca Westerfield and Moses Danby. Mrs. Iglehart was known as the Mother of the Baptist Church. For a few years previous to the founding of the church she had been conducting a Sunday School in her home, herself being the Superintendent. A marble tablet in the church built in 1875 commemorates her devotion.

The recognition of the church took place in the Methodist Episcopal Church April 29, 1858, and delegates from five churches in Chicago and Waukegan were present. Dr. Foster, president of the University, read the scripture and the Reverend A. J. Joslyn gave the charge to the church.

Northwestern University, in compliance with one of its rules, donated a lot to the Baptists for their church building, on the corner of Hinman Avenue and Church Street. More than that, it offered them the use of its chapel for their services until their church was completed. The first baptismal services of the church were in the lake, on the shore of which, and on the pier, stood nearly the whole village. Those baptized were Isaac Burroughs, Betsy Burroughs, his wife, Elmina Burroughs and Hannah Newell.

There was no regular preacher, the preachers being supplied either by the University or neighboring churches. In 1859, it was decided ''to suspend further efforts towards erecting a building for the church and also to give up public worship for the present.'' Prayer meetings and sociables kept the few members from giving up entirely. Mr. Iglehart, ever with the welfare of the church at heart, offered the use of a twenty by thirty foot building on his lot, near what is now Ridge Avenue and Oakton Street, for church services, as the Northwestern chapel had been given up, and the Congregationalists were occupying it. This building was intended originally for a billiard room, but when it was accepted for church services, it was christened ''Oakton Chapel.''

For a while the Baptists held four o'clock services in the University Chapel and evening prayer meeting at

Oakton Chapel. In 1861, they used the school house in the vicinity, instead of Oakton Chapel, with preaching only once a month.

In 1862 the Reverend J. S. Mahan came from Waukegan, but left after a few months as the compensation was but "$2.50 to $3.00 every two weeks." A few prayer meetings were held after that and then as the Iglehart family, which seemed to be the prime mover in the church, had gone to Chicago for a brief absence, all preaching and prayer meetings were suspended.

In the spring of 1863, an impetus seems to have been given to congregating again. Many had moved out from Chicago meanwhile. A meeting was held in June and ten persons were received into membership. Record was made of the former election of E. H. Mulford as deacon. In October trustees were elected. During the next few years the church grew in strength and membership. In June, 1865, they reported to the Fox River Baptist Association, "Our long night of anxiety has passed, and the full light of a new and, we trust, a better day, has dawned." And so, in truth, it had. Twenty-six had come into the church by letter and their new $6,500 home, free of debt, had been dedicated, February 16, 1865. In June, William J. Leonard accepted a call to the church at a salary of $1000.

By 1872 the congregation began to outgrow the small wooden church, so it was decided to move it to the rear of the lot at the northwest corner of Lake and Chicago Avenue and use it until the larger edifice on that lot was completed. Meanwhile, during the moving process, the services were to be held in Lyon's Hall. One Sunday evening, November 3, 1872, after the little church

18

had been moved, and the services were being held there temporarily, the preacher had just begun his discourse on "How David got a Whipping," when "nearly half the floor gave way and precipitated the congregation into the basement." No one was seriously hurt. A colored man, Nathan Branch, sitting at the side of the church in a pew fastened to the wall, felt the floor giving way and seeing the confusion, jumped straight to outdoors and safety through a window, breaking both glass and sash. The next morning he offered to make good the damage he had done in his fright. He was later the founder of the colored Baptist Church.

In February, 1875, the corporate name for the church adopted was the "First Baptist Church of Evanston." The new church was completed and dedicated November 21, 1875.

Mrs. Rebecca J. Mulford, one of the little group of six who founded the first little church in Evanston, of Baptist faith, is remembered by her name being placed in one of the windows beside a sheaf of ripe wheat. Nor had she forgotten the church in her will.

A church bell was made especially for the new church, and many citizens not belonging to the church made generous donations for it, in order to have a "church bell centrally located." On July 4, 1876, the bell was first rung, and in honor of its inauguration it was "consecrated to public services by being rung thirty minutes at sunrise, noon and sunset," according to the church records. In the metal of the bell is cast an appropriate motto consisting of thirty-two words.

In 1897, an invitation was extended to B. A. Greene, D.D., of Lynn, Massachusetts. He was engaged at a salary of $3,000. His years with the church were marked with harmony and prosperity, and an enlarged membership.

THE FIRST CONGREGATIONAL CHURCH

The First Congregational Church of Evanston had its first organization—first, because almost ten years later there was a second organization—December 8, 1859, in the chapel of Northwestern University, where five members met. The Reverend W. W. Patton, pastor of the First Church of Chicago, was appointed Moderator, E. W. Blatchford, scribe, A. T. Sherman, clerk and the deacons elected were S. S. Whitney and Isaac D. Guyer.

The membership reached eleven during the next six months, seven being Congregationalists and the other four from other denominations. This early organization was but short lived. Letters were granted to all who wished to withdraw from the church, as many were considering leaving Evanston at the time. The only one who did not take out his letter was the clerk, A. T. Sherman. Hoping the organization would gain strength in time, he paid the annual assessment to the Association for five years. Then seeing no hope of its reviving, he ceased these payments and the organization was suspended in 1865. Later, in the summer of that year, the suggestion was made by Dr. Bannister that a Congregational Church should be formed. A meeting was held at the home of Francis Bradley, and weekly prayer meetings were begun Out of these grew the "Lake Avenue Church," composed of Presbyterians and Congregationalists, from which the Congregationalists withdrew in 1869 to form a church of their own.

The Congregational Church was organized the second time, September 8, 1869, and recognized by council January 13, 1870. The first regular pastor was the Reverend Edward N. Packard of Syracuse, New York.

The services were held in the chapel of Northwestern University, the east room on the ground floor, a plain room, with stationary, drab colored, pine-wood pews, and blackboards around the walls.

Some of the early members were Francis Bradley, L. H. Boutell, the Reverend D. Crosby Green (afterward many years a missionary in Japan), Heman Powers, I. M. Williams and Orvis French.

Northwestern University granted this new church a lot, but this lot was a small park, originally given by the University to the village of Evanston for "Park purposes only." It was finally decided that the lot should revert to the University Trustees, upon the trustees of the church paying $600 to the Village Trustees. The University Trustees then deeded the property to the First Congregational Church, "without further compensation."

General Julius White, "moved that they (the church trustees), should proceed to build a church edifice costing not less than $10,000." The church cost $25,000, instead of $10,000, by the time it was completed. Its membership was less than fifty at the time.

The Chicago fire brought financial loss to many and a hard struggle followed, but the little church carried on and kept up the interest on its bonded debt, which was done only by the most careful management.

In 1879, the Reverend A. J. Scott succeeded Dr. Packard, who accepted a call to Boston.

In 1883, the church was enlarged and partly refurnished, at a cost of $5,000. There was but one service held in the renovated church. Immediately after this service, November 23, 1884, fire destroyed the whole building, and around the smoking ruins the following day pledges of money were made toward rebuilding. Before the embers of the fire were cold, invitations began to pour in from the Methodists, the Presbyterians and the Baptists, to use their buildings on Sunday afternoons and for social meetings. The Woman's Temperance Union offered Union Hall, and the University offered Heck Hall.

The new church, costing over $50,000 was completed and dedicated April 11, 1886. The Reverend Mr. Scott resigned in 1886. The Reverend Nathan H. Whittlesey, D.D., succeeded him and remained until May, 1892. The Reverend Jean Frederick Loba, D.D., was installed in November of that year.

The church has always stood for harmony, benevolence, and charity. It has always shown interest in civic improvement and been ready to cooperate with the sister churches in every religious and social movement.

THE EPISCOPAL CHURCH

The Episcopalians worshipped harmoniously with the Methodists for a number of years before founding a church of their own. It is said that this was probably due to the fact that there is much in common between the two communions. John Wesley never left the Church of England, even though that Father of Methodism authorized one Thomas Coke to go over to America and ordain Francis Asbury, the First Methodist Bishop.

A meeting was held at the home of Charles Comstock in the spring of 1864. Later notice was given in the chapel of the University, by the Reverend John Wilkinson, Chaplain to Bishop Whitehouse, that a church (Episcopal) would be organized in the Methodist Episcopal Church on April 20th. At this meeting, the new church was founded and the name chosen was St. Mark's Parish. It was never a mission. The church senior and junior wardens chosen were Charles Comstock and D. J. Crocker.

The first service of the church was held in the Methodist Church, the third Sunday in May, 1864, and was conducted by the Reverend Mr. Wilkinson. Familiar names, at least some of them, are appended to the constitution adopted, those of H. B. Hurd, John Lyman, J. H. Kedzie, F. M. Weller, J. S. Haywood, William C. Comstock, A. J. Wilder, John Lighthall and H. C. Cone.

The University offered the church the use of its chapel for services, and there the services were held until the first Episcopal church building in the village was erected, in 1865. The Reverend John Buckmaster was the first rector.

This church, a small wooden building, was built on a lot that Northwestern University had donated to the parish, 60 feet on the north side of Davis Street, between Ridge and Oak Avenues, with a depth of 150 feet.

Public services were suspended for several weeks during the spring of 1865, but the members must have kept the interest in the welfare of the church alive, as by September 15, 1865, the church was finished and free of debt, at which time it was consecrated by Bishop Whitehouse.

During the time the services were held in the University Chapel, the little melodeon used was carried every week to the chapel from the Avenue House, where the "Lady organist" boarded. William C. Comstock was chorister and sexton combined, and the Comstock carriage furnished the means of travel for the choir members to the chapel every Saturday evening for rehearsal.

When there was no regular rector, the pulpit was usually supplied by a temporary rector.

Under the second rector, the Reverend Thomas Lisle, of Philadelphia, 1867-1869, great progress was made in the church, and the people of the village began to realize that St. Mark's Parish had become an integral part of the place. The number of communicants in the parish during the Reverend Mr. Lisle's rectorship doubled. During these two years there were fourteen confirmations.

In 1868, the church building was enlarged, and Evanston's second church bell rang out from the new wooden tower, or rather belfry, this one to call the parishioners of St. Mark's to worship.

Three later additions were made to the little wooden church.

In 1873, plans for a new church began to be discussed. The vestry however, disapproved of building at this time, on the ground that the increased population was but temporary, as many who had moved from Chicago to Evanston after the Chicago fire, would return when their new homes were completed. The women of the church, however, were determined if a new church was not to be considered, to enlarge the church building at their own expense and it was resolved "unanimously" (according to the minutes of the vestry, July 11, 1875) that the ladies were to be allowed to enlarge the church building, but the vestry was not to be liable for any part of the cost. That they, the ladies, were to be entirely responsible for all expenses incurred, quenched their fire of enthusiasm not at all and their work resulted in the building of the "south aisle of the church." The Men's Guild, encouraged by this fine example of the ladies' work, later built the "north aisle."

The prophecy of the vestry proved a correct one. By 1874, many of the refugees from the Chicago fire had moved back to their former homes, and the congregation that once had filled the church, now comprised scarcely more than forty persons.

With the coming of the Reverend J. Stewart Smith in 1876, there began a marked change. The unattractive church building contained an altar that was nothing more than a wooden box, four feet long, with no cross, vases, altar lights or altar vestings; nor was there a full set of altar linens. Common bread was used in place of unleavened bread in celebrating the Holy Eucharist. The rector wore a long, white surplice, with black stole. Many feast and fast days were not observed.

The Reverend Mr. Smith remained as rector four years. By perseverance and tact, and in the face of some opposition, he brought about a new order of things, one marked by progress and prosperity not realized before. The building was given a more churchly appearance by repairing and decorating; a good cabinet organ replaced the little melodeon; a fitting altar with cross, vases and proper vestings for the various seasons of the Christian Year replaced the old wooden box affair; the rector appeared in proper vestments and all Holy Days were observed. The result was a brightness and attractiveness in the services that had not existed before.

Under the rectorship of the sixth minister, the Reverend Dr. Frederick S. Jewell (1880 to 1885), a mission in South Evanston was started. This mission became St. Luke's Church in 1891.

In 1882, the Men's Guild of St. Mark's Church was organized, its object being to promote fellowship in the parish, as well as to support the rector in his work.

The Reverend Richard Hayward was the seventh rector, a former chaplain in the U. S. Navy. He served the church from 1886 to 1888. During this time the scheme for building a new church was again given consideration and about ten thousand dollars pledged.

A six months' vacancy followed Mr. Hayward's term of serving, at the end of which time the Reverend Arthur W. Little's rectorship begins to date. Dr. Little began at once to push the building of a new church. This church, a beautiful stone building of early English type, was erected on the corner of Ridge Avenue and Grove Street. The corner stone had been laid by the bishop May 18, 1890. The first services were held Easter Sunday, March 29, 1891. On St. Mark's Day, April 25, 1895, the church being entirely free from debt was consecrated by the bishop.

Charles Comstock, connected with the church since its founding in 1865, attended public service for the last time, at the consecration of the new church. He had been Senior Warden of the church for thirty years, and in all the years of the existence of the church a generous benefactor. He died the following September, at the age of eighty-two years.

In the fall of 1901 the belfry in the tower was fitted with a chime of nine bells, the largest weighing 2,001 pounds. These were the gift of Arthur Orr. The value of the bells was over $9,000.

Under Dr. Little the church prospered, and grew not only in membership, but in far reaching influence. Its missions have increased and its charities have become manifold.

CHAPTER XV

CHURCHES—*(Continued)*

CATHOLIC CHURCH

THE few Catholic families living in Evanston in the early days, having no church of their own, were compelled to go either further west to Gross Point, or south to High Ridge (Kenmore). In 1864, there was an effort made to establish a church of the Catholic faith in the Village of Evanston, and a lot was purchased at the corner of Lake Street and Oak Avenue. The purchase of this lot, however, exhausted the available funds and the building of the church was postponed until 1866. The members meanwhile continued to attend services at Gross Point and High Ridge. In this year, 1866, a small twenty by forty foot wooden building was erected, and the Reverend Mr. Heskemann of Gross Point came to conduct the services every alternate Sunday, for a period of two years.

In 1869, the little church was moved to the south side of the lot and the second church was built. The Reverend Mr. Heamers succeeded the Reverend Mr. Heskemann, but he, too, came only on Sundays. During his time a school was established.

The Reverend Mr. Marshall, and later the Reverend Mr. Michels, succeeded to the pastorate in Rose Hill and attended Evanston only as a mission.

The first resident pastor was the Reverend M. Donohue, from Waukegan, who came in 1872. The second church was used for twenty years.

The new St. Mary's Church was begun in 1891, and was ready for use in May, 1892.

The German Catholic population had increased to such an extent it became possible to organize a new con-

THE REVEREND H. P. SMYTH
Pastor of St. Mary's Parish for thirty-five years

gregation. A two story building, to be used as a temporary church and a school, was erected on Ridge Avenue and Washington Street in 1887, and the Reverend Mr.

Greenebaum was installed as pastor. This building served for ten years.

In 1897, the church and school building burned to the ground during school hours, but the teachers and children escaped in safety. The congregation again attended services at St. Mary's Church, while the second building for the St. Nicholas' congregation was under construction. This church was ready for use the spring of the following year. An Academy for young ladies was established at the northeast corner of Davis Street and Wesley Avenue in 1897.

The Reverend H. P. Smyth and the Reverend Mr. Biermann of St. Nicholas Church, acting for the Franciscan Sisters, bought the Kirk residence on Ridge Avenue and fitted it up as a hospital in 1901, and "The St. Francis Hospital Auxiliary Association" was established by the parishes of both St. Mary's and St. Nicholas' Churches.

The Catholic population in Evanston, according to the census taken in 1900, was 3,400, and represented nearly all European nationalities.

The new Gothic Church building of St. Nicholas' parish was begun in the early years of the new century.

PRESBYTERIAN

In 1866, two years after the founding of the Episcopal Church, the Presbyterians and Congregationalists decided to withdraw from the Mother Church, the Methodist, and unite in forming an independent church, neither one being strong enough in numbers to branch out alone.

The Reverend James B. Duncan of the Presbyterian Church of Canada, was invited by the Presbyterians to come to Evanston. With the founding of this union church, July, 1866, began the ministry of the Reverend Mr. Duncan, which extended over a period of two years.

Northwestern University, true to its liberal policy, presented this new union church with a lot on the northwest corner of Hinman Avenue and Greenwood Boulevard, where later was built the Greenwood Inn. This lot was later exchanged for one at the corner of Lake "Avenue" and Chicago Avenue, and the simple wooden structure built upon it, seating about 250 persons, was called the "Lake Avenue Church."

Two years of harmony followed, during which time the attendance increased to such an extent that each denomination felt strong enough to organize a church of its own.

Accordingly, the Presbyterians purchased the interest of the Congregationalists and remained on the site, and the "First Presbyterian Church of Evanston" was organized July 27, 1868, by the Reverend Robert W. Patterson, D.D., and the Reverend James T. Matthews, its original members numbering thirty-eight, all but three of whom had been members of the "Lake Avenue Church."

The ruling elders chosen and ordained were Brainerd Kent, George E. Purrington, Lewis M. Angle and A. L. Winne.

Dr. George Clement Noyes of La Porte, Indiana, a cousin of Professor Henry E. Noyes of Northwestern University, began his long and useful pastorate, covering over twenty-one years of service, from November, 1868, until his death in January, 1889.

After he had served a year, the congregation had so greatly increased that it was necessary to enlarge the building. This was done and a lecture room was added. The church had a seating capacity for 350 persons, after it was enlarged.

In the spring of 1875, the little church and its contents were destroyed by fire, a serious loss to the congregation, following, as it did, so closely upon the Chicago fire, which had brought not only financial embarrassment to many of the business men of the church, but absolute ruin to some. The little congregation, however, rallied bravely to the work of rebuilding, and in a little more than six months—by Christmas time—services were held in the new lecture room. The following year, July, 1876, saw the new church completed, the cost of which was in the neighborhood of $22,000. While homeless, the congregation had held services in Lyon's Hall.

In "A Twenty Years' Pastorate," the Reverend Mr. Noyes says nine hundred and sixty-three persons were taken into the church during his ministry; he joined the hands of seventy-five couples in the holy bond of matrimony and christened one hundred and forty-five children. Had there been no losses by removal or by death, the membership would have reached 1,001, instead of four hundred and fifty or five hundred.

The church had a flourishing Sunday School, a strong Young People's Society of Christian Endeavor; a busy Ladies' Church Association; a "kitchen garden" where eighty-four poor girls were taught to sew and to do kitchen work; a church in South Evanston, the South Evanston Presbyterian Church, which had branched out from the Mother Presbyterian Church, with fifty members three years previous and now its membership had trebled. In short, the church was reaching out in its work in every direction and "carrying on." To use Dr. Noyes' words, "We are trying to do the work which belongs to us as a church." That the church succeeded so well in all its various undertakings was due to the splendid leadership of its pastor. His death occurred January 14, 1889, and he was deeply mourned not only by his own followers, but throughout the village.

For more than a year, the church had no regular pastor, then the Reverend Newell Dwight Hillis, of Peoria, accepted the invitation to take charge, February, 1890, and entered upon his work in April, 1890. His work immediately began to bear fruit and the membership increased almost seventy-five per cent in a few years.

In the fourth year of the Reverend Mr. Hillis' ministry, disaster again visited the church. February 24, 1894, on Sunday morning, the gathering members watched for the second time fire wipe out their place of worship. The membership had increased, and the building of a larger church had been under consideration for some time. Whether to tear the old one down and build an entirely new church, or add to the old one, was a question not yet decided. The fire answered the question. Work was begun at once on the old site, and the following October saw the laying of the corner stone. The building was completed and opened eleven months later, September 1, 1895. The new building of Lemont limestone, with red oak interior finishings and roof-beams of Georgia pine, was erected at a cost of $63,500; the organ cost $6,600 additional. The auditorium and gallery has a seating capacity of fourteen hundred. Two memorial windows commemorate two noble men of the Presbyterian faith, one, the Reverend Robert W. Patterson,

D.D., Father of Chicago Presbyterianism, and who, with the Reverend James T. Matthews was appointed to organize the "First Presbyterian Church of Evanston." The other window was dedicated to the memory of the beloved Reverend George Clement Noyes, D.D.

After Dr. Hillis retired in 1894 from the pastorate to accept an invitation to the Central Church (Independent), Chicago, the Reverend John H. Boyd, D.D., of Charlotte, North Carolina, accepted a call to the church. His persuasive powers were proved one Sunday in April, 1899, when the remaining church debt of $17,500 was wiped out by the congregation in a space of forty minutes, after an appeal by the pastor.

A prosperous church whose every pastor held a record for fine leadership; a church membership soaring toward the thousand mark—such was the First Presbyterian Church of Evanston, when the new century began.

GERMAN LUTHERAN

In the neighborhood of Clark Street and the Northwestern railroad, there was a settlement of German Lutherans in the early seventies who had come from their home in Mechlinburgh-Schwerin, to this "village in the woods," where they spent many homesick and unhappy hours without the solace of a church, where the gospel was preached in their own language. In 1872, the Reverend A. H. Reinke, who was later the pastor in Chicago of the largest German Lutheran congregation in America, agreed to come to Evanston on Sunday evenings and preach to the little group of German settlers gathered in one of the cabins, and occupying chairs, stools, boxes and even over-turned wash-tubs, so eager were these new countrymen to hear the gospel in their

19

native tongue. In this group were H. Voights, H. Witt, Joh. Witt, Joachim Witt, P. Claussen, Martin Becker, A. P. Handke, F. Lass, Joh. Vorbeck, and F. Strokey, and on August 8, 1875, these men founded the German Evangelical Lutheran Bethlehem Church of Evanston, Cook County, Illinois.

The first church of this denomination, a small frame building, was built on Florence Avenue near Lake Street. Their first ordained minister was the Reverend Edward Doring, who held the pastorate from 1874 to 1881.

The first school was in an attic of a small dwelling in the prairie where the pastor, the Reverend Mr. Detzer, who took charge in 1881, taught a class of twelve children. Although the members of the German Lutheran population were paying taxes for public schools, they decided to build a school house of their own and erected a school building on Greenwood Boulevard.

In 1886, fourteen years after the founding of the church, the members put up a substantial church building at the corner of Wesley Avenue and Greenwood Boulevard.

In 1890 a two-story brick-veneered school house was completed and the class of pupils moved into its more spacious quarters. Soon after this, the Reverend Mr. Detzer, after nearly twenty years of faithful service, left this Evanston church to build up a German Lutheran mission in St. Paul. The Reverend Mr. Reinke again took under his care the little congregation and in September, 1890, his son-in-law, the Reverend J. D. Matthius of Chicago, was installed as minister, under whom the the church continued to prosper and the congregation to increase.

NORWEGIAN-DANISH METHODIST EPISCOPAL CHURCH

Karl Shou, a native of Denmark, who was a student in Northwestern University, in 1870 gathered together a few Scandinavian friends on Sunday afternoons in the Benson Avenue School, for the study of the Bible. At the Annual Conference in Milwaukee, October, 1871, he was appointed pastor of the church, which had grown out of his Bible class, and had a membership of thirty-three. The vacated First Methodist Episcopal Church building was moved to a lot on the south side of Church Street, between Orrington and Sherman Avenues, and taken over for the use of this church.

By 1900, the membership reached about one hundred, and the various pastors that had been engaged comprised four teachers in the theological school, two editors, and six students in educational institutions in Evanston.

Brother Haugan, appointed pastor in 1895, made the plans for the church building on Clark Street and superintended its erection.

SWEDISH METHODIST EPISCOPAL CHURCH

The Swedes were in the majority in the Scandinavian Methodist Episcopal Church, which Karl Shou had organized in 1870, but as they were denied meetings conducted in their language, they withdrew and formed a separate society, holding their meetings in Lyon's Hall, where in 1874 their church was formally organized.

During the pastorate of O. J. Stead, a theological student, the church building on the corner of Grove Street and Sherman Avenue was erected. It was dedicated June 11, 1876.

CENTRAL STREET METHODIST EPISCOPAL CHURCH

In August, 1870, North Evanston was set apart as a separate charge at the quarterly conference of the First Methodist Episcopal Church of Evanston, and the Second Methodist Episcopal Society of Evanston was organized September 6, 1870, by the Reverend E. G. W. Hall, and Mr. and Mrs. D. W. Warren, and John Culver, who had withdrawn from the First Methodist Episcopal Church to form a new church.

John Culver donated a lot on West Railroad Avenue near Lincoln Street. The Reverend Daniel P. Kidder made a very liberal contribution which encouraged others to do likewise. The church was dedicated August 11, 1872. The rear part of the building, however, already had been in use for services for some time. Another lot was purchased at the corner of Central Street and Prairie Avenue and a new building erected, which was dedicated December, 1891.

THE HEMENWAY METHODIST EPISCOPAL CHURCH

The Hemenway Methodist Episcopal Church of South Evanston was organized July 17, 1873, but it had had its beginning over a year previous, in the spring of 1872. For several months, regular services were held in a school house on Ridge Avenue, south of Lincoln Avenue (Main Street). Lots for a church building were secured at the corner of Lincoln Avenue (Main Street) and Benson Avenue (Elmwood), and ground was broken for the first building July 22, 1873. With only the basement finished, the church was dedicated November, 1873. On May 9, 1883, the entire building was destroyed by a cyclone. The pastor, Isaac Linebarger and his wife were approaching the church at the time the cyclone struck it and the flying boards fell all around them.

The second church building was dedicated November 11, 1883. A little over two years later, on Saturday morning, January 23, 1886, it was burned. As James Wigginton and his wife stood looking at the ashes of the church, he turned to her and remarked, "The church needs us now." Mr. and Mrs. Wigginton immediately became members, an act that marked the beginning of more than forty years of faithful church service.

The congregation then worshiped in Ducat's Hall, and began to make plans for rebuilding. A new site was selected on the east side of Chicago Avenue just north of Lincoln Avenue, a lot with 150 foot frontage. The new church was dedicated December 25, 1887, and named Hemenway Methodist Episcopal Church, in honor of the Reverend Francis Dana Hemenway, professor at Garrett Biblical Institute.

The trustees were Thomas Purnell, Pres., John W. Byam, Wesley L. Knox, W. H. Blake, M. D. Ewell, W. G. Miller and Edwin Benjamin. The stewards were Thomas Purnell, E. Benjamin, J. E. Hathaway, James H. Thomas, Thomas Blackler, J. Milhenning, F. W. Brown, James Wigginton. Charles O. Boring was Sunday School Superintendent. The Reverend A. G. Burton was the first pastor. He served until 1873. Others were W. H. Burns, W. X. Ninde, J. R. C. Layton, C. H. Zimmerman, F. D. Hemenway, S. H. Adams, I. Linebarger, H. B. Ridgaway, L. Curts, M. S. Terry, T. P. Marsh, W. H. Holmes, W. E. Wilkinson, and O. F. Matteson. The first four and the seventh, eighth and ninth of these were supplies.

SECOND PRESBYTERIAN CHURCH

The Reverend George Clement Noyes of the First Presbyterian Church of Evanston began to hold a series of neighborhood prayer meetings in South Evanston after he moved to the corner of Greenleaf Street and Judson Avenue, and out of these prayer meetings grew a desire among the Presbyterians in the south end of town for a church of their own. A call was sent out to all interested persons to attend a meeting February 24, 1884, at Ducat's Hall, that an effort might be made to organize either a Presbyterian or a Congregational Church. There had been a few preliminary meetings and these had been attended by Charles Randolph, General Julius White, A. H. Gunn, J. M. Brown, T. Lamkin, E. A. Downs, William M. R. Vose and George W. Hotchkiss.

At the February meeting were eighty-five persons. A meeting in March showed the movement had the approval of over two hundred adults. At the April meeting, over $6,000 was reported pledged, and it was decided the work of organization and building of a church should go forward as rapidly as possible.

The organization was to be known as "The Presbyterian Church of South Evanston." A lot was purchased for $3,500 at the corner of Hinman Avenue with 114 foot frontage, and Lincoln Avenue (Main Street), on which a church building was erected with a seating capacity for four hundred and fifty persons, the cost of the building being about $20,000. Holabird and Roche were the architects. The church was dedicated by the Reverend George C. Noyes, June 28, 1885. After the village of South Evanston was annexed to Evanston, the corporation became known as "The South Presbyterian Church of Evanston." In 1901 the name was again changed, and it became "The Second Presbyterian of Evanston."

The various ministers occupying the pulpit were the Reverend R. W. Patterson, pulpit supply to November, 1885; the Reverend William Smith of Hudson, New York, who served until his death, February, 1892; the Reverend John N. Milles of Beatrice, Nebraska, serving from June, 1892, to May, 1895; Professor M. Bross Thomas, pulpit supply, March, 1896; Dr. Ringland, April 5, 1896, to February, 1898, whose failing health compelled him to take a year's vacation, at the end of which time he resigned, the pulpit being supplied meanwhile by Professor Thomas again. The Reverend John W. Francis became pastor of the church, February, 1899, and continued to have charge for several years.

ST. LUKE'S PARISH

St. Luke's Parish had its beginning in a mission in July, 1885, the number of communicants being twenty-seven. The first service was held in Ducat's Hall. Later a store on Chicago Avenue was used and the priest in charge the first year was the Reverend Marcus Lane. He was succeeded by the Reverend Daniel F. Smith.

Ground was broken for the church October, 1886, at the northeast corner of Lincoln Avenue (Main Street) and Sherman Avenue. Services were held in the new frame structure the following spring. Twice the church was enlarged. It was consecrated November, 1889, being free from debt. In January, 1889, the corporation was reorganized as a parish.

The number of communicants increased in twenty-one years from twenty-seven to over four hundred, and the parish became a strong and active one in the diocese.

WHEADON METHODIST EPISCOPAL CHURCH

The Wheadon Methodist Episcopal Church was organized in 1888 by the Reverend Dr. Luke Hitchcock, Presiding Elder of the Chicago District and named in honor of its first pastor, the Reverend Edward D. Wheadon, lovingly called Father Wheadon by his congregation. The Reverend Mr. Wheadon formed a class in 1887, which met around in the homes. Then a tent was pitched in a lot on Foster Street and services were held there. In 1888, the services were transferred to a hall on the same street, where the church was organized.

A lot was bought on the corner of Ridge Avenue and Leon Street in 1889, and a chapel built on it costing $1,750. The chapel was dedicated February, 1890. By 1900 the church had a membership of nearly one hundred and a flourishing Sunday School.

EMMANUEL METHODIST EPISCOPAL CHURCH

A Sunday School organized March, 1889, in the High School building on Dempster Street was the beginning of the Emmanuel Methodist Episcopal Church, under control of the First Methodist Episcopal Church. Charles O. Boring was Superintendent, S. A. Kean, Assistant Superintendent, and Charles G. Haskins, Secretary and Treasurer. At the quarterly conference of the First Methodist Episcopal Church, November, 1889, the resolution was offered and adopted, whereas the time had arrived for the purchase of a lot for the ultimate erection of a church thereon, that a committee be appointed to take care of the matter. Accordingly, a lot was purchased at the corner of Greenwood Boulevard and Oak Avenue at a cost of $11,500.

The church building was finished and dedicated August, 1892, the total cost of the property being $80,000.

Among the first Stewards of the church we see the names of H. B. Hurd, S. A. Kean, J. J. Shutterly, C. O. Boring, George S. Baker, John Freeman and George A. Bass. The first pastor appointed for this church was the Reverend Sylvestor F. Jones, brother to Professor William Jones, founder of the Northwestern Female College.

NORWEGIAN-DANISH LUTHERAN CHURCH

The Norwegian-Danish Lutheran Church was organized July 29, 1891. Services were held in rented rooms until a church building, which had belonged first to the German and later to the Swedish Lutheran congregation, was bought and moved to Greenwood Boulevard between Sherman and Benson Avenues.

THE SWEDISH EVANGELICAL LUTHERAN CHURCH

The Reverend S. A. Sandahl of Lake View organized this church with thirty-four communicants in 1888. The first minister was the Reverend J. Edgren. While the Reverend C. Solmonson was pastor, the church and parsonage at Sherman Avenue and Lake Street were built.

FIRST CHURCH OF CHRIST, SCIENTIST

The First Church of Christ, Scientist, began with a membership of twenty-six in January, 1895. The meetings were held in homes in the beginning, the congregation occupying larger quarters as the membership increased, until the church on the southwest corner of

Chicago Avenue and Grove Street was ready for use. This church was destroyed by fire about 1897, and the one hundred members immediately set about erecting a new church at a cost of $25,000. They wiped out the debt in three years.

EVANSTON CHRISTIAN CHURCH

The Evanston Christian Church is the outgrowth of the Reformation movement, which began in western Pennsylvania about the beginning of the nineteenth century, and has followed wherever emigration has gone.

On November 24, 1895, there was a meeting held at the home of Milton O. Naramore, at No. 925 Main Street, to discuss organizing a church. Attending this meeting, besides a few disciples, were City Evangelist E. W. Darst, W. B. Taylor, pastor of the North Side Christian Church of Chicago, and E. S. Ames of the Disciples' Divinity House of the University of Chicago. Several meetings were held in homes, after which a series of meetings were held in Union Hall, No. 807 Davis Street, beginning January 5, 1896. On this date the inaugural sermon was preached by the Reverend W. F. Black of the Central Church of Chicago. Meetings were held daily, except Saturday, for eleven consecutive weeks, at the end of which time, there was a membership of seventy-six persons.

Edward Scribner Ames was the first pastor, appointed May, 1896.

The church continued to grow and prosper and in 1900 a building fund was begun. The property known as the Plymouth Congregational Church was bought and five years later the church property was clear of all indebtedness, with an increasing congregation, an active

Sunday School, Ladies' Aid Society and Woman's Missionary Society.

The Free Methodist Church was organized in 1881, with the Reverend J. D. Kelsey as pastor.

The African Methodist Church was organized in 1882 by the Reverend George H. Hann. It had three members in the beginning. Before 1900 the membership had increased to ninety, and the society owned a house of worship on Benson Avenue.

The Second Baptist Church (colored) was organized in 1883 with twenty members, Nathan Branch being one of its founders. In less than ten years its membership was tripled. The church building which had burned was rebuilt in 1890.

CHAPTER XVI

SCHOOLS

DIVISION OF DISTRICTS. HISTORY OF DISTRICT No. 2

IN 1787, Congress passed an ordinance declaring "schools and the means of education shall be forever encouraged." In 1818, Congress passed an act enabling the people of Illinois to form a constitution of their own, and Section 16 in every township was granted to the state for use of the inhabitants for the support of schools.

Alas! Evanston occupied only the west side of Township 41 north, Range 14 east, and Section 16 lay deep under the waters of Lake Michigan. The provision was that if Section 16 were not obtainable, a section in close proximity should be chosen, so a tract of land in Section 12, Township 41 north, Range 13 east, was chosen, in place of the watery Section 16 of Range 14 east. This tract of land, 153.48 acres, was in Niles Township, lying within the boundaries of the present Simpson and Grant Streets, and Dodge and Hartrey Avenues. In 1847, the school trustees very unwisely parted with this land at the minimum government price of $1.25 per acre. Then, "insult was added to injury" when one Samuel Greene, School Treasurer, disappeared with this and other money in 1873. The money, $5,397.10, appropriated by him, was paid back by his bondsmen "apparently" in 1876, according to Harvey B. Hurd.

The earliest record of schools in "Ridgeville" is under date of 1846 when township trustees for school

A Representation of the Old Log Schoolhouse
on the Ridge

Oakton School
Sketch from memory by J. Seymour Currey

purposes were elected. This election took place at Ridge Road House four years before officials for the Town of Ridgeville were elected, and eleven years before the Illinois school laws were framed. Before 1857, the public schools were not free schools in Illinois, but were subscription schools.

The Township Trustees constituted the Board of Education. In 1848, we find the trustees for this township were O. A. Crain, E. Bennett, M. Dunlap, O. Munn, Jr., and George M. Huntoon, Secretary and Treasurer, whose bond was fixed at $400.

The school land sold to the township by Henry Clarke, December 1, 1846, was part of 80 acres, for which Mr. Clarke had paid the government $100. It had a frontage on Ridge of sixty-six feet, a depth of three hundred and fifty feet, and contained a little more than half an acre. The little log school house stood on the northwest corner of Ridge Avenue, and where Greenleaf Street was later cut through. Thirty-three feet were taken from the school and cemetery ground in 1874 to make Greenleaf Street the proper width.

The burial-ground was back (west) of the school house. This cemetery continued in use until 1872 when the last burial took place, there having been up to that time about a hundred burials in the "grave-yard." Among the burials were those of the Burroughs, Crains and Mr. Munn, Sr. In 1859 Rose Hill had been opened for use. In her memoirs, Mrs. Crain says that the log school house had been built by Samuel Reed and other pioneers before she came to Grosse Point in 1842. The ground was deeded to the township by Henry Clarke.

The homes nearest the school were those of Charles

and Ozro Crain. The Charles Crain home was on the southwest corner of where Greenleaf Street crosses Ridge Avenue. Across Greenleaf Street on the northwest corner stood the old log school house. On the southeast corner of Greenleaf and Ridge was Charles Crain's cooperage shop.

In 1844, Mrs. Marshall taught a private or subscription school in a cooper shop, presumably Ozro Crain's, as it was across from his residence on Ridge Avenue.

Throughout the length and breadth of the country, the one-room school house which in most cases was built of logs, was the forerunner of the great institutions of today.

The little school house served not only as a place of learning, but was the "meetin' house," and the center of social activities as well; its pump and tin cup in the yard; a water-pail and dipper requisites of the interior. The poor lone "school marm" had a hard time of it, trying to teach the "young ideas how to shoot." The ages of the pupils ranged from four to sixteen or eighteen, and the subjects taught were mainly the three R's. A great fire place at one side of the room furnished the comforting warmth during the cold weather. In later years the huge, round, cast-iron drum-stove stood out strong against the gleaming white-washed walls, and happy was the pupil who was allowed to feed its fiery interior.

Those were the days of apple-rolling; the days of the noisy slate and screeching pencil; the days of such games as "Double Scrub," "Rotation," "Chase the crowd," "Bull-pen," and "Run, Sheepie, run;" the days when each boy carved his autograph deep in the top of his desk, that all who came later might learn the identity of its former occupant.

Friday afternoons were times to be looked forward to with eager anticipation, when some embryo statesman, with great gusto, spoke his "piece" from the "Piece-book," or a future suffragette brought tears to the eyes of the audience, as she recited, "Curfew Shall Not Ring Tonight."

The Spelling Bees were occasions of great joy, the contestants being lined up on either side of the small room, and it was, perhaps, as much of an honor in those days for one to prove himself the best speller in a community, as it is today to be the proven foot-ball star.

The Singing School had its singing master who, after going through a song several times, struck the pitch, sometimes by voice, sometimes by tuning fork, and the very rafters resounded to the response of the gladsome young voices. Usually no notes accompanied the words in the song books to guide the singers; the singing master loudly carried the tune, while he beat time with his arms and his whole body swayed in rhythmic motion.

The evenings of the pie-suppers and box-suppers were popular with the young people, the boxes being sold to the highest bidders. The young men very soon discovered that the fanciest box did not always contain the best prepared supper and they made their bids accordingly.

The day of mental discipline had not yet arrived; there were sterner measures taken to enforce the rules. There is a tradition that an early teacher in the old school house on the Ridge bumped the heads of the unruly pupils against the walls.

The exact date that the log school house on the Ridge was erected is not on record, but it was about 1841 or 1842, according to Mrs. Crain, who lived opposite it. However, there is a record of its needing repairs in 1846, but when the trustees had their meeting, the repairs asked for were voted down. But the trustees voted at that meeting that a water pail and dipper should be furnished.

As previously stated, the public schools in Illinois at this time were not free schools. A careful schedule was kept of attendance and of all expenses, teachers' wages, fuel, light, repairs, etc., and the head of each family paid according to the number of children in his family attending school. Sometimes the poorest man paid the highest tax, if his family of children were the largest. The parents were required to board the teacher —"boarding around," it was termed. The tuition bill of a family varied from three-quarters of a cent to six cents per day, according to the number of children from a family and the wages of the teacher.

The first teacher in the log school house was James Baker. The second one was a Mr. Satchell, who taught the a b c's to William Carney, son of Pioneer John Carney. William Carney was on Evanston's police force in later years. The third teacher was a man by the name of Smith, said to be a "rough handler, who used to bang the boys' heads against the walls."

A few years ago, Charles S. Raddin was giving a lecture on early Evanston. He threw a view of the log school house on the screen, when a man in the audience very audibly remarked, "Many a good thrashing I got there."

20

The first teacher employed by the trustees was Miss Cornelia Wheadon (later Mrs. C. A. Churcher), daughter of Father Wheadon, so beloved by his Methodist congregation. Her license to teach was signed by George M. Huntoon, Treasurer, dated June 1, 1846, and is at Evanston's Historical Library. Miss Wheadon's salary was $1.25 per week, which was considered a very fair "wage" in those days. Her salary in the same school, previous to the time of her being employed by the trustees was six shillings (seventy-five cents) per week for five weeks. Before the days of the trustees employing the teachers, Miss Elmina Burroughs and Mr. T. H. Ballard also had taught in the little school house.

Miss Wheadon's successor was Miss H. W. Barnes, who continued teaching for two years after her marriage to Sylvester Hill. Her salary was somewhat higher than that of her predecessors, being the munificent sum of $2.00 per week.

During the winter of 1846, the fire place of the little one-room, log school house burned nine cords of wood.

One teacher by the name of Stiles thought the pupils should speak louder than was their custom and in order to insure this, he insisted on the pupils shouting their recitations that he might hear the words plainly from across the street where he had taken his stand. There probably was much merriment in the school during this performance and these times were probably hailed with joy by the mischievous ones.

That the log-house had a floor is proved by the fact that one time a wild animal took up its lodging beneath the boards of the floor and it is said there was great difficulty in getting it to take up other quarters.

The school also had a black-board, which, it seems, was something to boast of in those days.

In March, 1848, it was voted to divide the township into two school districts, all the township north of the south line of Section 19 to be incorporated in District No. 1. There is no record of the result of the vote on this question. In February, 1852, four years later, the division was legally made. District No. 1 comprised the south part of the township and District No. 2 extended "from the south line of Eli Gaffield's farm" to the north boundary line. A later vote, however, made the north District No. 1, "with its south boundary the middle line east and west of Section 19," and the southern part, which had been District No. 1 was made District No. 2.

The book used by the Directors of School District No. 2, beginning with the date of September 2, 1859, tells an interesting story, although the entries consist only of orders on the treasurer for money to be paid out, and brief reports of meetings. The old log school house now served only for church services, a new one-room building having been erected on a lot on the west side of the Ridge, south of Main Street, that was bought of George M. Huntoon for $250.

A "true" copy from the Poll Book is the first entry. Philip Petry, Peter Muno and Henry Hepworth were Judges of Election. Henry Hepworth acted as clerk. School Directors elected were Henry Hepworth, Albert Dart, Peter Muno and W. B. Huntoon. The sum of $200 was to be levied on all taxable property for school purposes.

Thirteen years before this date, Miss Wheadon had

been paid at the rate of $5.00 per month for teaching.
In 1859, the rate was considerably higher, being almost
four times that amount.

A stove now was in use, evidently, as an entry shows
the stove pipe was cleaned and fixed: a fire shovel bought.
Although cord wood was still used, a shovel was needed
for taking up ashes. With new blinds for the windows
and the walls freshly white-washed, the place was ready
for the opening of the fall term.

Harvey B. Hurd's name now appears as school treasurer. An order on the treasurer in 1861 shows that Miss
Minnie Holcomb received $18.00 per month. In Novem-
ber, a man teacher was employed, William Wheeler, at
$25.00 per month. By 1862, the wages of the man teacher
had risen to $30.00 per month. The women still received
less than the men. Phidelia Burroughs in 1863 received
$20.00 per month.

In this year charges of cruelty were preferred
against a man teacher, but the case was dismissed, as
proof was not sufficiently satisfactory.

A well was dug and curbed.

Cornelia Wheeler received $20.00 per month for
teaching, in 1865.

Six cords of wood were bought at $36.00. The same
were sawed at $1.00 per cord.

Under Miss Bartlett's tutelage, the curriculum was
extended, and a globe was needed and furnished.

Notices of election of directors were posted on the
school house, Oakton Depot and on the oak tree in front
of Peter Muno's house, the election to take place July
12, 1865.

In 1866, G. M. Huntoon took the school census.

O. F. Gibbs insured the school house January, 1866. The premium on the policy was $4.50.

In September, 1866, the school taxes were raised to $400.

In 1867, it was recommended school should be kept open ten months during the ensuing year, and the school taxes should not exceed $800.

Eight hundred fifty dollars was needed for repairs on the school, and bonds were issued. One was issued to Superintendent of Public Schools of Cook County at 10% per annum, six months' interest to be paid in advance and deducted.

Desks were bought for $322.00, and two stoves at $32.50, with $13.00 added for setting them up. Cedar posts came from Mears, Bales and Company.

Although the directors talked of selecting a more central site, the idea was abandoned and the little one-room school house was moved back and another room added. Two teachers' services were now required, the woman, Arelia Ferry, received $36.00 per month, and the man teacher, M. R. Brewster, $75.00 per month.

The janitor was paid the princely sum of one dollar per week.

School taxes rose to $1,200 in 1868.

New wood boxes were needed and made.

In 1869, James S. Kirk's name appears as one of the directors.

Children attending school from outside the district were required to pay fifty cents per month.

Mr. Brewster's salary now reached $90.00 per month.

Blackboard and chalk were bought.

In 1870, the names of F. M. McLaughlin, O. F. Gibbs, N. G. Iglehart and S. Goodenow appear as directors.

A. W. Shuman's salary reached the top notch of salaries in the old record book. He received an even $100.00 per month in 1871. Josephine Gibbs received $35.00 per month in 1873.

Samuel Greene's name appears as treasurer in 1870. He was elected in 1868.

In 1873, there was a balance in the treasurer's hands of $1,185.79. The story is cut short as a dozen or more leaves have been clipped from the book, but from another book we learn Samuel Greene disappeared with over $5,000.00, which amount was afterwards paid back. This amount was probably paid by his bondsmen.

The first regular school tax was levied in 1856, fifty cents on each hundred dollars of taxable property.

The first recorded school census was in 1857. All white children under 21 were enumerated. C. Thomas took the census, receiving six dollars for the work.

In the year of 1871, a four-room, brick building was erected on Lincoln Avenue (now Main Street), and Benson Avenue (now Elmwood Avenue), and called Central School. The cost of the building was $18,000. In 1890, it was enlarged at a cost of $10,000.00.

In 1893, during a school session, fire broke out and completely destroyed the building. Several persons were injured, but no one was killed. By great presence of mind and heroic efforts on the part of the teachers, the children were marched from the schoolrooms to safety. Miss Jenny Foster taught the first grade children at the time. She formed them in line and guided them without mishap through the smoke and out of the burning building. Sam

Mack, who ran an express business in the south end of town, caught several of the children who jumped from the second story, thus saving them not only from broken arms and legs, but probably from death. He was injured and taken to the hospital. Samuel Harrison, in later years Justice of the Peace in Evanston, made a heroic dash into the burning building and saved a little girl scarcely a moment before the roof caved in. A fountain erected in 1901 stands in the school yard, a memorial to the bravery of the teachers and to the men who gave such noble assistance.

Another building was immediately put up costing $47,000.00, the pupils under eighth grade occupying rented rooms during the construction, and the eighth grade pupils going to the High School building on Dempster Street.

The Lincoln School was erected in 1886 on Lincoln Avenue, as Main Street was then called. In 1891, Lincoln Avenue became Evanston Avenue and this was changed to Main Street probably when South Evanston was annexed to Evanston in 1892.

In 1895, the four rooms becoming inadequate for the increased number of pupils in the neighborhood, the beautiful Lincoln School building, similar in architecture to the Central School building, was erected, the cost being the same as that of the Central School, $47,000.00.

Lincoln School probably received its name, as did several other schools in Evanston, from the street on which it was located, and most likely retained it, when the name of the street was changed, by suggestion of Miss Nellie Sickles, a teacher in the south end schools.[1]

(1)   Miss Sickles died in 1925.   She had been a teacher in Evanston for over thirty-five years.

On the northwest corner of Ashland Avenue and Main Street, in 1900, another school building was built. This was Washington School, whose cost was $35,000.00.

These school buildings can scarcely be improved upon, either in architecture or equipment.

FREDERICK W. NICHOLS

Lyndon Evans was elected superintendent of South Evanston school in 1884. The superintendent in charge of the schools of District No. 2, preceding Mr. Nichols, was Professor Scudder. Professor Frederick W. Nichols came to the Evanston schools in the capacity of superintendent of District No. 2 in September, 1886, from the

Kensington School (now in Chicago), where he had been superintendent from 1883 to 1886. He remained in Evanston until 1893, when he took charge of the Springer School in Hyde Park, remaining four years. In 1897, Professor Nichols was again induced to return to Evanston, and is still at the head of District No. 76, which comprises four schools, Central, Lincoln, Washington and Oakton. These schools have reached a high plane of efficiency under his wise direction, many families taking up their residence in Evanston that their children might take advantage of the fine school system inaugurated by him. His love for the artistic shows itself in the surroundings of the school buildings, as well as in the interior decorations. The pupils have been encouraged in the line of art, and their work has been placed on exhibition many times at the Woman's Club and other places.

There is yet another school of the south end of town to be mentioned, the Illinois Industrial School for Girls, which was situated at the corner of Main Street and Sheridan Road. This school was organized in 1877 and while it received girls from all parts of the state, it was not a state organization, but was maintained by charity. A bill was passed in 1879, which insured it legal protection. The surplus funds of the Woman's Centennial Association of Illinois were used for the benefit of destitute girls and the school was a direct outgrowth of this organization. Mrs. John L. Beveridge was an active promoter in the organizing of the school, and its first president, Mrs. R. M. Wallace (wife of General Wallace) was president in the nineties. Each county paid $10 per month for each girl it sent. There were one hundred and fifteen girls in the school in the early nineties. If a reliable family desired one of the girls to assist in the housework it paid $1.25 per week to the home, and the total amount paid for her work was carefully credited to the girl's account and presented to her upon her discharge from the school.

Permanent buildings were erected in Park Ridge a little after 1900, and the home was moved to this location. This building had been previously the Soldiers' Home, which was moved to Quincy, Illinois.

CHAPTER XVII

SCHOOLS—*(Continued)*

DISTRICT No. 1
VILLAGE HIGH SCHOOL. EVANSTON TOWNSHIP HIGH SCHOOL

ALL the school records of District No. 1, previous to 1872, were destroyed in the Chicago fire. The first school house in District No. 1, later District 75, was built in 1842, and antedated the log school house on the Ridge, according to Benjamin Franklin Hill in his talk before the Evanston Historical Society on May 31, 1902. This school was a one-story building north of the line of Church Street and east of the present Maple Avenue. After a time another story was added to the school, but even the two rooms proved inadequate in a few years and in 1859 or 1860 the little building was replaced by a two-story structure on Benson Avenue between Clark and Church Streets, and became known as the Benson Avenue School. Its location was said to be in the exact geographical center of the district. Henry M. Bannister, son of the Reverend Henry Bannister of Garrett Biblical Institute, tells us that the school building was moved a block south a short time later and raised on posts, where a semi-tornado blew it off its supporting pillars. He also tells us of a teacher in the original school who would toss a ruler to a disorderly pupil and request him to return it, when he would receive a sharp slap on the palm of the hand with it.

After the tornado, the building was repaired and

served until about 1870, when wings were added to the
north and south sides. When the Milwaukee and St. Paul
Railroad bought the ground in 1888, the school had to be
moved, as it stood directly in the right of way. It was
necessary to divide it for the moving process into three
sections and the main part of the building was destroyed
at this time. Its new location was on the south side of
Emerson Street, west of Maple Avenue. The first little
building was moved to 1618 Orrington Avenue, where it
stood many years, the first floor used as a Chinese laun-
dry, and the upper story serving as a polling place. The
Haven School was erected at Church Street and Sherman Avenue, to take the place of the Benson Avenue
School.

In the Benson Avenue School many persons of more
than local renown taught. Among them were Frances
Willard, in 1862; Mary Bannister, who married Frances
Willard's brother Oliver, editor of the *Chicago Evening
Post;* Mary E. Willard, who supplied for a few weeks;
Jenny L. Wells (Mrs. Thomas Craven); Mary Woodford
(Mrs. Merrill).

Frances Willard said that teaching in this school
was the hardest work she had ever done. Many of the
pupils were mischievous and she had to resort to the use
of the stick. One day she started toward two unruly boys
with it, when they vaulted through an open window and
never returned. One man teacher was said to quell the
spirits of the rebellious ones by tossing them to the ceil-
ing. However, teaching in the school had its compensa-
tions. Miss Willard said that the sweetest music she
heard during her teaching years was the song her pupils
sang of the patter of the raindrops, while they accom-

DEMPSTER STREET SCHOOL, 1875
Sketch from pencil drawing made by Miss Jessie Bradley from memory
(Inset) MISS SARGENT

HINMAN AVENUE SCHOOL

panied themselves with drumming of their fingers on their desks, in imitation of the falling rain.

Not far from this school stood Ben Peeney's saw-mill, the gentle hum of which could be heard for blocks around. No more welcome sound ever reached the ears of the Benson Avenue School pupils than the shrill whistle of the saw mill at noon. Books and slates were instantly laid aside, as their owners suddenly realized that there was "an empty sort of feeling" in the neighborhood of the stomach that could only be done away with by partaking of the contents of one of Mother's well-filled baskets, or by indulging in one of her substantial and home-cooked dinners.

"Jim" Tait's wagon shop and "Dan" Bowdish's blacksmith shop were also in the same block with the school.

In 1870, two school lots were purchased one on Noyes Street where the North Ridge School was built, and one on Hinman Avenue and Dempster Street, the site of the old Dempster Street School. The Noyes Street School, or North Ridge School, as it was called, was a one-story, two-room wooden building, which was removed in 1892 to give place to a two-story, eight-room building. George Romyne Kline won a prize in the old North Ridge School for being the best speller. He was very proud of his prize, the picture of George Washington, and took great pleasure in exhibiting it in later years. Mr. Kline was Tax Collector in Evanston in 1898, 1899 and 1900. His father, Simon Veder Kline, had also held public office in Evanston at various times, being Township Assessor, Township Collector and Village Trustee. The Kline home was across the road from Buck-Eye Hotel.

There is no record of the names of the earliest teachers of the district. The names of Echenbracht and Edwards are found among the early principals. Under the administration of Charles Raymond, who was the first to bear the title of superintendent, the schools were first graded and order was brought out of chaos. He was succeeded by Otis E. Haven, son of Bishop Haven, in 1873, "under whose nine years' administration the schools were brought to their utmost efficiency," according to the report of District No. 1 published in 1892. Mr. Haven taught the highest grade in the Benson Avenue School, his room being called the High School, which he is credited with having organized. Strenuous objection was raised by some of the tax payers to organizing a public High School, as they said that anyone wishing a higher education than the grade schools afforded could go into his own pocket to pay for it. Dr. Haven had forty pupils enrolled in his room in 1873. The High School term was three years only, but before Mr. Haven left the school he had arranged a four-year program, which went into effect the last year of the Village High School. The science classes were all under one teacher in the early years. In 1876, Dr. Haven graduated two pupils, Ellen Pryor and Thomas S. Noyes.

In 1873 the grammer grades and High School were in the Benson Avenue building, and all the primary grades were housed in the Dempster Street building, there being 380 enrolled in the lower grades at Benson Avenue, and forty-nine in the primary grades at the Dempster Street School. In 1877, owing to the crowded condition of the Benson Avenue School, the High School classes were removed to Jones Hall on Davis Street.

J. Scott Clark became the first principal of the High School in 1879. Miss Ellen White was engaged in 1879, the first German teacher. The first writing teacher was A. J. Cole, hired in 1881. There were eight teachers in the two schools.

Returning to the early days of these two schools, we find Miss Celia Sargent began teaching in the Dempster Street School in 1873. She continued to teach for fifty years, without one year of absence, numbering among her pupils many whose names are known the world over. She was well loved by her young charges, who recalled in later years that her gentle methods of ruling were extremely original and thoroughly effective, and no harsh measures were necessary.

Miss Nanny Hines began teaching in the Benson Avenue School in 1873.

By 1879 the three schools were inadequate to accommodate the increasing number of children in the district, and a lot was purchased on Wesley Avenue, on which a large, one-story brick building was erected in 1882. This was known as the Wesley Avenue School until 1900, when the name was changed to David B. Dewey School, in honor of one of Evanston's prominent citizens and a member of the Board of Education for many years.

In 1881, the old Dempster Street School building was removed to Benson Avenue near Clark Street, and used as a church by the Second Baptist congregation until it was destroyed by fire in 1889. A second school house having four rooms was built on the original site of the Dempster Street School in the same year, 1881, and was known as the Hinman Avenue School. Miss Nanny Hines was transferred from the Benson Avenue School to the new Hinman Avenue School and made principal, in 1881. In 1891, two rooms were added to the building and in 1898 another larger building was erected on the site. As the building was not finished by September, it was necessary to house the pupils elsewhere. Several of the grades went to the Withington School, formerly a private school, and later a cafeteria. Miss Hines taught her class in a hall on Davis Street, and Miss Sargent took her class to Lincoln School, the children who lived at a distance being taken to the latter place in a bus, which met them at the Avenue House. This school received its third name in 1910, at the death of Mr. Miller, a member of the School Board for twenty-seven years, and became the H. H. C. Miller School. Mr. Miller was the first president of the board to be chosen by popular election.

Miss Nanny Hines resigned in 1909, after having served twenty-eight consecutive years in the same school, and eight years in the Benson Avenue School, a record of thirty-six years of faithful work. Harry P. Pearsons, a former pupil of Miss Hines, and later a mayor of Evanston for ten years, says of Miss Hines, "My thankfulness steadily increases as I come more and more to realize what a force she has been, not only in my life, but in the life of Evanston, for Evanston is now known as the Athens of the West, largely because of what Miss Hines has made of Evanston children."

The Larimer School, named for Joseph Larimer, a member of the School Board, was erected on Crain Street in 1894. Miss Jessie L. Luther was the first principal.

The pamphlet on the "Regulations and Course of Study for the Government of the Public Schools of Evanston, Illinois, Revised June 1879," shows O. E.

Haven, M. A., Superintendent; High School teachers, E. J. James, Ph. D., Principal, and Miss Jennie P. Fisk, Assistant; teachers in Grammar Schools, Miss Helen E. Amos, Eighth Grade; Miss Agnes S. Hinman, Seventh Grade; Miss Nannie M. Hines, Sixth Grade; Miss Alice Kitchell, Fifth Grade; teachers in Primary Schools, Miss Mary C. Adams, Third and Fourth Grades; Miss M. E. Offutt, First and Second Grades; Miss Celia Sargent, First and Second Grades. Slates were used in the first grade, and physical exercises were part of the day's work. Among the text-books, Monteith's Elementary Geography was used in the fourth and fifth grades, Robinson's Arithmetic in fifth, sixth and seventh grades, and Greene's Grammar in sixth, seventh and eighth grades.

The pamphlet on the course of study, published in 1884, shows George S. Baker, superintendent. He resigned after four years to take up law. Homer H. Kingsley succeeded Mr. Baker in 1886.

Credit is due Mr. Kingsley, to a large extent, for the introduction of the kindergarten in 1892, manual training in 1897, and domestic science about the same time. The kindergarten in connection with the public schools was a new idea, and Evanston was one of the first cities to try out the plan.

Mrs. Louise P. Stanwood was the first woman to serve on the School Board in District No. 1.

Before resuming the history of the High School, which was not organized as a Village High School until 1876, an early private school must be mentioned that had an existence of but four years. This school, called the Grove Street School, was founded in 1863, and was opened January 6, 1864. Edwin Haskin, the founder, felt that the old Benson Avenue School, with its two ungraded rooms, did not afford the educational facilities that he wished his own six children to have. Other children in the neighborhood attended this school and shared its advantages with the Haskin children. The first principal was Miss Minerva Bruce, and her assistant was Miss Susan Warner. The Reverend Henry Bannister, John Clough and Edwin Haskin were the directors. The school derived its name from the beautiful grove of gigantic oak trees that grew within the block bounded by Grove and Davis Streets and Hinman and Judson Avenues, where the school was located. Frances Willard, Kate Kidder, Kate Jackson, Anna Fisk and Emma B. White were some of the teachers. Numbered among its pupils were Ella Bannister, Lizzie White, Alice Judson, Rebecca Hoag, Annie Marcy, Charlie and Walter Haskin, Addison DeCoudries, George Bragdon, Henry Ten Eyck White, Will Somers and Frank Dennison, who was killed by the cars on his way home from school one evening. The school building was remodeled and turned into a residence after having served in its original capacity four years.

The district lost its name of District No. 1 in 1901, and became District 75 of Cook County, Illinois.

The Village High School was legally established in 1875. However, previous to this date, Dr. Haven had introduced high school studies in the eighth grade. There had been strong opposition to the idea of a high school, as it was thought that the Northwestern Academy could accomplish all that a high school could do to prepare pupils for college. For several years the school had no regular accommodations, being first housed in Lyons'

Hall,[1] then going from hall to hall, where its work was greatly hampered by cramped and uncomfortable quarters entirely unsuited to school purposes. From the beginning its scholarship had a high standard, and its graduates entered several of the best colleges. Among its early teachers was Dr. E. J. James, later President of the University of Illinois. In 1879 he was succeeded by J. Scott Clark, later Professor of English in Northwestern University.

In less than a half dozen years, Evanston realized the value of a High School. When a Township High School was suggested in 1881, the suggestion was received with great favor. A meeting was called, headed by John L. Beveridge, L. C. Pitner and H. A. Pearsons, to discuss the matter. The question of establishing a Township High School was submitted to the legal voters of the township, with the result of 611 votes cast in favor of it and 147 against it.

Henry Leonidas Boltwood is known as the Father of the Township High School in Illinois. He organized the first school of its kind in Princeton, Bureau County, in 1867, and another township high school in Ottawa, La Salle County, in 1878. In 1883, he organized his third township high school, which was in Evanston, where he remained as principal until his death twenty-two years later. He had been appointed a member of the Illinois State Board of Education in 1876 and served for eight years. In 1891 he was elected President of the State Teachers' Association. At the time of his death he had been a teacher in the east and middle west fifty-three years.

---

(1)   Named for Joseph McGee Lyons, a banker, who was a resident of Evanston for forty-two years.

The site proposed for the Evanston Township High School was at the corner of Benson Avenue (Elmwood Avenue) and Dempster Street, 250 feet on Benson Avenue and 200 feet on Dempster Street. The question of site was put to vote and there were 176 votes cast in favor of the site to two against it. The cost of the ground was sixteen dollars per front foot, which amounted to

EVANSTON TOWNSHIP HIGH SCHOOL

$4,000. The ground was very low—it had been a cow pasture—and the work of filling in cost $2,000. The contract price of the building was $32,500. The entire bond issue for the purchase of the land, erection of the building and equipment of the same with furniture was $40,000, as shown by the records of that time. Ground was broken October 18, 1882, and the completed building was dedicated August 31, 1883, less than a year later. School opened September 3, 1883, with the following teachers: Henry L. Boltwood, Principal; Lyndon Evans, A. B. (Knox), Science; Eva S. Edwards, Mathematics; Mary L. Barrie, Latin and English; Ellen L. White, German and History; O. H. Merwin, Music. Music was retained in the school only three years.

Two days before the Christmas vacation in 1883, the first year the school was occupied, it was found that there was a fire raging in each of the three flues in the west half of the building. Miss Eveline S. Edwards, a teacher in the old Village High School and for thirty-five years a member of the faculty of the Evanston Township High School, gives a fine account in a *News-Index* article of December 3, 1924, of the way the pupils conducted themselves at the time of the fire. She says there was no fire drill in those days, yet there was no excitement, no crowding. Each one quietly secured his possessions and went out, while the older boys tried to save the few pieces of apparatus in the school room. The Evanston Fire Department did all it could, but Chicago was called upon for help. The fire was so hidden in the partitions that it was three o'clock in the morning before the firemen dared to leave. Repairs were not completed when vacation was over, but all the classes were taken care of in the east half of the building, two teachers sometimes hearing recitations in the same room.

The enrollment for the year of 1883-1884 was one hundred fifty-five.

In 1885, five sets of examination papers were sent to the State Fair exhibit. Three of these took first prizes of five dollars each. In 1886, eight out of ten took first prizes and the other two took seconds, besides two "sweep-stake" prizes for the best six and best ten sets. In seven successive years the school carried off the highest honors, and the cash received, $424, was used for buying pictures, casts, and books for the library. The system of awarding prizes was then changed, and the school has not competed since.

New Trier Township paid a tuition of $1,525 for pupils attending the Evanston Township High School from Wilmette, Winnetka, Kenilworth, and Glencoe, while its own school building was under construction.

Manual training was introduced in the school in 1886, with equipment for a class of twelve, and twenty enrolled in the class! Each pupil paid twenty-five cents per week for instruction outside of school hours to T. E. Skinner. Short daylight hours interfered with the work in winter, and athletics interfered with it in mild weather, so the work was dropped for several years. In 1900 it was made a part of the school curriculum. Typewriting was introduced, but the study of it was left to the option of the pupil. Clay modeling had been introduced in 1885 and later dropped for lack of space. It was taken up again in 1889. Great interest was shown in the citizenship classes. On two presidential election days, the students went through the form of holding elections. Historic Art was introduced in 1887 and it has proved itself to be one of the most satisfactory studies of the course. The drawing department, under Miss Edwards in the early days, was a success from its beginning.

In 1891, an addition was built to the High School. The cost of this was $22,000.

WILFRED FITCH BEARDSLEY

HENRY LEONIDAS BOLTWOOD

In 1893 there was a vacancy in the High School for a Greek and Latin instructor. A young man called on Mr. Boltwood in regard to the position. "Pretty young?" queried Mrs. Boltwood after the applicant had gone. Yes, he was pretty young, thought Mr. Boltwood, but well qualified for the place. Thirty-four years have proved that Mr. Boltwood was right in his choice of an instructor, who was Wilfred Fitch Beardsley, present Principal of the High School. The following is taken from the (Northwestern) College Alumni Record, page 233: "Wilfred Fitch Beardsley. Born at Albion, Wisconsin. Prepared in Northwestern University Academy. A. B. Beta Theta Pi; Phi Beta Kappa. Deering Prize. Graduate student, Johns Hopkins University, 1898-99. Instructor in Greek and Latin, Evanston Township High School, 1893-98; Assistant Principal, 1899-1900; Associate Principal, 1900—" Mr. Beardsley[2] was Associate Principal until 1906, when he became Principal at the death of Mr. Boltwood.

The enrollment of the High School in 1903 was four hundred twenty.

---

(2) In June, 1927, the honorary degree of Doctor of Humane Letters was awarded Mr. Beardsley by Northwestern University.

Chapter XVIII

LIBRARIES

TO a rude cabin 'mongst the primeval forest trees, in 1837, came the first collection of books to this region, brought from the east by a woman of education, Mrs. Rebecca Mulford, wife of Major Mulford, the "gentleman pioneer." The early settlers brought to their new homes only necessities, but books to Mrs. Mulford came under that head, and not under the head of luxuries.

The first Sunday School library was a collection of fifty books presented to the Methodist Episcopal Sunday School, about 1854, by the same lady. This Sunday School had been started in the old Mulford cabin and was later moved to the log school-house on the Ridge. Mrs. Mulford—later prominent in the Baptist Church—was at one time superintendent, librarian and choir leader. Among the books of Major Mulford's private library were *John Quincy Adams*, by W. H. Seward; Macaulay's *History of England; Wabun,* by Mrs. John Kinzie; the old family Bible, dated 1813, the date of Major Mulford's marriage, and other good books.

In Major Mulford's handwriting in Murray's *English Reader,* Wordsworth's poem, "Pet Lamb," is marked, "learned by Ann at the age of seven years for her father, who was to pay her 25c."

Ann Mulford's name appears in one of the books, followed by "Monticello Female Seminary," and in one of the books, "Mary Mulford, Kemper Hall, Kenosha, Wis.," which reveal their places of schooling.

The *Laws of Illinois*, published in Vandalia, in 1833, which belonged to Major Mulford, is now the property of the Evanston Historical Society. Mary B. Lindsay in Hurd's *History of Evanston* says that this book probably furnished Justice Mulford all the legal lore necessary for him at the time. Major Mulford held the first court in Cook County in 1833. Chicago at that time had only twenty-nine voters.

Judge Harvey B. Hurd, who came to Evanston in 1855, had a very fine library which was destroyed by fire in later years.

In *The Index* of December 18, 1897, Dr. Henry B. Hemenway calls Dr. Edward Eggleston the "Father of the Public Library."

About 1867, Dr. Eggleston, according to Dr. Hemenway in Hurd's History, organized a class of boys (not from any particular church) to meet at his house, 1017 Davis Street, once a week. He was at that time superintendent of the Methodist Sunday School. After a short religious service and a social hour, the boys were invited into his library, there each one was to select books for his home reading for the week. No objection was made to books of adventure, but Dr. Eggleston tried to instill into the young minds a taste for books of value. Dr. Hemenway gives a graphic picture of this fine man sitting in a great, easy chair, his heavy brown hair pushed back and his face lighting up as he looks first to one and then to another of his hearers while he tells stories of frontier life, or stories of his own boyhood. A boy sat on each knee, others on the arms of the chair, more were hanging over the back, and the rest sat at his feet on the floor, or on low stools. Such a picture! Would that it could be duplicated wherever there are boys! The class in time became so large that he had to use the Kindergarten building, which he had built for his sister in the yard east of the house. Bigger plans began to form themselves in the mind of the man who later wrote *Hoosier School-master, Roxy,* and other famous books, and he appealed to various public spirited citizens, Luther L. Greenleaf, among them, to form a public library.

The first meeting to organize "The Evanston Library Association," out of which grew the Evanston Public Library, was held at the home of William T. Shepherd, 1738 Chicago Avenue, and was attended by the following persons: L. L. Greenleaf, the Reverend M. G. Clarke, Dr. E. O. Haven, A. L. Winne, William P. Kimball and William T. Shepherd. (No date recorded.)

A second meeting was held at the same home, August 26, 1870, at which were present L. L. Greenleaf, A. L. Winne, the Reverend E. N. Packard, H. C. Tillinghast and William T. Shepherd.

The constitution and by-laws were drafted by an appointed committee. On October 18, 1870, the constitution was adopted at a meeting held in the Methodist Church. The name according to the constitution became *The Evanston Library Association* and the object of the association was "to establish and maintain a public library and reading room, and in connection with this, by all suitable means to awaken a desire for sound knowledge and a correct taste, and to provide for the gratification of the same among all classes of the community."

There were two classes of membership, Ordinary and

Life. The Ordinary was open to all residents upon the payment of five dollars per annum. The Life was open to all residents upon payment of thirty dollars for the gentlemen, and twenty dollars for the ladies. L. L. Greenleaf was elected president and H. G. Powers, vice-president.

Many donations of money were made, the largest coming from L. L. Greenleaf, $575. Donations of books were made by H. G. Powers, Andrew Shuman, I. S. Jewell, L. J. Gage and others. It was voted December 3, 1870, that books to the amount of $1,000 should be bought by the Book Committee.

The library was in rooms on the second floor of Dr. W. S. Scott's building—later this building had the number of 513 on Davis Street—and was formally opened February 9, 1871. The Association was incorporated under the laws of the State of Illinois, February 23, 1871.

In the spring election of April, 1873, the town residents voted unanimously to have the library transferred to the town. The transfer was authorized to be made May 22, 1873. The first meeting of the Board of Directors of *The Free Library of the Village of Evanston* was held June 21, 1873, in the library rooms, at which time officers were elected. The transfer of 913 volumes and other property was made July 3, 1873.

J. H. Kedzie was the first president of The Free Public Library, and L. H. Boutell was the second president. Mr. Boutell served on the board for twenty-nine years— until his death in 1899. Thomas J. Kellam was the first librarian. The librarian's salary was to be five dollars per week, which included any expense incurred in the care of the room. City Treasurer John R. Lindgren generously turned over his year's salary for 1891 to the library for a book fund. This amount, $1,502.36, made possible a larger purchase of books than could be made in previous years.

In December, 1893, it was decided a trained librarian was needed and Miss Mary A. Lindsay was appointed She entered upon her duties June 1, 1894.

The work of classifying and cataloguing the books under the Dewey Decimal System was begun in March, 1896, and completed in December, 1896, without closing the library or interfering with its routine of work.

In 1896, the *Library Extension* was suggested by Mr. F. W. Nichols, Superintendent of School District No. 2. This consisted of one hundred books, sent to District No. 2, to be distributed under the direction of the teachers. A system of separate school libraries was put in operation the following year, wherein a hundred books were sent to each of the schools furthest from the main library. A Director on the Board, Richard C. Lake. donated one of these libraries of one hundred books.

In October, 1898, the *Children's Corner* in the library reading room was established.

The reference department already established was made of greater value by creating the position of assistant librarian for reference and children's work.

Library Day was inaugurated December 10, 1897. This was dispensed with two years later on account of lack of space to hold the number of persons attending.

From the small beginning of 913 books, owned by the Evanston Library Association, the number of books increased to 114,551 volumes reported for the year ending June 1, 1901, by The Free Public Library. In 1874, the amount of money paid out for books purchased during the year was $260. For the year ending 1901, the amount paid out for books was $2,459.49.

The Inter-State Library Conference was held in Evanston in February, 1898, at which there were 170 delegates representing eleven states.

The library was moved from the Scott Building to the first floor of the Anton Block Building, 522 Sherman Avenue. In 1892, it was moved again, this time to the second floor of the City Hall, upon the completion of that building.

As early as 1884, the erection of a library building was contemplated. Three years later, in 1887, Mr. William Deering offered $5,000 toward the work. During the next ten years the Board was unceasing in its efforts to arouse interest in the subject. In 1897, Charles F. Grey offered $10,000 toward a $100,000 building. The city was asked by the Board in 1899 to appropriate $35,000 for a site for the library. The appropriation was not granted. Charles F. Grey then offered to give $100,-000 for a library building, but the condition was that a site should be furnished, free of incumbrance, and furthermore that the premises should be exempt from taxation.

In June, 1900, the Board sent out circular letters explaining the need of money to buy ground. Voluntary contributions came in, but only to the amount of a little over $2,000, when $40,000 was needed. The money was returned to the donors.

April 6, 1901, a state law was passed, which gave to cities the power to levy a tax for the purpose of purchasing sites for public library buildings. The Board passed resolutions to purchase a site at an estimated cost of $45,000 and sent them to the City Council. The City Council approved the resolutions, but—alas!—the City of Evanston was already in debt to its full legal limit and the action of the Council had to be rescinded.

There were later and other unsuccessful attempts to raise money. In June, 1904, the city purchased the site at the corner of Orrington Avenue and Church Street. On this site of 198 feet facing Orrington Avenue, and 210 feet on Church Street, there stood six dwelling houses which had to be removed before the Library building could be erected. Thirty years before this the first church built in the city had been located on this site.

The city paid for this piece of ground $31,600, issuing bonds in order to be able to do so. Also the city agreed to furnish $25,000 toward the cost of the building. Mr. Andrew Carnegie, god-father of libraries, offered $40,000 and later added $10,000, making a sum of $50,000 toward the cost of the building. Success at last! The corner stone of the Evanston Public Library was laid June 2, 1906, and a beautiful building was erected on the site facing Orrington Avenue. This building is of pure classic design, with a portico supported by Grecian columns. The frame work of the building is of steel, with Bedford stone on the exterior walls.

Mr. J. Seymour Currey tells of making the trip to the R. A. Franks bank in Hoboken, N. J., one time when he was in New York, for the express purpose of thanking Mr. Carnegie for his gift to Evanston. The R. A. Franks bank was in an out-of-the-way, quiet street, with only a clerk or two in sight, a banking establishment, with one depositor only, whose sole business was to distribute the numerous gifts of Mr. Carnegie to libraries, the number of which at that time, in the building and completed, was over 1,800. When a library was named after Mr. Carnegie, it was done solely to honor this generous man and was never the result of a request on his part.

The date of the beginning of Northwestern University Library is almost as early as the beginning of the University itself. In 1856, the University Trustees

LUTHER L. GREENLEAF   J. SEYMOUR CURREY

decided to make an appropriation during the current year for books. This library was for the use of the students, and Miss Willard says the policy was a University library used but not abused. Dr. Foster, who had just been elected to the presidency of the University, asked for a leave of absence for one year in order to continue his work in the Trinity Methodist Episcopal Church of

22

New York for that length of time. This request was granted by the Trustees, and his year's salary of $2,000 was added to the library book fund.

In 1868, the catalogue shows the library contained 3,000 volumes. In 1891, the bound volumes numbered 24,116, and in 1903 this number had increased to 51,658 volumes, and 35,000 pamphlets.

In 1869, Luther L. Greenleaf presented to the University the library of Honorable Johann Schulze, Ph. D., Member of Prussian Ministry of Public Instruction. Mr. Greenleaf had purchased this library from the heirs of Johann Schulze. This collection, containing 11,246 volumes, besides unbound publications, is known as the Greenleaf Library.

A portion of Oliver A. Willard's library, devoted to local and state histories and political science, was bought by William Deering and Lyman J. Gage and presented to the University in 1878.

The library of Professor Henry S. Noyes was purchased by the University after Professor Noyes' death in 1872. This consisted of 1,500 bound volumes.

A gift of 500 volumes, mostly biblical and philosophical, from the library of the Reverend R. W. Patterson, D. D., was made to the University, by his widow, in 1895.

In 1898, a library of 2,533 volumes by German authors was collected by Geheimer Regierungsrath and presented to the University.

In 1903, the collection of documents received from the United States government—a generous donor to the library—contained 6,740 volumes and 10,154 pamphlets.

In 1870, the library was open only four hours each day of the week, Sunday excepted. In 1903, the library record shows the hours the library was open were thirteen each week day during the college year. A room in Old College was used until 1869 for the library, when it was transferred to University Hall, where it remained until 1894, when it was moved to the Orrington Lunt Library building. In 1865, Orrington Lunt deeded to the University 157 acres of land, in what was then North Evanston. Part of this was sold. The remaining part of the property in 1906 was valued at $90,000.

In 1891, Mr. Lunt offered $50,000 toward a library building. Other friends contributed $15,000, Mrs. Robert M. Hatfield contributing $5,000 of this amount in memory of her husband, the Reverend Robert M. Hatfield, who had been a trustee of the University for years.

By an appropriation from the funds of the University the amount was raised to $100,000. The beautiful Orrington Lunt Library building covers an area of ground, 73 by 162 feet, and faces Sheridan Road. It is Italian Renaissance in style of architecture; the outer walls are of Bedford limestone, and the roof is of red tile. Ionic columns support the large semi-circular porch. This building was dedicated September 26, 1894. The presentation speech was made by Orrington Lunt, and the address of acceptance was made by President Henry Wade Rogers, L.L.D.; the dedication ode was written and read by Mrs. Emily Huntington Miller.

In the early years some one of the professors was appointed librarian. Among the librarians of those days, we find the names of W. D. Godman, David H. Wheeler, Louis Kistler and Charles W. Pearson. Horace G. Lunt was librarian from 1876 to 1886, giving his services free, as did his father.

The Garrett Biblical Institute Library consists largely of theological books and was located in Memorial Hall until 1923, when it was removed to the new Administration Building. Dr. H. B. Hemenway was librarian for a number of years, holding that position up to the time of his death.

In 1906, the library contained 16,260 volumes, and 2,200 pamphlets. Throughout the city could be found in the early days—and the same is true today—in private homes wonderful collections of books, histories, classics, essays, rare old first editions, libraries of 4,000 and 5,000 volumes and over, whose owners oftentimes invited the youth of the day to their homes—there to indulge in a true literary feast.

Chapter XIX

GOVERNMENT

WHEN the pioneers arrived in this region, some coming by foot, others in ox-carts or by schooners, they found Cook County under a form of government known as "County government," all community business being supervised by a Board of County Commissioners, and this form existed until 1849. The pioneers were, for the most part, God-loving and God-fearing people who would have proved themselves fine citizens in any locality. Among the first to arrive were Major Mulford and Edward Murphy, whose opinions were regarded as authority and who were looked up to in all matters for the good of the community, their education being superior to that of their neighbors and their wide knowledge of public affairs of great benefit to the young settlement, in the government of which they took an active part.

Though there was no township government, townships were indicated in the United States Survey and designated by numbers, which were used before 1849. The records of Township 41, in which Evanston is located, show the election of trustees for school purposes, May 9, 1846, four years before officers were elected for the Town of Ridgeville. In the minutes of the meeting, May 20, 1846, at Ridge Road House, Mulford's tavern, it was ordered that Miss Cornelia Wheadon should be hired to teach the school, and repairs were asked for the school house.

By Act of February 12, 1849, the people were permitted to divide their counties into towns or townships and choose a name, and the name of Ridgeville was chosen by residents of Fractional Town 41 North, Range 14 East.[1]

The following is taken from Andreas' History: The Town of Ridgeville—in old records Ridgevill—was one of the first to be organized under the Act of 1849 and took effect April, 1850. The first election was held April 2, 1850, Moderator Ebenezer Bennett making proclamation in a loud voice at the door of George Reed's house that the polls were open ready for the reception of votes. Up to the time of closing, 6 P. M., 93 votes were cast and elections made as follows, familiar names, most of them: Edward Murphy, Supervisor; S. S. Billings, Town Clerk; Peter Smith and E. H. Mulford, Justices of the Peace; Philip Rogers, Assessor; Jacob Smith, Collector; Otis Munn, Overseer of the Poor; David Wood, Charles Miller, and Martin Young, Commissioners of Highway; Andrew Faber and Jacob Smith, Constables.

Paul Pratt, George W. Huntoon, Isaac Burroughs, Edward Murphy and Jacob Smith, the commissioners on "animals running at large," reported that to the best of their judgment all cattle and horses should be shut up during December, January and February, and hogs and geese the year around.

---

(1)   Ranges are rows of townships running north and south and have their start from some principal meridian.   The First Principal Meridian (there are others east of this) is a line running north and south along the boundary line between Ohio and Indiana.   The Second Principal Meridian runs through the state of Indiana.   The Third Principal Meridian—from which the ranges of townships, in which Range 14 lies, begin numbering—passes through a point at the mouth of the Ohio river at Cairo, Illinois.   Range 14 is the fourteenth row of townships east of the line that runs north and south through Cairo.
    Townships begin their numbering north or south of certain longitudes used as base lines.

There were two pounds established and David W. Burroughs and David Hood were appointed Pound Masters.

When taking oath for office, each man had to swear he had not fought a duel, sent or accepted a challenge to fight, or been a second to either party, or in any manner aided or assisted in such a duel; that he would not be so engaged or concerned, directly or indirectly, in or about any such duel during continuance in office. The taking of this oath was deemed necessary, as duels were fought occasionally as late as 1860. Abraham Lincoln was at one time challenged to fight a duel, which challenge he did not accept.

Philip Rogers made the first recorded assessment of the Township, in 1853, and the value of taxable property was placed at $6,000, and among the property owners taxed were William Foster, Eli Gaffield, Paul Pratt, Mrs. George Pratt, O. A. Crain, Charles Crain, G. W. Huntoon, Peter Monroe, John O'Leary, Patrick Goodwin, Jacob Phillips, Peter Smith, Sr., Anton Haskamp and John Georges.

The region, later given the name of Evanston, was platted in 1854 by Philo Judson.

By Act of Legislature February 15, 1857, the name was changed to Evanston Township and enlarged by addition of a tier of sections from Niles Township on the west; the Archange Reservation and several sections in Township 42 from New Trier on the north. This Act reads, "The name of Ridgeville shall be changed to Evanston and the Town of Evanston shall comprise all of fractional Township 41 North, Range 14 East, Sections 12, 13, 24, 25 and 36, Township 41 North, Range 13

East, the Archange Reservation and fractional Sections 22, 26 and 27, Township 42 North, Range 14 East, and the same shall form and constitute a township for school purposes and be known as Town 41 North, Range 14 East."[2]

Evanston existed under a loose form of county and township government until 1863. In December, 1863, the residents of Evanston decided that Evanston should be incorporated as a town. By general statute, a town could not include within its limits a territory of more than one mile square. This territory lay between a line just south of the Biblical Institute building and Foster Avenue on the north, and Dempster Street on the south; and between the lake on the east and Wesley Avenue on the west.

Five trustees for the town were elected January, 1864, H. B. Hurd, president, C. Comstock, E. Haskins, Professor H. S. Noyes and J. Clough.

In July town rules and ordinances were adopted and in addition an ordinance was passed enforcing the provision of the University charter, in regard to the sale of liquor. The offices created were trustees, clerk, treasurer, attorney, street commissioner and constable.

L. L. Greenleaf, town treasurer, let the first important contract for public improvement, October, 1864—grading and graveling Hinman Avenue from Davis Street to University Place.

E. Haskins was president of the town from 1865 to 1867. In 1867, J. F. Willard was elected president. He

---

(2)   When the territory of the city of Evanston was embraced in a single township in 1903 it was under the name of Ridgeville with boundaries identical with those of the city. This was a great step forward. The territory previously included portions of three townships, Niles, Evanston and New Trier, and each township had its own officials. This meant for part of Evanston three sets of Highway Commissioners, three sets of Collectors, and three sets of Town Clerks. Each of the three townships placed a different valuation on property, which called for much book-keeping and resulted in dissatisfaction.

was succeeded in 1868 by Eli A. Gage, and in 1869, E. R. Paul was elected president. This year, 1869, the town, still satisfied with its simple form of government, voted against a city charter, permitted to Evanston by Act of Legislature, which would mean incorporation as a city. The adoption of a city charter was voted down, there being 197 votes against it and 87 in favor of it. John L. Beveridge was elected president 1870; H. G. Powers 1871; C. G. Gilbert 1872.

The territory east of North Evanston and north of the original town was annexed in 1872.

Within three years—in 1872—after the Act of Legislature of 1869 giving permission to Evanston to incorporate as a city, the townsmen organized under the Act for Cities and Villages, and Evanston became a village, but made no change in the form of government. Trustees were elected from the village at large and a village president, in place of aldermen for wards and a mayor.

The first election of village trustees for Evanston took place April 1873, when C. G. Gilbert was made president again.

In June, 1874, the first Board of Health was appointed.

In this same year, 1874, North Evanston petitioned for annexation to Evanston and was voted into the village. The original owners and promoters of North Evanston were C. E. Browne, C. L. Jenks and Dr. Kidder, who sold its tracts either in acreage or in small parcels, subdividing the land and making improvements. There was a general opinion among north shore residents that the prices were inflated and that the bubble would burst, when an advertisement appeared in a Chicago paper offering lots a little north of the Biblical Institute at $200 per acre and an eighty acre lot of choice, fertile prairie, one mile north of the village, at $75 per acre.

The territory lying between Hamilton and Greenleaf Streets, the lake and Chicago Avenue was included by petition the same year, 1874. By Act of May 23, 1877 (and amended in 1903) all the territory in the Village of Evanston was changed into a township, under the old name of Ridgeville, making the boundaries of village and township identical and consolidating the village and township government. The new township embraced the southern part of New Trier Township and a northeast corner of Niles Township. The remaining portion of the former township, a small tract of land south of the limits and a tract west of the south end of the village, under the name of Evanston Township, is part of the City of Chicago.

The president's office was filled, following Mr. Gilbert's term of office, successively by Obadiah Huse, N. S. Davis, J. M. Williams, Thomas J. Frost, T. A. Cosgrove and J. S. Parkhurst.

In 1883, South Evanston, through its trustees, petitioned to be annexed to Evanston. The annexation did not take place at that time.

In 1884, Evanston had a population of 5,000, "among the most intelligent in the state," to quote Andreas, "and of progressive disposition," fine system of water works— a pumping station had been installed in 1872—fire department, organized in 1881, consisting of Babcock chemical engine, eight men; hose company of thirty men (hook and ladder company), wide and clean avenues and streets, lighted with gas, a fine public library, a well conducted newspaper, *The Evanston Index,* a first class hotel, the Avenue House, prosperous looking business houses and churches of several denominations. Lake Shore Drive from the city was under construction and when completed, it was expected to be one of the finest carriage ways in the world.

April, 1886, the territory embraced by Church and Crain Streets, Wesley and McDaniel Avenues was annexed.

In 1892, South Evanston's petition for annexation had been pending for nine years, since 1883. March 29, 1892, the question of annexation was put to the vote of both villages. Neither village seemed very favorably inclined toward annexation, as it was approved by only a small majority, after a hotly contested campaign. Evanston deemed it necessary to enlarge its bonding and taxing area, as municipal indebtedness was not allowed in excess of 5% of its property. The Village of South Evanston, organized in 1873, now found it necessary to make a change in regard to its water supply, as the sewer emptied into the lake only about 600 feet from the pumping station, thus contaminating the supply of water. Also, South Evanston was already deeply in debt and felt it dared not incur greater indebtedness by going to the expense of pushing the inlet further into the lake. Therefore annexation was the only solution to the problem. In short, annexation to Evanston meant pure water, as it would then receive its supply of water through Evanston's mains.

Before the inlet at Main Street had been constructed and the water tower and pumping station built (at a cost of $20,000) South Evanston obtained its water supply by means of an artesian well, at Chicago Avenue and Washington Street. This well was bored to the depth of 2,600 feet, "which spurted up like an oil gusher, sixty feet above the surface, the water so hard it could not be cut with an axe." The residents were not satisfied with this and asked for lake water.

South Evanston received its first settler in 1836, Major Mulford. He, however, did not occupy his board cabin for a year after preempting the land and building the cabin to hold the title, but rented it to Arunah Hill. He returned in 1837 to take possession himself. After him, came the Gaffields, the Burroughs, the Crains and many others, long before Evanston proper began to be settled. Its first subdivision was made by General Julius White, about 1871. General White subdivided eighty acres adjoining Evanston on the north and lying east of the Northwestern railroad tracks. Merrill Ladd, O. F. Gibbs, Judge Adams and L. C. Pitner also operated in South Evanston lands, Adams and Pitner operating west of the railroad track, where land sold at $15 and $20 per front foot.

In 1873, South Evanston acquired the status of village. At that time it occupied 1,000 acres of territory mostly in Section 19, Evanston Township. The village extended from the lake one and a half miles westward and one mile from north to south boundaries, with spacious streets, and all lots of good depth, with an allowance for alleys.

The firm of Warren, Keeney & Co., with Mr. Kedzie of Evanston, bought 55 acres south of General White's subdivision. Of the fifty-five acres, thirty-five were bought of John Klein and twenty of Jacob Rinn, at the price of $1,350 per acre. This tract was named Kedzie and Keeney's Addition and was graded and fenced in. The following May, this firm bought thirty-seven acres of high land, heavily timbered, along the lake shore at $1,350 per acre. The firm's expenditures were over $100,000 and the sales amounted to over $200,000 the first season. Sewers to the lake were laid through the principal east and west streets. Many of the houses were supplied with gas from the Evanston Gas Works. The population in 1874 was 1,300, and the number of houses 250.

Evanston, though not quite fully grown, was fast reaching maturity, standing firmly on its feet, its streets running rigidly straight, truly symbolic of the character of its early founders, who rejoiced in treading the straight and narrow path. It was quite enough grown up to realize its own importance, and South Evanston, with all its fine independence, was compelled to recognize Evanston's supremacy, and in 1892 it became a part of Evanston proper.

With South Evanston annexed, the three villages, now become one, weighed the question of adoption of city organization and looked on it favorably. It was submitted to the people by vote March 29, 1892. That the village was now fully ready and desirous to put on city garb is proved by the overwhelming number of votes in its favor, which numbered 784 to 26.

The first election of the full fledged City of Evanston took place April 29, 1892, and Dr. Oscar H. Mann became the first mayor of Evanston. The city was divided into seven wards and fourteen aldermen were elected, two for each ward. Its population was 15,967.

CHAPTER XX

EVANSTON'S THOROUGHFARES

THE natural ridges were the first thoroughfares through Evanston. The Drainage Commission excavating ditches for drainage between the ridges, Ridge Avenue and the Dutch Ridge further west, created other roads, Mulford Road, Church Street, Emerson Street and Indian Boundary Line, which was established by treaty, 1816, with the Potawatomi, Chippewa, and Ottawa Indians.

The names of most of the streets commemorate early and honored citizens and other persons of distinction, especially Methodists.

When one thinks of Evanston, a picture of Fountain Square comes to mind,—Fountain Square, very appropriately called by W. C. Levere, in one of his newspaper articles, the Heart of Evanston. The streets radiating from it to all parts of the city, he likens to the arteries of the heart. Probably no part of Evanston, not excepting the University buildings themselves, remains clearer in the memories of both Evanstonians and visitors than Fountain Square, with its lofty trees beneath whose outspreading branches several cranes nobly take their stand. The fountain, which was originally surmounted by the figure of a crane,[1] was dedicated July 4, 1876, Centennial year, and was called Centennial Fountain. It was presented to the city by a number of residents to commem-

---

[1]   This old crane may be seen at the Evanston Historical Society rooms.

orate the nation's birthday. The village trustees were
petitioned to accept the fountain and appropriate a sum

DEDICATION OF THE FOUNTAIN, JULY 4, 1876

of money to construct a base. The signers of the petition
were Lyman J. Gage, H. G. Powers, J. H. Kedzie, S. B.

Raymond, O. H. Mann, Merrill Ladd, Archibald Winne, H. T. Tillinghast and J. F. Keeney. Edwin Lee Brown and his son, Edwin F. Brown, were generous contributors to this, as they were to every public-spirited enterprise. When the street car company was building its line through Evanston, Mayor Mann gave his consent to have the fountain taken out and the plot of ground around it

THE FOUNTAIN REMODELED

to be used. Indignant citizens, not least among whom was Norman Williams, called upon the mayor, who seeing the imprudence of his action, recalled his consent and the fountain was saved.

There are a few streets whose names are misnomers and do not have any particular reference to their locations, for instance, Central Street is in the extreme north end of town, and Main Street, which previously bore the names of both Lincoln Avenue and Evanston Avenue, is located in the south end of town.

Evanston's thoroughfares are called Avenues, Streets, Courts and Places. The avenues and courts run north and south while streets and places run east and west. Sheridan Road, running north and south, is an exception.

The house numbering begins at the south end of the city on the avenues and courts. The house numbering of the streets and places begins at the lake and runs westward. The numbering in every block commences with the even hundred. The streets and places run about twelve hundred to the mile, while the avenues and courts, having longer blocks, run about eight hundred to the mile.

The names of the thoroughfares, with their derivations, follow; also a few facts concerning some of the best known thoroughfares:

ARNOLD STREET. Isaac N. Arnold, Chicagoan and a member of Congress.

ASBURY AVENUE. Francis Asbury, first American Methodist Episcopal Bishop.

AYARS PLACE. James Ayars, President of Board of Village (Evanston) Trustees. This was formerly Ayars Court.

BENNETT AVENUE. Mrs. C. C. Bennett (nee Culver), Chicago Public School teacher.

BENSON AVENUE. Francis H. Benson, early Evanstonian.

BOOMER PLACE. Norton W. Boomer, Chicago Public School Principal.

23

BOTSFORD STREET. J. K. Botsford, Chicagoan, North-western University Trustee.

BROWNE AVENUE. Charles E. Browne, North Evans-ton property owner.

CHANCELLOR STREET. Chancellor L. Jenks, early resident of Evanston.

CHICAGO AVENUE received its name when North Avenue was the northern boundary line of Chicago. It is the low ridge to the east of Ridge Avenue and is a branch of Green Bay Trail. Green Bay Trail followed the line of Clark Street in Chicago to Rose Hill, where it divided, one part going over Chicago Avenue and the other over the Ridge, the two parts joining again at a point north of the Lighthouse, after being divided for four miles.

The long stretch of country road joining Chicago Avenue in Evanston with North Clark Street at Chicago's north boundary, North Avenue, ran through farms and market gardens. It was sandy and in such bad condition that in 1859 a corporation, called the Rose Hill and Evanston Road Company, with C. Billings president, was formed to grade it. After the grading was done, it became Gravel Road. There were three toll-gates on it several miles apart, at which each team was charged a small fee for the privilege of using it. The keepers lived in small toll-houses near the toll-gates. One toll-gate was at the intersection of Indian Boundary Line and another further south at Graceland.

South Evanston had the cedar block paving craze, and Chicago Avenue came in for its share in 1891, when it was paved with cedar blocks from the north limit of Hamilton Street to the south limit of the village. The first brick pavement laid in Evanston was in 1891, on Chicago Avenue from Davis Street to University Place.

This low ridge, Chicago Avenue, was under water part of the year, in the early days. A narrow bridge made of single planks laid across crotched sticks was built for the convenience of children going from the east ridge to school over on the west ridge, Ridge Avenue. A number of poles were kept at either end of the bridge, for use as balancing poles for those crossing.

From the cupola of Edward S. Taylor's home on the corner of Chicago Avenue and Grove Street a group of Evanstonians watched the flames of the Chicago fire on the night of October 9, 1871. Rest Cottage, once the home of Frances Willard, on Chicago Avenue, is said to bring annually over 14,000 persons to Evanston from all over the world to visit the place, where once dwelt one who was widely known through her temperance work.

A little grey and green house just north of Davis Street on the west side of the avenue was once the village post office, and here Edward Eggleston, the author of *Hoosier Schoolmaster*, Bishop Randolph Foster, Bishop Matthew Simpson, and other great lights no doubt met and discussed the topics of the day.

General Nelson A. Miles once lived at the southeast corner of Chicago Avenue and Clark Street. Here also, at one time, lived John L. Beveridge, later Governor of Illinois. James A. Patten occupied the house for several years. Others who lived in this house were William Raymond, the opera singer, Kuehne Beveridge, the sculptor, and President Abram W. Harris of Northwestern University.

CHURCH STREET. The first church building in Evanston was on this street, the First Methodist Episcopal Church, on the site of the Public Library.

CLARK STREET. The Reverend John Clark, minister of Clark Street Church, Chicago.

COLFAX STREET. United States Vice-President Schuyler Colfax.

COLLEGE STREET. Now Davis Street. College Street was the original name of Davis Street west of Sherman Avenue; changed to Davis Street in 1871.

COOK STREET. Origin of name not known. Cook Street is now Garrett Place.

CRAIN STREET. Ozro and Charles Crain, early settlers.

DARROW AVENUE. A prominent colored Mason of Chicago.

DAVIS STREET. Nathan S. Davis, M. D., one of the Trustees of Northwestern University, a man not only of nation-wide reputation, but also well known in the medical profession in Europe. He was one of the few medical practitioners of the day who refused to use alcoholics in his practice of medicine.

It was said, in regard to Dr. Davis, that he cared more for his work than for his dress, and it required the greatest diplomacy on the part of his wife to make him change to a new suit. Up to the time of his death in 1904, he persisted in wearing the old-fashioned dress coat, or claw-hammers. It is also related of him that he was careful to treat all his patients alike, rich or poor. A story is told that shows his ready wit and keen sense of humor. A young man, son of a bishop, who had no appointment rushed into his office and was told he would have to wait his turn, as the doctor was busy. Rushing past the office attendant, he entered the doctor's private office. The doctor very politely told him to have a seat. "But," he exclaimed, "I am So-and-So," trying to impress the doctor with his importance.

"Ah, Sir," the doctor said, bowing low, "have two seats."

In 1855, this street was called Davis Street only from Fountain Square east, being College Street west of Fountain Square. When the Village Board voted for street improvement, clay was used to the depth of several inches, with a covering of gravel. The first paving of Davis Street was of clay and gravel. The owners of the lots fronting on this street decided that the contractor should give them plenty of clay and when the work was begun they braved the tortures of a hot July sun beating down on their heads, while they bossed the job. One wonders whether that particular contractor may not have had a little bit of Irish in his make-up and knew what the result of an abundance of clay would be, for he gave them plenty—six or eight inches—and over this he spread the gravel, and woe was theirs for the next year and a half! Davis Street became a veritable hog-wallow the greater part of the year!

The next pavement was of macadam, and being found unsatisfactory, it became the foundation for the brick pavement laid on top of it. The first University Building, Old College, and the only one for five years, was built in Block 20, on Davis Street, near Hinman Avenue. In 1871, the west end of the street changed its name from College Street to Davis Street.

The home of H. B. Hurd stood out conspicuously at Ridge Avenue and Davis Street. This beautiful residence, with its spacious rooms, winding driveway and great trees shading the well-kept lawn, was built in 1854, and was one of the earliest of the fine houses in Evanston.

Danks Hotel was built on the site of the North Shore Hotel. A visitor in 1855 found every room in Danks Hotel taken and people sleeping on the dining room tables and on cots between the tables.

DEMPSTER STREET. Dr. John Dempster, Professor at Garrett Biblical Institute.[2] Two real estate men, William Vose and William P. Kimball, saw the possibility of a new center being created, if the street could be opened up to cross the railroad tracks, in the neighborhood of where Dempster Street later was laid out. Accordingly, in 1882, these men began to buy property, the first being three hundred feet west of Chicago Avenue. The old Snyder house stood at the point where the proposed new thoroughfare intersected Chicago Avenue.[3] This house had to be moved out of the way. The necessary application was made to the village government to open the street. While waiting for this to go through, Vose and Kimball bought the site of the Jones School (Northwestern Female College), and land from Obadiah Huse, between the railroad track and Benson Avenue, south to Crain Street. This included the block where the Boltwood School stood, which piece of land was a cow pasture, with a wide ditch running through it, and the entire tract held but one house, which belonged to the first Chinese resident and land owner. After buying 1,500 feet to the west, reaching to Maple Avenue, the real

(2)   Upon coming to Evanston, Dr. Dempster built a house on the edge of the bluff at the foot of Cook Street, which might be called the first apartment house in Evanston, as it contained four suites.

(3)   In 1844 Abraham Snyder bought ninety-six acres between Greenleaf and Dempster Streets, which he sold in the early sixties to Hurd and Brown.

estate men started to lay out their territory. Dempster Street was not opened through to Benson Avenue until 1883. The first train stopped at Dempster Street Station about 1885.

DEWEY AVENUE. Two Chicago school teachers in the Jones School, sisters, Electa E. Dewey and Mary J. Dewey.

DODGE AVENUE. Kate Dodge, teacher in Jones School, Chicago.

EMERSON STREET. Benjamin Emmerson, who came here in 1839 and at the time of his death, had lived here nearly sixty years. William C. Levere says of him, in one of his articles, "He found Evanston a wilderness and when he died, it was the most civilized city in the world."

Emerson Street, at its west end, runs through land that was formerly the Emmerson farm, which was west of the railroad tracks. Two neighbors of Emmerson, Pratt and Gaffield, as well as Emmerson himself, were anxious to have the north end of town developed and the three united in their efforts to get a vote from the village board to open the street. The board voted favorably and the street received its present name. The family name was spelled with two m's, but the street name has but one.

EWING AVENUE. Adlai Ewing, who controlled Ewing's Addition to Evanston, and was one of the World's Fair Commissioners from Illinois.

FLORENCE AVENUE. Florence Tullis, teacher in the Jones School, Chicago.

FOREST AVENUE. Thomas L. Forrest, thirty years cashier of the Hide and Leather Bank in Chicago. He owned some property in Evanston. The beautiful trees lining either side of this street cause many people to think Forest Avenue was named after them. The dropping of one of the r's, too, would give rise to that idea. Mr. Forrest never lived on his property, through which the street passes, but was a resident of Chicago.

The first map of Evanston, made soon after the town was laid out in 1854, by an early surveyor, Mr. Van Vechten, showed Forest Avenue as a straight street, running directly north across Davis Street. This map was taken to a lithographer in Chicago, to have copies made from it, shortly before the Chicago fire, and was burned with many other valuable documents that memorable October 9th, 1871. Allan Vane owned several lots on the north side of Davis Street, and not knowing the exact boundary line of these lots he built on the ground at the head of Forest Avenue, which made a jog in the street, causing it to run about 100 feet to the east, and making it scarcely recognizable as a continuation of the street. This continuation is called Forest Place.[4]

One of the most historic houses built on Forest Avenue was a grey grout house, originally the home of Stephen Lunt, and later of Robert M. Hatfield, and more recently of the late Daniel Burnham. Once this house was surrounded by a marsh. Henry Kidder, calling there at one time, left his horse tied to the fence and made his way home on foot, as the swamps were full of dangers.

In 1872, a petition was sent to the Board of Trustees of the Village of Evanston, from owners and lessees, fronting on the east side of Forest Avenue, requesting a plank sidewalk, five feet four inches wide, extending from Davis Street to the south side of Greenleaf Street. This

---

(4)   Places run east and west in Evanston. This is an exception.

petition was signed by Andrew Shuman, Isaac H. Taylor, H. G. Powers, Arthur C. Ducat and T. C. Hoag. L. L. Greenleaf reserved the right to build his own. This width of sidewalk was used all over the city in accordance with an ordinance passed by city council, as boards coming in sixteen foot lengths could be cut in three pieces, without an inch of waste.

FOSTER STREET. Randolph S. Foster, second president of Northwestern University.

GAFFIELD PLACE. Eli Gaffield, pioneer.

GRANT STREET. General U. S. Grant.

GREENLEAF STREET. Luther L. Greenleaf, citizen of Evanston 1860 to 1875.

GREY AVENUE. Charles F. Grey, resident of Evanston; village trustee.

GROVE STREET. Received its name probably from the grove of gigantic oak trees which grew abundantly along the way. This street begins at Dodge Avenue and runs east almost to the lake, joining Lake Street at Judson Avenue. Frances Willard made her first public address in the First Congregational Church, which stood on Grove Street.

Aldin J. Grover, a citizen well known in early days, had his home on this street. He was the father of Frank Grover, the writer of many valuable pamphlets on early Evanston history.

HAMILTON STREET. James G. Hamilton, Secretary of the Board of Trustees of Northwestern University.

HAMLIN STREET. Leonidas L. Hamline, Bishop of the Methodist Episcopal Church. This street, too, has lost a letter (e).

HARTZELL STREET. Joseph C. Hartzell, one of the

heroes at the time of the wreck of the schooner, *Storm,* May, 1864. He was later Methodist Bishop of Africa.

HAVEN STREET.   Erastus O. Haven, Northwestern University President; later Methodist Bishop.

HINMAN AVENUE.   Clark T. Hinman, first president of Northwestern University.   Dr. Hinman bought land where the National Headquarters of the Sigma Alpha Epsilon Fraternity now are located (1927), 1856 Sheridan Road, but he never built a home on the ground. What the populace wants and what is good for it, are two different things.   This was demonstrated a second time when James Ayars attempted to pave Hinman Avenue. Some of the property owners wanted the street kept like a country village street; others wanted it paved, and so the discussions for and against it went back and forth, until Mr. Ayars finally gave up in despair and declared Hinman Avenue could never be paved, there was "too much brains on the street!"

ISABELLA STREET.   Isabella Browne, daughter of Charles E. Browne.

JACKSON AVENUE.   A. B. Jackson, Rogers Park resident.

JENKS STREET.   Chancellor L. Jenks, lawyer.   In 1860, during the stormy days preceding the war, when the whole country was stirred over the slavery question, an incident occurred that showed Chancellor Jenks' antislavery tendencies that gained him national fame.   A comely colored girl of about twenty had escaped from bondage and had been in hiding for a few weeks in Chicago.   One of her own race, hoping to obtain the reward offered, had betrayed her hiding place.   An agent of her owner and a United States Marshal had captured her and were about to return her to slavery. The little party attracted the notice of the passersby and was soon surrounded by perhaps a thousand persons, who were intensely interested in the affair and about equally divided in their sympathies. The slowly moving procession was suddenly stopped at the corner of Clark and Van Buren Streets, as a determined man of middle age seized the burly slave driver and hurled him backward. Then grasping the girl, he was soon lost in the crowd. In this heroic and dramatic manner, Mr. Jenks secured the release of the slave-girl. Later he was tried in the United States court and fined $1,000. A few years afterward he and the southerner met, and that gentleman told him he would have shot him (Jenks), had not the suddenness and daring of the rescue surprised him and before he had recovered, Jenks and the girl had disappeared.

JUDSON AVENUE. Philo Judson, pioneer of Evanston, and Business Agent of Northwestern University.

KEDZIE STREET. John H. Kedzie, forty-two years a resident of Evanston.

KEENEY STREET. James F. Keeney, resident of Evanston.

KIRK STREET. James S. Kirk, resident of Evanston for twenty-seven years; prominent soap manufacturer.

LEE STREET. Lee J. Pitner, son of L. C. Pitner. This name was given to the street in 1871, when Union Addition was laid out.

LEON STREET. A part of Louis Leonhardt's name.

LIBRARY PLACE. This name was given to part of Hamlin Street, between Orrington Avenue and Sheridan Road, by city ordinance, 1904, on account of its nearness to the Lunt Library.

LIVINGSTON STREET. Probably the middle name of Chancellor Livingston Jenks.

LYONS STREET. Joseph M. Lyons, of Evanston.

MCDANIEL AVENUE. Alexander McDaniel, pioneer of Evanston; a forty-niner; Postmaster of Wilmette for nineteen years, 1870 to 1889.

MULFORD STREET. Edward H. Mulford, pioneer.

NATE STREET. The Reverend John Nate. Changed to Clinton Place.

NOYES STREET. Henry S. Noyes, Acting President of Northwestern University from 1860 to 1869.

ORRINGTON AVENUE. Orrington Lunt, one of the founders of Northwestern University. Miss Cornelia Lunt, his daughter, told the following story of how the name of Orrington originated. Near the little town of Bowdoinham, Maine, where her father was born, was the Town of Orrington, which was settled by men from Orange County, Ireland. Wishing to have the settlement incorporated as a town, one of its prominent men, who knew more about farming than spelling, wrote to the Legislature in regard to the matter, intending to give the town a name that would perpetuate the name of the place from which these North of Ireland men came, "Orange-town." The name was spelled *Orrington,* and Orrington it went on record, and Orrington it has remained. Miss Lunt said her father would not vouch for the truth of the story, but traditions of this kind usually have truth for foundation.

William C. Levere, in one of his articles in the News-Index, made the statement that Orrington Avenue in Evanston was the only street in America carrying the name, and that a letter addressed to a number on Orrington Avenue, without city or state name, would reach its destination. A gentleman, reading the article, decided to make the test, and arranged to have a letter mailed to him from Hornell, New York, having only his name, street and number on the envelope. Within thirty-six hours after being mailed, the letter was delivered to him at his Orrington Avenue address.

PAYNE STREET. Henry M. Payne, resident of Chicago.

PITNER AVENUE. Levi C. Pitner, Evanston resident, and real estate broker.

PRATT COURT. Paul and George Pratt, pioneers coming to Evanston in 1839.

REBA PLACE. Reba Poor, daughter of John E. Poor.

REESE AVENUE. Theodore Reese, surveyor, living in Evanston.

RIDGE AVENUE. The oldest thoroughfare in Evanston, a natural ridge.

RINN STREET (Now South Boulevard). Jacob Rinn, an early resident of Evanston.

SHERIDAN ROAD. General Philip H. Sheridan. Formerly there was no thoroughfare east of Calvary Cemetery between Evanston and Chicago. Early in the sixties an attempt was made to extend Evanston Avenue (now Broadway) north through Calvary. The Archbishop of that day objected to the plan. In 1887, the North Shore Improvement Association was formed for the purpose, chiefly, of making a driveway along the lake shore. The matter met with general favor, and Archbishop Feehan generously donated one hundred feet of the east border of Calvary Cemetery. Evanston citizens, headed by

Volney W. Foster, raised $3,000 for leveling the sand hills, and claying and grading the road.

In 1890, Sheridan Square was Warren Court. Part of Sheridan Road was called Congress Street at one time, and a part was called Michigan Avenue, from Greenwood to University Place. Sheridan Road also bore the name of Raymond Avenue on the block between Hamilton and Greenleaf Streets. In the south end, 1883, between Lincoln Avenue (Main Street) and Calvary Cemetery, Sheridan Road was Arnold Avenue.

SHERMAN AVENUE. Alson Smith Sherman, one of the incorporators of Northwestern University and first vice-president. He was elected mayor of Chicago, 1844. Mr. Sherman walked into Chicago from St. Joseph, Michigan, in 1836, having reached that city by wagon from Detroit, to which place he had come by boat on canal and lake from his Vermont home.

South of Fountain Square the legal name of the street is Orrington Avenue on the east side of the street to the slight bend, while the west side is Sherman Avenue.

One of the best photographers of the day had his studio on Sherman Avenue, Alexander Hesler. His pictures of Abraham Lincoln are among the best of the Lincoln pictures, and have won for him a place in American history. His photograph of one of the old residents of Evanston, George Montieth, labeled "The Old Rustic," won the first prize at the Centennial Exposition in Philadelphia, 1876. One of Hesler's pictures of Minnehaha Falls inspired Longfellow to write Hiawatha. In 1851 Mr. Hesler was taking pictures in the Mississippi Valley region, and saw the beautiful cascade a few miles from St. Paul, then but a small town. He photographed the cascade, and on his return home he presented the picture to the brother of Charles Sumner, who took it east and gave it to Longfellow.   When the poem was published, Longfellow sent a copy of it to Hesler, with his compliments.

President McKinley was entertained by the members of his college fraternity, the Sigma Alpha Epsilon, at their fraternity house at 2031 Sherman Avenue.   His fraternity brothers were anxious to make a good impres-

"The Old Rustic"

sion on him and borrowed all the fine furniture, statues and ornaments that could be borrowed within a radius of a quarter of a mile.   They felt they had accomplished their purpose, when the president spoke with admiration of their fine furnishings.   That night, however, more than one brother slept with an eye open, so fearful were they that something would happen to the valued belongings of their kind neighbors.

Shuman Street.   Andrew Shuman, editor *Chicago*

Evening Journal. Lieutenant-Governor of Illinois, 1877-1881.

SIMPSON STREET. Bishop Matthew Simpson, President of Garrett Biblical Institute.

STANLEY AVENUE. B. F. Stanley. Name given by C. L. Jenks.

STEWART AVENUE. John W. Stewart, property owner in North Evanston.

STOCKHAM PLACE. Mrs. Alice B. Stockham, Evanston resident. (Now Burnham Place.)

THAYER STREET. John Culver's wife, whose maiden name was Thayer.

WARREN STREET. Henry A. Warren, former resident of Evanston.

WESLEY AVENUE. John Wesley, Founder of Methodism.

WILDER STREET. Aldin G. Wilder, lumber dealer in Evanston. He also subdivided lands in the western part of the city.

WILLARD PLACE. Frances E. Willard, President of Woman's College; President of Woman's Christian Temperance Union and President of World's Christian Temperance Union.

Although the Illinois, Miami and Potawatomi Indians had their home on this site for so many years, there is not an Indian name given to any thoroughfare to commemorate either a tribe or a chief.

A few items gleaned from one of the dusty record books in the city hall, show some interesting facts. Main Street was called Lincoln Avenue for a number of years. It was changed to Evanston Avenue in 1891, and later received its present name. In 1890, Ashland was Simpson

Street. The present Michigan Avenue was Wheeler Street in 1890, then received the name of Congress, changing to Michigan Avenue later. Forest Avenue, also, was Wheeler at one time.

There was an ordinance passed to clay and gravel Lee Street from Forest Avenue east in 1889. Benson Avenue was ordered improved in 1889. In 1890 Ridge Avenue was paved with cedar blocks from Crain Street to Howard Street. Lincoln Avenue (Main Street) was paved with cedar blocks from Chicago Avenue to the Ridge, in 1890.

Wheeler Street (Michigan Avenue) was macadamized in 1891.

The first sidewalks were made of clay and gravel in the business section. Later a single plank was laid lengthwise. Then Obadiah Huse suggested laying two planks parallel to each other, with space between. This style of walk served until the walks of boards laid crosswise came into use. The length of these boards, which was the width of the sidewalk, was determined by village ordinance.

The triangle south of Fountain Square was a haymarket until a street railway began to be considered in the eighties. Here hay could be bought by the ton (not baled), and wood by the cord. There was a drinking trough for horses, and later a huge flag pole, donated by Fort Dearborn Chapter, Daughters of the American Revolution, which attracted the lightning and was finally taken away. There was a chestnut tree of immense proportions in the triangle that had to be removed to give space for street cars. This was taken up with great care and planted in Raymond Park.

24

On July 4, 1876, the fountain was dedicated in commemoration of the one hundredth anniversary of American Independence. Edward S. Taylor, a prominent early citizen of Evanston, made the dedicatory speech, entitled "The Ministry of Water," of which the following is an excerpt: "Evanston is a cold water town, and in that fountain, with its sparkling water, we see a symbol of a prosperous, peaceful and law abiding people, and what is more wonderful to contemplate than the ministry of water. It antagonizes and quenches the destructive conflagration; it floats the commerce of the world, and its latent power developed gives added impulse to that commerce, and the same power moves your burdened train across the continent, connecting ocean and ocean." The fountain itself was but a crude affair, with but a wooden foundation. There were no shade trees and no shrubbery around it. A few years previous to this time, there was marshy ground all around, with a tiny island a block south of the square, where the police station was built later. The water was so deep, an early settler had to use a boat, in going after his cattle that had swum to a little island in the marsh, to get them back on high ground on the ridge. The only way of crossing the slough was a roadway built where Fountain Square now stands. The roadway was made of rails and hay.

Samuel Reed, one of the pioneers of Evanston, held the office of street commissioner for over forty years.

(The list of street names, with origins, is taken mostly from Hurd's *History of Evanston*, Munsell Publishing Company, by permission of William P. Munsell.)

CHAPTER XXI

TRANSPORTATION

BEGINNING with the earliest mode of transportation, we see the early explorers,—Marquette, Joliet, LaSalle, Tonti,—swiftly covering great distances in their birchbark canoes over the surface of a smooth and smiling lake, or battling with the angry waves of a storm-tossed sea, with that grim determination that marked the every act of those brave and fearless men. Then, as the shadows lengthened and the keen wind cut across their faces, they drew their canoes out of the waters of the lake and, shouldering them, began their perilous journey across the ice-floes and snow, to make a landing and camp overnight on the shore of the "Lake of Illinois," as it came to be called, on account of the Illinois Indians frequenting its shores. We see the Indian, with his sure and steady stroke, shooting his canoe through the water; tramping through the forests, his canoe well balanced on his shoulder, as he crossed the portage, sometimes from the Wisconsin to the Fox River, or between the Des Plaines and the Chicago Rivers.

Cattle were introduced into this country by the Spaniards in the sixteenth century. Previous to the introduction of cattle, under which head comes the horse, the Indian traveled by foot or by using the waterways. When Charlevoix visited the Indian villages along the Mississippi River, in 1721, he found no horses north of the Missouri River.

Some of the early settlers came to Evanston, or
Grosse Pointe, as it was then called, in the "prairie
schooner" or "covered wagon," drawn by a yoke of
oxen, the men of the party oftentimes walking along beside the team, urging the oxen to greater speed—if speed
it could be called—and one or two dogs, belonging to the
families en route, running along barking and snapping at
the patient oxen's heels, while the passengers inside the
wagon were jostled and bumped over the rough roads in
no very comfortable manner, but enduring the hardships
uncomplainingly for the sake of the new life they were
entering.

Among the early settlers who arrived in this manner
were Arunah Hill, his wife and seven children; George
Washington Huntoon and his family; David Norton Burroughs, his wife and three children—the parents, brothers
and sister of Sarah Burroughs (later Mrs. Charles
Crain) who had preceded them, arriving in 1842 with her
sister, Captain Beckwith's wife, and her brother, Alonzo
Burroughs. They, also, had made the trip from Ashtabula, Ohio, in a covered wagon, but one drawn by
horses instead of oxen.

In those days, there were no concrete bridges of
architectural beauty to cross, but the covered or hooded
bridges of pioneer days, that the traveler encountered
along his route. The covered bridge was as artistic to
the eye as the later, modern structure—the long, covered
bridge, half hidden among the trees that always mark the
course of the smaller streams. Those old-time bridges
were eagerly watched for and hailed with delight by the
younger members of the families. The tread of the oxen
hoof, the rumble of the great cart wheels and the sound

of the lusty young voices echoing throughout the bridge's length and breadth gave zest to the children's enjoyment. A sign at either end of the covered bridge read, "$5 Fine for driving faster than a walk over this bridge."

In Mrs. Crain's memoirs, which touch only on the bright and happy side of those early days—perhaps those stood out clearer in her memory than the hardships, or perhaps her kindly nature would spare us a recital of the dark side—she speaks of the lumber wagon being used on festal occasions. The lumber wagon evidently did triple duty. It served in the hauling of lumber; it was turned into a conveyance for a merry group of both old and young bound for the usual picnic grounds, the old oak grove on the site that later became the University grounds. There the very useful lumber wagon's great box was lifted from its supports, inverted and set on the ground to be used as a dinner table for the merry-makers, a snowy cloth spread thereon and a goodly supply of edibles piled high, making a veritable banquet.

Over the Green Bay Road traveled the early mail carriers on foot in the winter seasons for twenty years, beginning in 1816. In the summer the mail was carried by sailing vessels.

The road from Chicago to Green Bay dates its beginning from an act of Congress approved June 15, 1832, for the establishment of a road between these points. The first stage service between Chicago and Milwaukee was along the Milwaukee Avenue route, according to the best records, about the spring of 1836, the proprietor of the line being one Lathrop Johnson, who used an open lumber wagon for transporting mail and "such passengers as might choose to entrust themselves to his oversight."

To give dignity to his service he used four horses instead of two. Later Frink and Walker began business in the Chicago area, got the contract for carrying mail and were scheduled to run daily in winter and tri-weekly in summer, making the journey between Milwaukee and Chicago in one and a half days, stopping at Kenosha over night. Occasionally the stage coach used the Chicago Avenue route through Evanston instead of Ridge Avenue.

The Frink and Walker stage coach was a very elaborate affair, compared with the early lumber wagon used by Johnson. These four-horse coaches, traveling between Chicago and Green Bay, stopped at Baer's Tavern—Seven-Mile House—now Rose Hill; Mulford's, the Ten-Mile House, and farther north at Buck-Eye Hotel, and Wigglesworth's Tavern. Sometimes the east ridge (Chicago Avenue route) was chosen instead of Green Bay Road, as it was said to be "less horrible" at some seasons of the year. With the exception of the stage coach, private conveyances were the only means the early settlers had of traveling to and from Grosse Pointe.

William Cullen Bryant, after riding in one of the stage coaches between Waukegan and Chicago, describes it "Built after the fashion of the English post coach, set high upon springs; the most absurd kind of carriage that could be devised for Illinois roads. It seemed to be set high in the air, that it might be the more easily overturned." He refused to make the return trip in the stage and hired a private conveyance.

James K. Calhoun tells an interesting story of the old stage coaches in his History of Glencoe. A man asked the price of the fare to Chicago and was given the information, first, second and third class. Seeing all the passengers together, mystified, he asked where he should sit and was told anywhere. Soon the muddy roads were reached and the driver called out, "First class passengers sit still; second class get out and walk and third class get out and push."

The low, wide and roomy phaeton came into use in the sixties, and the ladies carried the small "carriage parasol," a parasol about fourteen inches in diameter.

The carry-all, the trap, the shining fringed-top surrey, and the Democrat—a light-bodied express wagon with four crosswise seats, to carry the family to and from church and other places—each held prominent place.

Still in use was the chaise (pronounced shay) an open or covered two-wheeled carriage drawn by one horse. Who has not read Oliver Wendell Holmes' "One Hoss Shay" that "ran a hundred years to a day"?

In the eighties came the rubber-tired "Hug-me-tight" buggies, probably so named from the narrowness of the vehicle.

In winter, there was no greater sport for the young folks, than to skim over the snow in the light-weight sleighs, tucked warmly in buffalo robes, which in those days cost no more than the commonest horse blankets, or to be packed closely together in a bob-sled, which was nothing more than a big wagon-box on runners, its floor covered to a depth of a foot or more with hay or straw.

In the seventies, sleighing and skating parties made the trip from Evanston, following the Big Ditch to the point where it flowed into the north branch of the Chicago River. At some places, the Big Ditch was twelve feet wide.

Sailing vessels were a big feature in transportation, as many, to avoid the poor traveling over bad roads, would embark in a sailing vessel. Just when one would reach his destination, traveling this way, depended on the wind—and the wind was not dependable. Fewer sailing vessels were used after the railroad went through Evanston in 1854, but still much freight was carried on the lake.

Communication between the east and west was mainly carried on by means of the lake steamers, which did an enormous business. In the season of open navigation (May to November) before the advent of the railroads, many preferred the lake steamers to the prairie schooners for traveling. Western products were transported by water to the east, and the steamers returned laden with needful supplies for the west, such as coal, salt, etc., and lumber from the north.

In the sixties, the Davis Street pier held a place of great importance. This pier was built in 1857 by the Evanston Pier Company, of which George F. Foster was president, and John L. Beveridge, secretary, William Judson, son of Philo Judson, superintending the building of it. Extending out twelve hundred feet into the lake,—about a quarter of a mile,—with a width of fifty feet, this pier must have afforded an interesting sight to the townspeople and their visitors, with steamers and sailing vessels flanking it on three sides; men busily engaged in the unloading of the cargoes; two-horse wagons and carriages moving in a steady line over its broad surface.

Casting the eye farther out over the bosom of the lake, one could sight sailing vessels, sometimes to the number of seventy-five, their sails gracefully bending and dipping in the lake breezes. Fishermen had their shanties, boats and nets on the sandy beach near the Davis Street pier.

The principal business of the sailing vessels was hauling lumber. The bulk of the lumber business in Evanston was done by I. P. DeCoudries and James Currey, father of J. Seymour Currey. DeCoudries received his lumber from saw-mills in which he had interest, situated along the northern shores of Lake Michigan. James Currey purchased his supplies from the lumber market in Chicago. Lumber was brought from Chicago in vessels and towed to the Davis Street pier by tugs. An ordinary schooner load averaged 70,000 feet of lumber, two-thirds of which was stowed in the hold, and the remaining third piled on the deck of the vessel to a height of six or eight feet, secured by stanchions. Oftentimes the lumber on the decks was swept overboard and lost during heavy storms. DeCoudries sold out, in 1871, to Asa Milton Allen.

Mr. Peeney was a carpenter, as well as a saw-mill owner, and did work on some of the University buildings.

John A. Pearsons' house was built in 1854, three years before the first pier was built in Evanston. The lumber for this house was unloaded directly on the shore.

At times, lumber was thrown off vessels as near to shore as possible, and men waded into the lake waist deep, and the lumber was passed from man to man, until finally landed. The arrival of a vessel was hailed with joy by students in the Old College Building. When a lumber vessel was sighted, the professor would dismiss the class and the students would rush out and leap aboard the vessel as soon as it was tied to the pier, and begin to pass the lumber ashore, accompanying their work with joyous shouts and merry songs. A happy sight it was, and the work brought many a needed dollar to the young men's pockets, welcome financial aid, as a goodly proportion of the students was self-supporting in those days.

Foster pier, the pier at Dempster Street, was built some years later than the Davis Street pier, by John Foster, son of "Uncle Billy." It was used principally for unloading coal from ports on Lake Erie. This pier was never as popular for sightseers as the Davis Street pier. During the World's Fair, and for a few years after, both piers were used for excursion steamers. Excursion steamers made the trip out from Chicago every Fourth of July. When Heck Hall was dedicated in 1867 —July 4—the steamers, Orion and Seabird, made frequent trips between Chicago and Evanston to bring crowds of visitors for the "Educational and Patriotic Jubilee at Evanston," as announced in the Chicago Tribune, and Goodrich's Side-Wheelers, chartered exclusively for the occasion, made seven round trips to Evanston Pier.

In later years, after 1900, even had the piers not fallen into decay, the vessels could no longer have reached them, as land extended considerably farther into the lake than in the latter part of the 19th century.

The west was making great strides in progress and Evanston was coming in for its share. The first railroad train passed through Evanston on its way to Waukegan, December 19, 1854. Ah, proud the day and proud the people, through whose towns the bravely puffing, little wood-burning engine drew its tender and one lone coach, amid the cheers of its admirers!

Only a little more than a quarter of a century—twenty-six years—had passed since the first spade of earth had been turned for the first passenger railroad in America, (1828) and the man to perform that ceremony was Charles Carroll of Carrollton, ninety years old, the last living signer of the Declaration of Independence.

The little, ten-ton, wood-burning engine that blazed the trail that winter day, though a very crude affair, was a far cry, in the way of development, from the horse-propelled cars of 1830—the first passenger car in America—where a horse was placed in the center of the car to run a tread-mill, which formed the motive power; the passengers arranged along the sides of the car, and across its top words announced in large letters that this was the "Flying Dutchman." The Flying Dutchman had a speed of thirteen miles per hour.[1] Evanston's first car was a far cry from the invention of 1840, a car that looked like an immense baby-carriage on wheels, carrying sails; or the cars the first steam engine drew, which were merely stage-coach bodies set on car trucks. Far removed from any of these was that proud, little engine, with its clear-toned bell, which was, in itself, almost an innovation at the time.

Conductor Charles George, who traveled for years on the train through Evanston, tells the following interesting story in regard to the bell, in his "Forty Years on the Railroad." In the early days, the only way the conductor had of signaling the engineer was to send word by the

_____

[1] Sixty-three years later the No. 999 engine exhibited at the World's Fair in Chicago in 1893 had broken all records with a speed of 112 miles per hour.

brakeman, who sometimes had to climb over a dozen freight cars to reach him. An old conductor, Ayers, in the east grew tired of this poor system and invented one of his own, out of which the bell-cord system grew. "Pappy" Ayers hung a stick that would dangle in front of the engineer's face, and carried the rope attached to it over the whole length of cars. In this way, he could signal the engineer in a moment, and the train could be brought to a standstill very shortly. However, he had reckoned without his engineer, who stubbornly refused to use the invention, whereupon "Pappy" Ayers promptly gave him a "good licking" and all went smoothly thereafter. As conductors were allowed to cater to their own taste in the matter of dress, the tall, silk hat and Prince Albert coat were chosen as most befitting their calling. It must have been an awesome sight to see "Pappy" Ayers discard his long coat and lay aside his high hat, with its leather band across the front carrying in silver letters the word "Conductor"— lay these aside, tenderly and solemnly, and prepare to subdue his rebellious engineer.

The Chicago and Galena Union Railroad was the original road, from which the great corporation—the Chicago and North Western Railroad—may claim descent, and as such must have some mention. When this road was constructed, railroad building was in its infancy in the west and not much more than that anywhere in the United States. In 1835, there was not a railroad built, nor a corporation chartered to build a road in Northern Illinois. Chicago was but a little village looking for its prosperity to come by boats. When subscription books were opened to build a road, "certain business men in

Chicago opposed the construction of the road, on the ground that it might divert business from Chicago to other points along the line,'' according to Stennett's history of the road. Not very far-seeing, those business men, as today Chicago is the greatest railroad center in the country.

The ''Pioneer'' was the first engine bought by the Chicago and Galena Union Railroad, and it was one of the first engines to run through Evanston. This engine may be seen at the Field Museum.

An item from a Chicago paper, dated December 11, 1849, states, in regard to the first train to run from Chicago to St. Charles: ''Owing to the hasty manner in which the track was laid, it was announced that the trains would be drawn by horses for the present.''

The name of the first railroad that ran through Evanston, in 1854, was the Chicago and Milwaukee. It continued under this name until it was merged with the Chicago and North Western by permanent lease in 1866. It was ultimately bought and consolidated with this railroad.

A Chicago paper of February 10, 1855, states that ''the Chicago and Milwaukee Railroad passes through the newly laid out towns of Chittenden, Evanston, Winnetka, and Port Clinton.'' Rose Hill was formerly Chittenden, and Highland Park was Port Clinton. The end of the road was the state line, nine miles north of Waukegan, but no station is mentioned as being there. Later the Milwaukee and Chicago Railroad was constructed, and met the Chicago and Milwaukee at the state line and the passengers were transferred from one train to the other. The two roads eventually merged under one management and became a part of the Chicago and North Western system.

The rate of fare, in 1874, from Chicago to Evanston was fourteen cents on a hundred-ride ticket.

An excursion train ran from Chicago to Milwaukee, June 21, 1855, according to a letter written by A. Z. Blodgett, an employe of the old railroad when it first started. The excursion train consisted of five flat cars, with seats around the sides. There were about two hundred persons on board. "We stopped the train where Zion City is now," he writes, "and cut pine trees and put them in the sockets for shade."

The new road brought more settlers to the vicinity. The location of the station determined the business section of the town. A young man by the name of Kearney was contractor for the construction of the road. He was accompanied by his brother George, who decided to remain. George Kearney built a house north of Emerson Street, west of the Ridge.

Andrew J. Brown had bought the Carney farm in 1853. This farm lay west of the present site of the railroad. When the railroad was completed to Evanston, Mr. Brown donated to the railroad company land necessary for the right-of-way, and for the station, from Davis Street to Church Street. It might be mentioned here that Andrew Brown was a citizen of whom Evanston might well be proud. He was elected Probate Judge in DeKalb County, in 1840, on his twenty-first birthday.

For a number of years the railroad between Chicago and Evanston consisted of a single track. In 1882 the double track was completed. As all know, Evanston has always been a "prohibition town" but there was plenty of liquor to be obtained outside the realms of Evanston; also, some engineers did not hail from Evanston, and thereby hangs a tale. In 1855, three trainloads of children were being brought from Chicago to Evanston for a picnic. At that time, as stated, there was only the single track. The train reached town, but failed to stop at the station, whereupon the conductor and brakeman brought the train to a standstill as soon as they could by means of the brakes, just in the nick of time, it proved, as another train was already in sight, coming towards them on the same track. When the half-intoxicated engineer was questioned, he answered, "I was thinking what a lot of little angels there would be, if I should hit that train."

Evanston was the first station north of Chicago. When a train was about half a mile from the station, the engineer would give a long whistle, a signal to the brakeman to apply the brakes and bring the train to a standstill. If the train had not quite reached the station, it was necessary to apply more steam; the train shot past the station if too much steam had been turned on. The horses were frightened by the unusual sight and the drivers invariably had to stand at their heads and keep a tight rein on them.

After the trains had been running a few years over the suburban route north, the directors of the road held a meeting to decide whether it would pay to continue the service, which consisted of but one accommodation train a day, stopping morning and evening. Charles George, who had been invited to attend this meeting, strongly urged them to continue to run this train and even made the suggestion that they give better service, predicting

that this suburban line would one day be the best patron-
ized line of the company. The directors decided to follow
his advice, and also to give better service. Time proved
Conductor George was right and the directors had no
reason to regret their course of action.

C. T. Bartlett tells of taking the train at Davis Street
station at four in the morning, in order to reach his office
in the city at seven. He arrived home in the evening at
half past seven. A lantern was a necessity to find the
road to and from the station.

In 1872 W. G. Norkett became station agent in South
Evanston, and has served in that capacity for fifty-five
years.

Before the date, December 31, 1864, arrived, to turn
in the eighteenth annual report, the great consolidation
of the Galena and Chicago Union Railroad with the Chicago and North Western Railroad had taken place and
the Galena and Chicago Union Railroad had passed out of
existence. The name, Galena and Chicago Union Railroad was a misnomer, as that railroad did not touch
Galena.

In 1856 coal was introduced for use in the engines.
The important experiment of burning soft coal was tried
on the Galena Road. Bituminous coal was used in place
of wood and two locomotives were purchased. The
engines were not to be paid for unless they "were successful with Illinois soft coal."

One of the heaviest snows of years occurred in 1856.
The snow buried the tracks twenty feet in places. At
Rose Hill, Conductor George's train got stuck in a snow
drift so deep that the four little ten-ton engines that
came to the rescue failed, and a heavier engine had to be

borrowed from another road. A crew of 200 men was put to work to clear the track, but it was two weeks before traffic could be resumed.

February 9, 1885, was the date of another heavy snow-fall. The Evanston train got no further than Summerdale, and at three in the afternoon another engine drew it back to Evanston. From Chicago, the trains got no further than Clybourn Junction. The side-walks in Evanston could not be seen, as the snow was hip-deep, and they remained impassable until the latter part of March. The people objected to the use of the two snow-plows the village owned, as they were afraid the heavy horses would damage the plank side-walks then in use.

The first Pullman cars went into service in the fall of 1858. They cost $1,000 each and were upholstered in plush, lighted by oil lamps, heated with box stoves and mounted on four-wheel trucks with iron wheels. The berth rate was fifty cents a night and, there being no porter, the brakeman made up the berths. Each car had ten sleeping car sections, a linen locker and two wash-rooms. These cars had flat tops like box cars.

Formerly all locomotives had names instead of numbers. Indian names were used, also names of towns and names of railroad officials. Cloud, Kehotaw, Black Hawk, Walking Thunder and Shabbona were some of the Indian names. So much could be told of Shabbona, whose "skin was tawny; but his soul was white." He had always been a friend of the white people. When the Indian tribes moved west, he was urged to go, but he did not wish to leave his white friends. At last he consented to leave. Growing homesick, he returned, only to find his land had been sold. He was told he had forfeited his land by his absence. This discouraged him and he took to intoxicating drinks (he was a teetotaler up to that time) and his mind became affected. He was very fond of the engine that was named in his honor and, knowing the time it was due to arrive in the Chicago station, he would be on hand and standing proudly by its side, would inform all who went by that the engine bore his name. "Shabbona, me; Shabbona, me," he would say over and over again, pointing to himself.

In 1864, Orrington Lunt, John Evans, and a few other persons, formed a corporation under the name of Chicago and Evanston Railroad Company. The railroad to be constructed was to be either for steam or horse cars and to connect with the horse cars at Fullerton Avenue in Chicago. Nothing came of this until 1887, when the Chicago, Evanston and Lake Superior Railway Company, a new corporation, pushed the project to completion as far as Calvary Cemetery, and obtained rights to construct the road through South Evanston and Evanston. The Chicago, Milwaukee and St. Paul Railway Company then obtained control of the road and operated it as a local line.

In the seventies, a bus owned by the Powers and Schwall Livery and Bus Company, and later by Andrew Schwall, each day met the evening train. It also carried the ladies to their afternoon parties. The Schwall Livery Stable, located on Sherman Avenue between Davis and Lake Streets, was next door to the famous "Round House," which had degenerated into a tenement building, housing some of the colored population. "Andy" Schwall was a familiar figure sitting in front of his place of business or driving his well-kept horses from the high seat on the top of the old omnibus.

In 1892, the Chicago and North Shore Street Railway Company was formed. Their electric cars connected with the cable cars in Chicago at the Wrightwood Avenue barns, Wrightwood and Sheffield Avenues, where another fare, five cents, was demanded to carry the passenger to Dempster Street. In 1893 the street cars ran north as far as Emerson Street. At that time Chicago's street cars were propelled either by cable or horses, no electric cars, as yet, being in use, so Evanston, made a city only that year, 1892, was already surpassing its larger sister city to the south, in having an electrified street railway system.

In the late nineties the automobile came into existence. Horses shied at its appearance and their drivers had to stand by their heads until the "devil-wagon" had passed. Bicyclists felt that the automobile drivers were trying to run them down. Not in those days were these conveyances ever designated as cars or machines. They were automobiles, the word being pronounced in various ways, with the accent on first, third or last syllable. One day Evanston opened its eyes—one of its own citizens, Edwin Brown, was the proud owner of an automobile, the first one owned in Evanston. This first automobile was on exhibit for many successive years at automobile shows, being on a raised platform in the center of the Coliseum building. It was finally burned when the house, in which it was stored at Mr. Brown's place in Evanston, burned. Mr. Brown was the first president of the Chicago Bicycle Club of Chicago. This club made a run to Canada at one time. Mr. Brown rode—before the safety came into existence—the high bicycle, large front wheel and small rear. Later the wheels of the machines were reversed, the small wheel being placed in front. Looking at these unwieldy shaped affairs, we do not wonder at the name safety being bestowed on the later machines, where the wheels were the same size.

CHAPTER XXII

DRAINAGE, WATER AND LIGHT

WITH the exception of the University grounds and the land along the Ridge, the site of Evanston was low, swampy ground. The children from the east ridge (Chicago Avenue) were forced to use rafts or boats to reach the log school house on the Ridge. Cows, which in those days were allowed to roam at will, frequently became mired and had to be pried out of the swampy ground by rails. The people on the two ridges found the swamp a barrier to neighborly relations.

The ridges running north and south through Grosse Pointe, and Dutch Ridge west of it, prevented drainage of the land lying between them. Wooden box drains emptying into the lake and into the North Branch of the Chicago River made the land between the ridges habitable.

Edward Mulford, living on the Ridge and what was later Mulford Street, and Edward Murphy, living at the Indian boundary line and the lake, noting the existing conditions, decided to construct a much needed ditch; consequently in the forties "Mulford's ditch" was constructed between the east and the west ridges, and this was the first attempt to drain and redeem the swamp land.

"Mulford's Ditch" consisted of a wooden box-drain, and ran half way between the east and west ridges (Chicago Avenue and Ridge Avenue), and emptied into the lake through a ravine between the college campus and the site of the first Biblical Institute building, Dempster Hall.

Dutch Ridge, according to Hurd's History, begins in Winnetka at the south end of the bluff along the shore, runs in a southwesterly direction toward the North Branch of the Chicago River and ends near Niles Center. Evanston's highest ridge, Ridge Avenue, begins at the Ridge and the lake, runs south to Bowmanville and terminates at the North Branch of the Chicago River. The east ridge, which is Chicago Avenue through Evanston, commences on the campus at the lake shore, runs south through Evanston and Lake View, and ends at Lincoln Park. There is yet another ridge running through Evanston, the low one on Forest Avenue.

Some parts of the land lying between the ridges were under water and impassable the year around.

The land just west of Ridge Road was prairie land. Further west, near Dutch Ridge, was timber land. This latter was called the Big Woods. To the south of the Big Woods, at Rose Hill, the land was almost barren of trees, and here again was prairie land. The road running through the prairie land south of Rose Hill was known as Prairie Road.

The Drainage Commission was formed February 15, 1855, especially for the purpose of draining the wet lands in Townships 41 and 42, Ranges 13 and 14, and certain sections in Township 40, of Range 13, and the commission was given power "to lay out, locate, construct, complete and alter ditches, embankments, culverts, bridges and roads, and maintain and keep the same in repair." The members of the commission were Harvey B. Hurd, George M. Huntoon, James B. Colvin, John Beveridge, and John H. Foster. A. G. Wilder was later put in Dr. Foster's place as he, Dr. Foster, resided in Chicago. Mr. Hurd was secretary, and he virtually controlled operation.

The only road leading to Chicago west of Evanston was one east of the Big Woods, running from Emmerson's barn through Bowmanville. This road could be used only part of the year, in the late summer and when the ground was frozen. The first work undertaken by the commissioners was making a ditch on the west side of it. The earth thrown up onto this road helped make it passable.

The next work was the construction of the Big Ditch. The Big Ditch was located between the Big Woods and the west ridge (Ridge Avenue). The description, in Hurd's History of the Big Ditch is as follows: "It was so shaped that the north end of it, from the north side of Center Street on the town line between Evanston and New Trier emptied into the lake, and from the south side of Center Street, the water was carried south, emptying into the North Branch at a point about three-fourths of a mile northwest of Bowmanville."

Cutting across the prairie due west, several ditches were constructed in such a manner as to create roads— Rogers Road beginning at the Rogers' home and running to Niles Center, Mulford Road (Church Street) running to the Big Woods, and Emmerson Road, now Emerson Street.

The Mulford Ditch, which had gone pretty much to decay by 1850, was enlarged and furnished fair drainage between the east and west ridges.

The north end of the Big Ditch was later enlarged

and extended toward the south so as to allow drainage toward the lake from Church Street. In time, the city installed the sewerage system to replace these crude attempts at draining.

All the roads constructed by the commission have been extended and improved and are not only principal highways, but legal highways, as the owners of the land through which the roads ran found them of such benefit, they showed no desire to fence them off before the twenty years expired, as they had a right to do. The law under which the roads were constructed was eventually declared void.

Drainage was first done in South Evanston by means of wooden box-drains both on Keeney Street and on Main Street from the railroad to the lake. At the east ridge, Chicago Avenue, the Main Street drain was cut deep enough to drain the land between the ridges. The drain at this place was constructed of brick.

When the first ditch was being constructed along the west side of the Big Woods Road, the Big Woods people came out with pitch forks and clubs and tried to drive off the engineer and his workers, but the engineer was firm and held to his purpose.

WATER

Before 1875, Evanston's water supply was obtained from wells and cisterns. Credit is due Charles J. Gilbert for his preseverance and persistence in the fight for a water plant. For his activity in the carrying through of this project, he became known as Father of the Evanston Water Works. In 1874, the first engine was purchased at a cost of $24,000, and installed, the water being carried from the bottom of the lake twelve hundred feet out through a 16 inch intake pipe. This engine was named C. J. Gilbert. In 1889, a 30 inch intake pipe ran 2,600 feet out into the lake to a submerged crib. In 1886, another engine was installed, and in 1897, a third engine

SOUTH EVANSTON WATER WORKS TOWER,
DEMOLISHED 1902

was added. The first engine was run continuously for seventeen years averaging 23.7 hours out of every 24 hours. An artesian well at Chicago Avenue and Washington Street, bored to the depth of 2,600 feet and gushing up 60 feet above the ground, furnished the water supply for South Evanston. This water was so hard that the residents of South Evanston soon grew tired of it, and desired lake water. The intake pipe for South Evanston's supply of water was situated only 600 feet from the place the Main Street sewer emptied into the lake, thus contaminating the water. In 1892, the question of annexation of South Evanston to the village of Evanston was put to the vote and carried. This annexation gave South Evanston pure water through the Evanston water mains.

LIGHT

Up to 1871, the only street lighting Evanston had was by means of kerosene lamps, not satisfactory at best. Then the Northwestern Gas Light and Coke Company erected a small plant and furnished gas to a limited number, but not until five years later was gas used in the street lamps. In 1890, South Evanston was lighted by electricity and was the only municipality so lighted between Chicago and Waukegan. The lighting plant was operated by the same crew of men and by the same boiler that operated the water tower. The artesian well tower just south of the fire house at Kedzie Avenue was 120 feet high, circular in shape, and 16 feet in diameter. The lower portion was made of brick and the upper 40 feet was an iron tank 15 feet in diameter. At first, the natural flow of water kept the tank full, but this diminished in time. After South Evanston was annexed to the village of Evanston in 1892, the tower's usefulness as part of the water works system was ended, and for the next ten years it was used solely for lighting. A cluster of powerful electric lights surrounded the tower, lighting the neighborhood for blocks around, and was plainly visible to mariners far out on the lake. The faithful light tenders performed their duties in all kinds of weather, climbing the stairs within the lower walls of the tower, then emerging through a small opening in the wall to a balcony at the base of the tank, and climbing the remaining forty feet, clinging to a line of rungs, on the outside of the tank. In the ten years this tower was used as a beacon, not once did the light tenders fail in their duty. In 1895, Evanston discontinued using the gas street lamps and substituted electricity for street lighting, having entered into a contract with the Evanston Electric Illuminating Company.

Chapter XXIII

PUBLICATIONS

PROFESSOR W. P. JONES, founder of the Northwestern Female College, is entitled to the distinction of having the first paper ever printed in Evanston. This was *The Casket and Budget,* a little four page sheet published by his students, dated December, 1858. This little paper tells more than is divulged by its printed words. The fact that the first page, only eight by ten inches in size, gives space in its three columns to two poems to "Mother," one quite a lengthy one, and on the second page, another "Mother" poem, makes one ponder for a moment on the loneliness and homesickness of the students, trying to lessen the ache in their hearts by this expression of love.

In 1864, *The Suburban Idea* appeared, a four page, four column paper, edited and published by the Reverend Nathan Sheppard, a man of high ideals. Later he was the author of a number of well-known books. His paper lived but one year and had no successor for seven years.

On June 8, 1872, *The Evanston Index,* a three column, fifteen by twenty page paper, began a useful and active existence, and became an important factor in Evanston's home life, as well as in its official and political life, for over thirty years. The idea of a community paper in Evanston originated with Alfred L. Sewell, who with John E. Miller had been publishing *The Little*

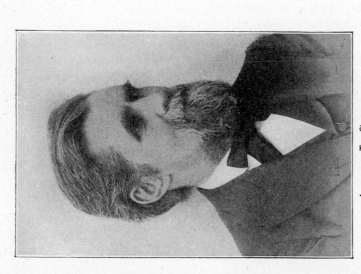

THE EVANSTON INDEX

ALFRED L. SEWELL

Corporal, a juvenile paper edited by Mrs. Emily Huntington Miller.   The first copy of *The Evanston Index* carries
on its first page the statement beneath its name, "Issued
every Saturday, at one o'clock P. M., for the convenience
of Evanston and adjacent villages."   The paper's office
in Evanston was at Mr. Sewell's residence; in Chicago,
the Steam Printing Rooms of Alfred L. Sewell and Company, 75 West Washington Street, corner of Jefferson
Street.   The price was one dollar a year in advance.   In
the same column that gives this information, are printed
the advertising rates and beneath them the following:
"The Index is not a newspaper, and therefore does not
attempt to rival the City Dailies. . . The question, 'What
then is this Stripling?' is answered, 'Simply a local *Index*
of the rapidly unfolding life of our beautiful triple village, its fluctuations and its vast concerns.' 'Small?' did
you say, Sir or Madam? Would you make an index larger
than the volume? This index is expected to grow as the
village grows, both in size and usefulness, so that in the
near future, which will give this triple Evanston—three
in one and one in three—a population of fifteen thousand
souls, the Index will be as large as the people desire to
have it."

The column to the left carries John Culver's real
estate advertisement, offering lots in North Evanston
50 x 150, with sidewalks, and ornamented with shade
trees, $500 to $1,000 each.   In the column to the right,
Huntoon and Gamble advertise groceries; L. C. Pitner,
real estate; I. B. Lampkin, boots and shoes.

Such was the beginning of the first family newspaper
in Evanston, the forerunner of the *Evanston News-Index.*
The *Index* had scarcely reached its first birthday, when

Mr. Sewell opened a printing plant in Evanston and *The Index* began to be published in its home town.

John A. Childs, who had been with the paper from its beginning, bought out Mr. Sewell's interest, together with David Cavan, in November, 1875, becoming sole owner two years later.

The Evanston Herald made its appearance in 1875, and the following spring it became part of *The Index.* This paper was published in a building on Davis Street, that in later years housed the Star Theater. One night fire broke out in the printing plant, and the citizens rushed to its rescue. Dumping the type matter in buckets, they carried it to safety. Even the youngest child printer in school can appreciate the *pi* that resulted from this kind act.

The Evanston Press had its birth January 5, 1889. Frances E. Willard contributed to this paper weekly for a year, *An Old Timer's Story of Evanston,* and so widespread did the interest in Miss Willard's articles become that the paper had one thousand paid subscribers before its third issue was printed. The publishers were two young men just out of college, Robert O. Vandercook and Edwin L. Shuman, the latter withdrawing at the end of one year. *The Evanston Press* grew out of a toy printing press received in trade for a "boyish knicknack" by an older brother. This toy printing press was traded for a larger and better one, which in time was turned over for a still better one. On leaving high school, Robert Vandercook, who had bought out the older brother in the beginning, had a $500 plant, and had earned all but forty dollars of the amount that went into it. He published *The High School Budget* for one year.

A corporation, with Robert Vandercook at the head, was formed and was known as *The University Press Company.* Good old Dr. Cummings, president of the University, strongly advised the founders to go slowly, in order to avoid disappointment to themselves and friends, fearing, with their slight experience, that their venture would result only in failure. In spite of his warning, the University Press Company refused to give up, and was incorporated under the State laws of Illinois. The University Trustees gave the new corporation space in the basement of the gymnasium building, with lights, fuel and janitor service free.

Students earned money by setting type for *The Northwestern,* and doing catalogue and other necessary printing for the college. Two years after the birth of the *Evanston Press,* the corporation changed its name to The Evanston Press Company.

The Press was published for six years in the Simpson Market Building, southeast corner of Fountain Square, and the next five years in the Park building on Davis Street.

During the Spanish-American war, the Chicago papers were compelled to suspend publication on account of a strike in the mechanical departments, and the *Index* and the *Press* were sold on Chicago streets. *The Press* had a special correspondent at Washington, and got out three editions a day.

Milton A. Smith published *The Evanston Daily News,* which lived only from November, 1897, to February, 1898.

L. C. Pitner published, after the Chicago fire in 1871, *The Real Estate News,* a four page paper.

Harry W. Taylor published *The Lake Breeze,* in 1875.

A weekly newspaper, *The Evanston Citizen,* a strong prohibition paper, was published in 1882 by William Duffell. Its last number appeared nine years later, December, 1891.

The Northwestern grew out of two University papers, *The Tripod* and *The Vidette,* in 1881. *The Tripod* was first issued in 1871, a three column, twelve page, monthly magazine. *The Vidette* was semi-monthly, published by the entire student body.

The Northwestern was published by the fraternity students. Their rivals, the non-frats, began a paper of their own called *The Northwestern World,* a weekly, living from October, 1890, to June, 1892, when it went out of existence, as its editor became a fraternity brother.

A war broke out in 1890 between the frats and the non-frats. Each side worked hard for the advertising patronage of the local business houses. One day a dry-goods man announced he could advertise in but one of the college papers and that one would be the paper that brought the best results to an advertisement he would insert in each paper the following Saturday for a special sale. In the frat organ, *The Northwestern,* he would advertise underwear; in the non-frat paper, *The Northwestern World,* kid gloves. Before the doors of the store opened for business on the day of the sale, each side had rallied its forces, relatives, friends and acquaintances, and a long line of students was waiting. The first pair of gloves was bought by the veteran Captain of the Life Saving Crew, who being a non-fraternity man, felt he must stand by that side.

26

Each side felt confident of winning as the sales went merrily on, until the frat men saw a long line of *Bibs* (Biblical students),—more than a hundred of them lined up to buy gloves,—and then the frat men began to see defeat. Never before in the history of Evanston, nor probably since, has there been a day of such tremendous sale of kid gloves and underwear. The contest was won by the *Barbs*—the non-frats—and the triumphant cry that went up from their throats when the dry-goods man made the announcement, could be heard for blocks around.

The first periodical of the colored citizens was *The Afro-American Budget,* a monthly magazine published in 1889.

In 1900, William Lord published *The Noon,* a poetry magazine, which ran for two years.

Such were the various publications, each one frail and weak in the beginning, gaining in strength as time went on; some struggling on alone, some joining with others, "growing as the city grew, both in size and usefulness, rapidly unfolding the city's life, its fluctuations and its vast concerns,"—to borrow Mr. Sewell's words.

Chapter XXIV

EVANSTON PARKS

IN THE days before Northwestern University came into existence, and for a few years after, the townspeople used the beautiful grove on Dr. Foster's land—later the campus—as picnic grounds and a pleasure park. The high ground overlooking the lake, covered by luxuriant trees, and easily reached during the summer months, made an ideal playground for young and old.

Evanston was platted by Philo Judson, business agent of the University, and Andrew J. Brown in the winter of 1853 and 1854. With a spacious campus planned for the University, these men began to lay out a real City Beautiful, which could be accomplished only by leaving open spaces for parks. As a shore beautified into parks adds immeasurably to the attractions of a town, a large part of the land along the lake was laid out for park purposes.

Each of the three parks along the lake front was given the name of Lake Front Park. *Lake Front Park,* extending from University Place to Greenwood Boulevard, contains fifteen acres. *Lake Front Park,* lying between Greenwood Boulevard and Hamilton, contains a little more than one and a half acres. *Lake Front Park,* between Greenleaf and Lee Streets, contains one and a quarter acres.

There are a number of small parks scattered over

Evanston—*Ackerman Park, Commercial Park, Elling-wood Park, Howell Park, Quinlan Park.*

Bell Park is a park of less than half an acre, located at the end of Davis Street on Forest Place. It was named for Captain Bell, a steamboat captain, who retired in 1876, and resided in Evanston until his death in 1899.

Boltwood Park, sixteen and one-fourth acres, lying north of Main Street, between Dodge and Florence Avenues, was named, in 1918, in honor of Professor Henry Leonidas Boltwood, who established the Evanston Township High School.

The Chicago and North Western Railway Park lies west of Dewey Avenue, between Davis and Church Streets.

Clark Square, the first park in South Evanston, was named for Alexander Clark. It is three and one-quarter acres in size, and lies between Main and Kedzie Streets, and east of Sheridan Road. The lake was gradually eating up the land of this block along the shore. Some men from the east who had gained control of the block by foreclosure, fearing they would lose all of the land by the erosion of water, parted with it to the village of South Evanston for $1,600. There was a lake frontage of eight hundred feet. Special assessment was levied on every lot from the Ridge east, amounting to $7,000. This amount was spent on breakwaters, grading the land, and setting out trees upon it. Before the end of the century, the ground had nearly doubled by accretion. This park was secured for the city through the efforts of Alexander Clark. Alexander Clark, attorney, was one of the earliest residents of South Evanston, a man public-spirited, generous and efficient. It was largely through his influence that the three villages were merged into one; that South Evanston secured its supply of water from the lake, when the artesian well water proved unsatisfactory; that cement sidewalks were introduced; that Evanston connects by electric railway with Chicago. In his brain originated the idea of a union loop in Chicago for the elevated railway, all of its legal phases being carried out in accordance with plans he had formed. These are but a few of the things with which he may be credited. He well deserves the honor bestowed on him in regard to the naming of Clark Square.

Congregational Park was originally given to the village by the University Trustees, for *park purposes only.* When the Congregational Church was founded, the church trustees paid $600 to the village trustees for enough ground for their purpose, whereupon the village trustees deeded the ground back to the University Trustees, who, in turn, deeded it to the church trustees.

Elliott Park, comprising two and a half acres, lies between Hamilton and Greenleaf Streets.

Fountain Square, in the center of the city at the intersection of Davis Street, Sherman and Orrington Avenues, contains eighty-seven hundredths of an acre.

Grey Park was named in honor of Charles F. Grey, who donated the land, one and one-half acres, at the northeast corner of Main Street and the Ridge.

Housel Park is the land lying between the Chicago and Northwestern Railway and the Elevated Railway tracks, bounded on the north and south by Church and Davis Streets. This park was named for Benjamin Housel, who was Superintendent of Streets for twenty-four years. During his term of office he added twenty-two acres to the Lake Front parks by means of dumping.

Mason Park, containing two and three-fourths acres, is bounded by Davis and Church Streets, Florence and Dewey Avenues, and was donated by William S. Mason.

Michigan Park, a piece of land lying between Michigan Avenue—now Sheridan Road—and the lake, gained its name from its location. The thoroughfare called Michigan Avenue extended from University Place to Greenwood Boulevard. The park contains about one and three-quarter acres.

Raymond Park, one and nine-tenths acres of land, bounded by Chicago and Hinman Avenues, Grove and Lake Streets, perpetuates the name of the Reverend Miner Raymond, D.D., L.L.D., pastor of the First M. E. Church, Professor of Theology in Garrett, with which institution he was connected for thirty years, and President of the Village Board of Education. He was called "the greatest mathematical teacher on God's earth," by one of his students who was later a lawyer in New York City. The name *Raymond Park* was not bestowed on this ground until the City Council voted to that effect in 1901. The only thoroughfare in Evanston bearing Dr. Raymond's name—Raymond Avenue, one block long, between Hamilton and Greenleaf Streets nearest the lake—had been swallowed up by Sheridan Road. At the meeting, the name of Grant Goodrich was proposed for the name of the park, but he was not a resident, whereas Dr. Miner Raymond was. Grant Goodrich was entitled to the high honor on account of his participation in the founding of Northwestern University. Dr. Raymond's name was proposed by Andrew J. Brown and was heartily endorsed by the members of the council. Dr. Miner Raymond's home was at the southeast corner of Hinman Avenue and Davis Street, where the Georgian Hotel now stands.

Land adjoining the right of way of the St. Paul Railroad Company, which formerly ran trains from Chicago to Evanston, was converted into two small parks, each bearing the name *St. Paul Park*. One is south of Main Street, on the west side of Chicago Avenue, and the other south of Lake Street, west of Sherman Avenue.

Evanston, a City of Homes, is one great park in itself, whose wide streets are tree-lined, the result of the foresight of a few early residents—Josiah F. Willard, W. B. Kimball, Alonzo Burroughs, John A. Pearsons, Dr. F. D. Hemenway and others—who set out young trees, in the early days, which have grown tall and strong and add materially to the grandeur of the *City Beautiful*.

CHAPTER XXV

EVANSTON IN THE CIVIL WAR

IN July the Ordinance of 1787, one clause of which prohibited slavery in the Northwest Territory, was passed by congress—two months before the Constitution of the United States was framed. The clauses of this Ordinance[1] were mainly supplied by Dr. Manasseh Cutler, who had studied successively law, theology and medicine; was an eminent scientist and had served as chaplain during the Revolutionary War. With such a man back of it, we are not surprised at the wisdom shown in its clauses. The clause prohibiting slavery in the Northwest Territory, which was then a wilderness, has been a priceless heritage to the five great states[2] composing that territory, especially in the stormy days preceding the Civil War.

When the news of the attack on Fort Sumter reached Evanston that April day in 1861, Evanston, no less than every other city in the United States, was appalled, but its citizens felt that the war would be of short duration—three months would see its finish. They had watched the storm brew, a storm whose original cause dated its beginning nearly two hundred and fifty years before, when in 1619 a Dutch man-of-war brought "20 Negars" to our shores and sold them. It is true, at

---

(1) There is no legal distinction between ordinance, act and statute. After the ratification of the Constitution in 1789, either of the terms, act or statute, was used in regard to measures passed by congress, and the term ordinance was limited to measures passed in the city councils.

(2) Ohio, Indiana, Illinois, Michigan and Wisconsin.

that time, traffic in slavery was not condemned, nor did any serious trouble result from it in the United States until the early nineteenth century, when the free states began to voice their disapproval of slave-holding and the southern states retaliated by trying to secede from the Union. In utter disregard of the admonition contained in Washington's *Farewell Address* in 1796, when he called upon the people indignantly to "frown upon the first dawning of every attempt to alienate any portion of our country from the rest," seven southern states had formed a new government under the title of "Confederate States of America," and Evanston's citizens realized that the time had come when they must take up arms to preserve the Union.

In 1861 Evanston's population numbered less than twelve hundred, including the students at the University and the Biblical Institute, yet it contributed to the cause four general officers, twenty-four other officers, fifty-four enlisted men, besides the services of several women in the management of the Soldiers' Fairs held in Chicago. Two men, University students, southern-born, joined the Confederate army.

The morning after the fall of Fort Sumter Bishop Simpson preached a rousing sermon which awoke in the citizens of Evanston a spirit of patriotism that could be surpassed nowhere.

The Sunday following the defeat of Bull Run, July 21, 1861, Julius White stood up in his pew near the altar and made an impassioned appeal to the congregation, calling on all the patriots to convene in the church the following evening and declare what they were going to do to save the country. And the following evening the

GENERAL JULIUS WHITE   GENERAL WILLIAM GAMBLE

GENERAL JOHN L. BEVERIDGE

CAPTAIN H. A. PEARSONS   COLONEL JAMES MULLIGAN

patriots came and showed their intentions by putting their names on the muster roll. Subscriptions were started for the support of the families of men enlisting who were not overburdened with this world's goods. Dr. Evans put his name down for hundreds of dollars and others followed for smaller sums, many of whom were young women earning small salaries.

Evanston's list of men in the war is very incomplete. One who reached the highest rank was General John L. Beveridge (later governor of Illinois) who raised a company which became Company F in the Eighth Illinois Cavalry. He was appointed captain and in 1861 became major of the regiment. In 1864 he was promoted to the colonelcy of the Seventeenth Illinois Cavalry and was breveted Brigadier-General, February 7, 1865, for gallant services. General Julius White opened a recruiting office in Chicago and was at the head of the Thirty-seventh Illinois Infantry. He was appointed Brigadier-General on June 9, 1862, and Brevet Major-General on March 13, 1865. General William Gamble[3] drilled the Eighth Illinois Cavalry, and made it one of the most effective of the 178 Illinois regiments. He was appointed Brigadier-General on September 25, 1865.

Other officers were Colonel H. M. Kidder, Captain H. A. Pearsons, Major Edward Russell, Captain Joseph Clapp, Captain Alphonso C. Linn, Captain Milton C. Springer, Lieutenant George E. Strobridge, Corporal Thomas Strobridge, brother of George, and Sergeant George W. Huntoon.

Although Evanston proudly claims to have had three generals in the Civil War, there was no full general at

_____
(3) The Evanston Post of the Grand Army of the Republic was originally named Gamble Post, complimenting General William Gamble.

that time, the term being loosely used. Washington had rightly held the title, but army records tell us there was no other man on whom the title of general was bestowed until U. S. Grant was made general after the close of the Civil War.

Among the privates were Charles Bragdon, Charles McDaniel, George H. Reed, James A. Snyder, O. C. Foster, E. R. Lewis, Philo Judson, J. D. Ludlam, W. A. Spencer, Charles P. Westerfield, William R. Bailey, A. R. Bailey (died 1863), W. E. Smith (killed in action July, 1863), Harry Meacham, L. A. Sinclair (died in Washington, 1864), W. J. Kennicott (died of wounds 1863), Joseph E. Edsall (died 1863), Orsevius Coe, William Mickels, Chauncey Parker, James Balls, James Lemon, Harrison Pratt, son of Mrs. Eliza (Gaffield) Pratt, Eighty-ninth Illinois (died in a hospital in the south during the war), Willard Pratt, a son of Paul Pratt (one of the few exchanged from Libby Prison; died shortly after coming home), Charles Pratt, another son, Eighth Cavalry, Edward McSweeney, Edward Steele, Edwin Bailey, George Hide, Charles Wigglesworth, Dwight Bannister, George Kirby, A. Butterfield, K. S. Lewis, Joseph Milner, Peter Schutz, William Gamble (same name as general), Lyman K. Ayrault, Charles Baker, John C. Boggs, William C. Gray, Melvin Meigs, William F. Siebert, Morton Culver, William R. Wightman, Isaac R. Adams, Joseph Sears, and I. W. McCaskey.

Henry Leonidas Boltwood, ordained chaplain, engaged in the work of the United States Christian Commission, "which shared the hardships of the march, the trench, the battlefield, and cared for both bodies and souls; cheered the sick, comforted the dying and buried the dead,'' work similar to Red Cross work of today. Chaplain Boltwood was present at the last battle of the war, when Fort Blakely in Mobile Bay was taken only a few hours before Lee surrendered at Appomatox.

On Saturday, April 13, 1861, the day following the attack on Fort Sumter, many of the Northwestern University students, finding that the last train had gone, and there being no Sunday trains in those days, walked the distance into the city late Saturday night. They found the Chicago streets filled with people, flags flying from every house and great excitement everywhere. They were told there would surely be enlisting Monday morning, so they boarded a freight train and returned to Evanston. Monday morning they marched to the train, to find standing room only, the boys from the country being already on board. President Lincoln's first call for troops was made that day, Monday, April 15, 1861.

At several enlisting places the students found placards stating that no more men were wanted. The same thing met them at the Military Battery in Chicago, but they were let in through a back door quietly and told to get recommendations from some prominent person. This they did, but on their return they found that the desired number of men had been secured and the books closed. This information was received with a howl of disappointment. Thousands of young men were clamoring to enlist, but the Illinois quota had been filled. Not discouraged, however, they formed companies and commenced to drill and to prepare for a call.

The students, after seeing the fortunate men off to Cairo, began to be impatient and sent word to the military authorities that they would not wait any longer;

accordingly a sergeant was sent to escort them to the detachment to which they had been assigned.

The first student of Northwestern University[4] to enlist was A. W. Gray, serving first with Battery B, Chicago Artillery and later as lieutenant in Company G of the Fifty-first Illinois Volunteers.

Bunting could not be manufactured fast enough to meet the demand for flags. Mrs. Julia Atkins Miller, valedictorian of the class of 1860 of the Northwestern Female College, writes in Frances Willard's *Classic Town,* that Dr. Charles Jones happened to remember an old flag that was stored in Chicago, belonging to his brother Wesley. He brought it to Evanston and Mrs. Miller worked all day repairing that torn, mouse-eaten flag. At evening it floated over their college building, the first flag to wave in Evanston, to the great joy of Professor and Mrs. Jones; and Northwestern University students went wild with enthusiasm, when they saw it.

The students of Northwestern University then wished to raise a flag over their building to show their patriotism, but no flag could be procured, as the supply of bunting had been exhausted, so the girls set to work making a flag from calico. When the flag was hoisted to the peak of the flag-staff the whole population of the surrounding country was present, and the boys raised their right hands and swore to protect the honor of the flag with their lives.

"The First Gun Is Fired, May God Protect the Right," composed by George F. Root at this time, became the most popular song of the day.

The army career of John Henry Page, a southerner and a former slave-owner, was remarkable and his pro-

---

(4) Dr. A. W. Gray was born in Chicago, December 16, 1839, and died March 23. 1927.

motion was rapid. We are indebted to him for the account of the students' patriotism, for he was one of those who walked into Chicago that Saturday night.

Mr. Levere's scrap-book gives an incident of Page's early days. He was born at New Castle, Delaware, and the members of his family were slave-owners. When a boy he had been given a young Negro as a birthday present, who was "handsome, intelligent and powerful of limb." Young Page could knock the chip from the shoulder of any boy in town, as his Negro boy did the fighting for him. The Negro could pick up and conceal between his toes more marbles than any darkey in town—and he never bothered about anything less than twenty-five cent "alleys." As the boy belonged to Page, of course the marbles went into Page's bag. One day the two walked down to the wharf to meet a steamboat carrying peaches to Philadelphia. As the boat pushed off, a hand reached down, grabbed Negro Bill by the collar and swung him on board. That was the last young Page ever saw of Bill, nor did the $800, which the transportation company was obliged to pay for him, lessen Page's grief over his loss. With the loss of his "body-guard" Page lost his prestige among his school-mates.

The Northwestern University College Alumni Record for 1903 says, concerning Page's Civil War career:

"John Henry Page, from Baltimore, Md. Enlisted from freshman class 25 Aug. 1861, in 3rd U. S. Infantry. Promoted to 2nd Lieutenant."

The Official Records of the War of the Rebellion show that, as First Lieutenant, Page was in command of Company G, 3rd U. S. Infantry at the battles of Gaines Mills and Malvern Hill. While still First Lieutenant he was in command of Company I at the Second Battle of Bull Run, at the Battle of Fredericksburg, and in the three-days Battle of Gettysburg. He was in command of his regiment while yet First Lieutenant early in 1864 and was Captain and in command of the regiment at the close of the war.

It is a very unusual occurrence that a first lieutenant should have command of a regiment, and indicates the character of the fighting in which the regiment took part, since all the field officers and captains were either killed, wounded, or otherwise incapacitated.

Later Page became Colonel of the Third U. S. Infantry and served in the Spanish-American War, leading his regiment at Santiago and also in the Philippines.

The Battle of Gettysburg, July 1, 1863, was commenced by the Eighth Illinois Cavalry, the Evanston regiment being under command of Major Beveridge. Major Winfield S. Gamble, youngest of General Gamble's fifteen children, wrote a letter to the Evanston Historical Society, in which he says, "There is no question of the fact that the Battle of Gettysburg, July 1, 1863, the pivotal battle of the Rebellion, was won by the first three and a half hours stand of General Gamble's and Devin's brigades against the overwhelming forces of Heth's division [Confederate], while Meade was moving troops to Gettysburg and whipping chaos into battle formation. This stand of nine thousand dismounted cavalry against twenty-five thousand confederates of Lee's army deserves a place in history unequalled by any military action in the world's history and the Eighth Illinois Cavalry bore the most conspicuous part. Evanston can never adequately honor its heroic veterans, and the military records of John L.

Beveridge, Majors Edward Russell and James Ludlam, Captain Joseph Clapp and others deserve a high place on the roll of fame.''

General William Gamble was born in the North of Ireland. He enlisted in the First United States Dragoons, was in the Seminole War and in other Indian warfare on the western plains. He came to Evanston while he was in the service of the government as engineer, stationed at Chicago. In 1859 he occupied the "Wheeler house," north of the DeCoudries home on Hinman Avenue, between Clark Street and University Place, while erecting another home on the northeast corner of Hinman Avenue and Clark Street.

In a fight near Middleburg, Virginia, General Gamble's horse was shot under him and he was thrown headlong. At Malvern Hill he received a wound in the breast that nearly cost him his life. At one time his regiment was given a thirty day furlough, but the men had hardly reached home, when they were ordered to the front again. General Gamble posted a notice that the furlough was revoked, and that the regiment was ordered to active service in the field at once, where it had been continuously for the last two and a half years. He stated that it was a high compliment to the regiment, showing that it was two and a half times as efficient as other regiments who were allowed full furlough and longer.

In 1864, in Virginia, a citizen riding a mule came to Gamble's tent to make complaint that one of his horses had been taken by one of Gamble's men and brought to the camp. At the proper times, Colonel Gamble was quite as ready to play a joke on some one as were his men. While the complainant held the mule's halter firmly,

27

Colonel Gamble was having him describe the lost horse
very minutely. Meanwhile the soldiers were separating
the mule from the halter and the soldier commissioned to
hold the halter would give a jerk now and then, in imitation of the mule's actions. So intent had the man been on
presenting his claim that he did not know his mule had
been led away, and great was his surprise to find, when
the colonel gave him permission to search the camp for
his horse, that his mule, also, was missing. However,
Colonel Gamble sent him away happy, in possession of
both the lost horse and the mule.

General Gamble died of cholera, December 20, 1866,
in Central America, and was buried at Virgin Bay, on the
shore of Lake Nicaragua.

Another outstanding figure of the war was Colonel
James Mulligan, who, while not an Evanstonian, was a
close neighbor and deserves mention here. He lived on
a farm near Arunah Hill's place, west of the present
Gross Point. James Mulligan raised a company, which
was called Mulligan's Guards. This company, with other
companies, formed the Twenty-third Regiment of Illinois
Volunteers, of which Mulligan was made colonel, and
which was known as the "Irish Brigade."

Colonel Mulligan is probably best remembered by his
gallant defense of Lexington, Missouri, where, on August
20, 1861, with about 3,000 men, he was surrounded by
about 18,000 rebels under General Price and forced to
surrender. All of his officers and men were released on
parole, but he was kept a prisoner for several months and
finally exchanged. In Chicago and elsewhere Colonel
Mulligan was received with enthusiastic honors.

At the Battle of Winchester, Virginia, Mulligan was

struck by a bullet and mortally wounded. Lieutenant
James H. Nugent, his brother-in-law, ran to his aid, but
Mulligan, seeing the enemy advancing in overwhelming
numbers, called out for him to lay him down and save the
flag. Nugent rescued the colors and returned to Mulligan's side but fell almost instantly, mortally wounded.
Colonel Mulligan's brave words inspired George F. Root
to write the famous patriotic song, "Lay Me Down and
Save the Flag." Colonel Mulligan died July 26, 1864,
forty-eight hours after being wounded. After his death
his widow received from President Lincoln Colonel Mulligan's commission of Brevet Brigadier-General, U. S. V.
dated July 24, "for gallant and meritorious services at the
battle of Winchester."[5] He was buried in Calvary Cemetery near the entrance.

In the third year of the war, in the early part of 1864,
as it was thought the Confederacy was fast reaching the
limit of its endurance, military authorities decided that a
quickly raised temporary force might be used in guarding
railroads and important points, thus relieving the older
regiments employed in active service at the front. The
term of enlistment was to be one hundred days. Illinois
agreed to furnish thirteen regiments of such troops.
These regiments were called One Hundred Day Troops in
the Adjutant General's report. The One Hundred and
Thirty-fourth Regiment was composed mostly of men
from Chicago. Company A was known as the Board of
Trade Company, as that organization made some special
provisions for its maintenance and presented each member with thirty dollars by way of bounty. J. Seymour
Currey enlisted in this company, this being the second

---

(5) Vol. I, Battles and Leaders of the Civil War, published by the Century
Company.

time he had entered the Civil War. The first time he entered as a boy of sixteen at Joliet, his enlistment being for three months.

Company F was known as the University Guards, many of its members being residents of Evanston. Alphonso C. Linn, an instructor in Northwestern University, was its captain. He died in the south within a few months, and Milton C. Springer of Evanston (and, after the war, of Wilmette) succeeded him. George Strobridge[6] was a lieutenant. In the different companies of this regiment were many Evanston men, Corporal Thomas Strobridge, Gamble, Ayrault, Baker, Boggs, Gray, Meigs, Siebert, Culver, Wightman, Adams, and Sears. The One Hundred and Thirty-fourth Regiment was mustered in at Camp Fry, Chicago, May 31, 1864.

There is a very interesting bit of history connected with the lantern at the Gross Point Lighthouse. This lantern was one of three that the government bought from France before the Civil War, one to be sent to the Pacific coast and two to be used on the Florida coast.

During the second year of the war, the lenses, which were later installed in the Gross Point Lighthouse, disappeared from their place in a lighthouse on the Florida coast. In 1862 the keeper, himself a rebel, heard that the rebels were going to attack the lighthouse and destroy the lenses on a certain night. He wanted to help the southern cause, but he did not want the precious lenses destroyed, so he took them out and buried them in the sand. This caused the loss of the Yankee ships, as he had hoped, and helped the southern side. A Union gunboat came soon

---

(6) George Strobridge married the daughter of Dr. Kidder. His little daughter's grave is in the small Protestant cemetery in Rome, near the grave of the poet, John Keats, and near where the heart of Shelley is buried.

afterward and began a search for the missing lenses. The keeper at first denied knowledge of their whereabouts, but finally confessed that he had buried them. They were dug up and sent to Paris to be repaired. When they came back, they were installed in the Gross Point Lighthouse, where they have remained ever since.

Harvey B. Hurd of Evanston was once measured for a suit of clothes for John Brown, of anti-slavery fame. This happened a few years before the war. John Brown had come to Chicago, when he was under ban of the law, a price having been set on his head for having aided fugitive slaves to escape. Harvey B. Hurd looked him up and found him in clothes so ragged they were unfit to wear. As Mr. Hurd was about John Brown's size, he went to the tailor's and had a suit of clothes made to his own measure, which was turned over to Brown.[7]

During the Civil War the government issued paper money called greenbacks, because the backs of the bills were then first printed largely in green ink. These greenbacks in the summer of 1864 were much depreciated in value and were worth but about thirty-five cents on the dollar in gold.

Fractional currency, popularly called "shin-plasters," was also issued in denominations of five, ten, twenty-five and fifty cents, and for years was in general, if not exclusive, use. At the Evanston Historical Society rooms may be seen some of the shin-plasters. There may also be seen in these rooms Confederate money to the amount of $1,500 which Mr. W. C. Levere obtained from the government a few years ago.

In 1863 Congress passed an act for the enrollment of

_____

(7) A half-length portrait of John Brown was donated to the Evanston Historical Society by Mr. Hurd.

all men between the ages of twenty and forty-five. Evanston had a population of a little more than a thousand. The men subject to draft numbered 194, and the draft quota was eleven men. As Evanston had already furnished eighty volunteers, far exceeding its draft quota, no draft measures had to be taken. The total number drafted in Cook County was fifty-nine, and volunteers replaced these before they were mustered in. Cook County furnished, through volunteer enlistments, more than 22,000 of the 267,000 that the State of Illinois contributed to the Union armies.

Before the Emancipation Proclamation had been issued, an Evanston woman, Mrs. Hide, suggested that a petition with this in view, should be started, and be brought before the president as the voice of the women of the land. A petition was prepared and copies of it sent to the religious papers of different denominations, with requests for its publication. Nearly all the papers commended the movement, and women gladly circulated the petitions and obtained signatures. The *Northwestern Christian Advocate* in Chicago reported that a mammoth roll, almost beyond the capacity of a man to carry, was being daily added to the petition. Senator Harlan was engaged to present the petition to the president, but before this could be done, President Lincoln had issued the Emancipation Proclamation, September 22, 1862, which gave the rebels one hundred days to surrender or have the proclamation go into effect. The *Chicago Tribune* of September 23, 1862, says this was the grandest proclamation ever issued by man. The hundred days ended January 1, 1863, when the second and final Emancipation Proclamation was issued. January 1, 1863, was one of the coldest days of a cold winter and consequently the great event was very quietly celebrated.

The original draft of the Emancipation Proclamation was given by Lincoln to the Sanitary Fair. President Lincoln told the ladies who were conducting the Fair that he had intended it as a keepsake for his sons, but the soldier boys were dearer to him than anything else, so he presented it to the Fair for their sakes. Honorable Thomas B. Brian bought it for $3,000 and gave it, subsequently, to the Soldiers' Home in Chicago. At the time of the Chicago fire, it was in the rooms of the Chicago Historical Society and was destroyed. Facsimiles had been made of it, and these were sold for two dollars each. One of these is in the rooms of the Evanston Historical Society.

The ladies of Evanston were active in their work for the soldiers during the entire period of the war. The United States Sanitary Commission was formed for relief work among the soldiers of the Union army. Mrs. A. H. Hoge, of Evanston, was a member of the Sanitary Commission of Chicago and was the originator of the idea of a Soldiers' Fair. Frances Willard says that Mrs. Hoge shared with Mrs. Mary A. Livermore the distinction of having stood at the head of all the women of the war, whose record in caring for the sick and the wounded is as glorious as that of our soldiers on the fields.

In order to obtain money for the relief work of the Sanitary Commission, two fairs were held in Chicago, one in the fall of 1863, called the Pioneer Fair, and a second one in May, 1865, to relieve the pressing need of the families of those who had lost their lives at the front. Articles on sale at these fairs were generously donated, even the food for the guests. The prices obtained were high, in view of the object for which these funds were being raised. On the opening day came a long line of a hundred wagons from Waukegan and Libertyville, bearing a banner inscribed, ''The gift of Lake County to our brave boys in the hospitals through the great Northwestern Fair.'' Every wagon was filled to its capacity with vegetables and fruit, all of the largest and best specimens. *The Tribune* said this was a sight to bring tears to the eyes of any man but a confirmed copperhead.

It was hoped to clear at least $25,000, but the total amount raised for the Commission at the first fair far exceeded that amount. It reached a total beyond the wildest dreams of those in charge—more than $86,000.

In 1865 the Second Sanitary Fair was held in Dearborn Park (site of present Public Library), where a building four hundred feet in length was erected for the purpose. Mrs. Hoge and Mrs. Livermore were again the leaders, but this time they made plans on a more extensive scale, having grown wise through their former experience, and they entered into the work with confidence and enthusiasm.

Andrew Shuman, editor of the *Chicago Evening Journal,* and a resident of Evanston, published a daily paper, *The Voice of the Fair.* Alfred L. Sewell, a resident of Evanston, printed and sold in enormous quantities, cards bearing the picture of ''Old Abe,''[8] the war

(8) Old Abe, a fine specimen of the American bald eagle, was carried as a regimental standard by the Eighth Wisconsin Infantry during three years of the Civil War. This regiment was called the Eagle Regiment. The eagle was carried at the left of the color bearer, in the center of the regiment, by a man who had no other task than that of carrying the eagle. It had been captured by an Indian of the Chippewa tribe on the Flambeau river, before it could fly, and sold to Daniel McCann for a bushel of corn, who, in turn, sold it to a patriotic citizen for a company of men enlisting for the war. Old Abe went through the battles with eyes glistening, wings flapping and uttering screeches like war-whoops, and came through with only a few wing feathers missing. General Price said he would rather get

eagle, who was present at the Second Sanitary Fair, and giving accounts of his life. The sale of these cards netted the Fair $16,000.

The second fair brought $240,000. Mrs. Hoge's book, entitled *Boys in Blue,* gives good descriptions of the scenes at the "soldiers' fairs." Copies of Shuman's paper, *The Voice of the Fair,* are at the Evanston Historical rooms.

Joseph F. Ward, a later resident and one of the leading citizens of Evanston, was in the infantry at the Battle of Cedar Creek. He was the first to recognize Sheridan, as the latter rode upon his charger, in his thirteen mile gallop, arriving just in time to rally his disordered lines and lead the men to victory.

When the soldier boys returned to Evanston, after the close of the war, a great spread was made for them, a floor being laid over the pews of the old Methodist church and the tables set on it. Edward S. Taylor made a stirring speech on this occasion.

While feeling was running high in the anti-slavery cause, a young lady visiting in Evanston caught sight of the flag flying over the post office door—Edwin A. Clifford was postmaster at the time. Running up the steps, she tore the flag from its flagstaff, threw it on the ground and stamped it in the dust beneath her heel. Needless to say, in a place with Evanston's patriotism, an angry crowd soon gathered and she was saved from rough treatment only by the intervention of friends.

---

that bird than capture a whole regiment. At the end of the war Old Abe was presented to the State of Wisconsin, and the governor refused an offer of $20,000 for him from the show man, P. T. Barnum. When the State Capitol building of Wisconsin burned, Old Abe, who was being kept there, inhaled smoke, which caused his death in 1881. His body was mounted and put in the State House among war relics, where it remained for twenty-five years; a second fire took all that was left of the old war eagle, whose memory is a proud possession, not only of his state, but of the whole nation.

Chicago went wild with joy when the news came that the war was ended. Chicago's population at that time was about 178,000. J. Seymour Currey was a prescription clerk at the time, in the drug store of Bliss and Sharp, 144 Lake Street, and it was his turn to stay that night to take care of emergency calls. He says he was aroused out of a sound sleep by loud cries and shots and unusual noises and running quickly to the door to learn the cause of the commotion he was informed by passers-by of Lee's surrender. A great procession was formed with General Sweet, then in command at Camp Douglas, at the head with his staff following, after which came veteran reserves, the Fenians in their green jackets, prominent citizens riding horseback, great numbers of colored people who were loudly cheered, and lastly buggies and carriages. The procession took nearly an hour to pass a certain point. This was a time never to be forgotten by the residents of Chicago.

A few days later hearts were full of sorrow when the news of the president's assassination was flashed over the country.

Conductor Charles B. George, who has given us many incidents in regard to early days in his *Forty Years on the Railroad*, tells of receiving the news of Lincoln's assassination just as his train (the Waukegan Accommodation train on the Northwestern railroad) reached Evanston. In the smoking car was a jolly company, Judge Blodgett and Mr. Ferry being in the crowd. The party had just burst into a hearty laugh at someone's joke, when Conductor George entered with the telegram. In a moment there was not a dry eye in the car and a sadder lot of passengers never stepped from a train.

Chapter XXVI

GENERAL HISTORY FROM 1870 TO 1900

MIDWAY between the years 1840 and 1900 came the year which showed Evanston with almost phenomenal strides to its credit. In 1840 the place had been a dismal swamp, with scarcely a house within the whole vicinity. In 1870 the Civil War was a memory—a bitter one, although it had gained its end. During war days, the women had proved their ability to stand on a par with the men in their noble work. Also, they had edged their way into college, with a fine prospect of the doors of Northwestern University swinging open to them. Moreover, it was due to the women's perseverance that the debts of various churches were either wiped out entirely, or being gradually diminished. The past thirty years had seen the needful things come into existence—churches, schools and the proper village organization. The next thirty years were to see a full-fledged city, with a population of 20,344,[1] its north and south neighbors annexed, and its residents beginning to talk elevated service in addition to its fine train and street car service. There would be pleasure clubs, and societies, and the hard life of the pioneer would give way to the new order of city ways and city conventions.

The small boy was still picking up Indian darts and having sham battles with fake Indians along the lake shore.

---

[1] *Chicago Times Herald* Census of July, 1900.

The little old graveyard at the corner of Ridge Avenue and Greenleaf Street continued to receive its dead, although Rose Hill had been opened in 1859, and one of Evanston's most valued citizens was its first occupant, before it was formally dedicated. This was Dr. Jacob Ludlam, who came to Evanston in 1854 and bought a tract of land near Major Mulford's place on the Ridge. The last burial in the small graveyard took place in 1872, which made about 100 burials there. Right here might be mentioned a queer custom of the early days, one that was wisely dispensed with later. The silver name plate was taken from the coffin after the funeral services, framed and hung on the wall, there to remain a gruesome reminder of an unhappy day.

In the winter time the half-grown boys made ice sail boats, using ordinary ice skates, and borrowing mast and sail from the old boats laid up for the winter. On the lake there were large spaces of clear, smooth ice anchored between great jagged cakes of ice piled on the first and second sand bars, and over the smooth ice the boats flew with almost lightning speed.

In the summer the Goodrich people ran excursion steamers out from Chicago on special occasions.

Captain Charles H. Jennings, Chief of Police in Chicago in the seventies, lived at Indian Boundary Line and the lake. His family traded in Evanston's shopping district, Davis Street. One dark night, his son and the hired man were making a short cut across Calvary Cemetery, after a shopping trip, when in the middle of a very interesting story the hired man was telling he suddenly disappeared. The following seconds seemed like hours to young Jennings before he heard a voice come faintly from a yawning, newly-dug grave, into which his companion had stumbled.

The French House, now the Greenwood Inn, dated its beginning from the time of the Chicago fire. A double house was built in 1869 on Hinman Avenue at Greenwood Street. The north half of the house was occupied by the Reverend George Clement Noyes. The south half was occupied by Orvis French, who owned a hardware store on Lake Street in Chicago. Frederick E. French, son of Orvis French, remembers hearing his father tell of the sorrowful period immediately following the day of the great fire. For three days vehicles of every description, carrying household goods, went north on Chicago Avenue, the procession resembling a long funeral train. The French family, like nearly every other family in the village, hospitably threw open the doors of its home to the fire victims. Mr. French's guests were made comfortable, and having no other shelter in sight they asked their host to allow them to remain. Mr. French, seeing a means of livelihood in the arrangement, consented, as his hardware store had been burned. In the early nineties, Benjamin Bayless bought the property, and the French House became the Greenwood Inn.

Ogden House, the only house left standing in the fire-swept district, was saved by wet blankets being put on it. In this work Andrew J. Brown[2] of Evanston helped. He said the park to the south lessened the danger from the fire.

The first book published about the Chicago fire was written by Alfred L. Sewell of Evanston, and came out one month after the event.

---

(2) Henry Brown, father of Andrew, wrote *History of Illinois.*

Among those who came to Evanston shortly after the fire were the Orrington Lunts. When Orrington Lunt saw his home in Chicago threatened by the flames, he made haste to save the books belonging to Northwestern University, before he gave a thought to his own possessions. By the addition of the Lunts, Evanston was to gain far more than could be realized at the time. There was Horace, a graduate of Harvard, who later gave freely of his services to the library, and started the Village Improvement Society; George, of the class of 1878, Northwestern University, who with Will Evans, son of Dr. Evans, organized the Yacht Club and the Country Club; and Miss Nina (Cornelia), with her love of music and her ability to organize music clubs and give concerts. Those were happy days for Miss Nina, although there were happier ones yet to come, as she says the happiest and busiest years of her life were between the ages of thirty-five and sixty. During this period she organized the Woman's Guild, Evanston Amateur Concert Club, Fort Dearborn Chapter of the Daughters of the American Revolution, and was Chairman of Dormitories and Woman's Building. And of Orrington Lunt, what can one say to adequately express what he meant to the city? He was one of the founders of Northwestern University, and vice-president of its Board of Trustees; one of the incorporators of Garrett Biblical Institute, of which he was secretary and treasurer for over fifty years, and president of its Executive Board after Dr. Evans resigned. One might go on and on and fill pages telling of his work. His home, which had been the first stone house built in Chicago, had been ruined by the fire. No longer did the place by the lake have power to hold him, and Evanston was holding out a gracious welcome, which he accepted in 1874.

Evanston's first fire engine was neither large nor of attractive design—so states J. Seymour Currey in one of his newspaper articles. The small hand engine consisted of three parts, first, running gear of four small cast-iron wheels, eighteen inches in diameter, a draw-bar or tongue to pull by hand, and a bright red tank mounted on the running gear, three feet by six or eight feet long and two feet deep. Men worked the handles of the force pump on either side of the top of the tank. Hose about twice the size of ordinary garden hose protruded through the top. At one time fire wiped out the entire business center on the north side of Davis Street. The engine was in use the entire night, and the whole town looked on. W. S. Bailey was the first fire marshal. William C. Pocklington, who came to Evanston in 1875, was the city's first fire laddie. One of the leather buckets belonging to the first volunteer fire department is at the Evanston Historical Society rooms.

E. S. Taylor was a great fire fan. He urged the organizing of a volunteer fire department, and "ran with the boys" after it was started. On one occasion, when the Babcock extinguisher was frozen, Mr. Taylor ran up the ladder with the hose nozzle in his pocket, that his hands might be free to use in climbing. Some one turned on the water before he was ready, and in an instant he was thoroughly drenched from top to toe. Besides this, a fine sealskin cap he was wearing was scorched by the flames.

Many interesting anecdotes might be told of Mr. Taylor. Before he gave up the practice of law to go into politics, one of his most interesting cases had its climax in Evanston.   There had been a series of burglaries in Chicago that baffled the police.   The burglar always left a card in the mirror of one of the rooms, on which was written, "With the compliments of Handy Andy," and Handy Andy always managed to elude the police.   He was a distinguished looking man, and carried himself well.   Dressed in evening clothes, he would place himself in the foyer of one of Chicago's finest theatres, there to watch for the most diamond-bedecked lady.   With a few artfully put questions, he would obtain her name from her coachman, and before she had reached home later in the evening, he would be carefully hidden in one of the rooms, and when he left, several thousand dollars worth of jewelry would be in his possession.   He was finally landed in jail through the betrayal of an assistant, after the robbery of Mrs. Kate Daggett's jewels.   For several years he refused to tell where Mrs. Daggett's jewels were hidden, but his health beginning to fail, he sent for Mr. Taylor and offered to give the information if Mr. Taylor would secure his pardon.   John L. Beveridge was governor at the time.   Governor Beveridge at first did not look favorably on the proposition, but when convinced that the prisoner's life was threatened by disease, and assured of his reform, he relented.   The small negro boy, to whom Handy Andy had entrusted the box of jewels, refused to give it up to anyone but Handy Andy, and E. S. Taylor had to get permission from the governor to take Handy Andy to East St. Louis to secure the box of jewels.   The boy recognized the prisoner and immediately led the two men into his back yard, where he dug up the box from a place near the base of a tree.   The prisoner

was then returned to jail to await the governor's pardon.
Not long after this, Mr. Taylor was entertaining guests
at dinner, when the door-bell rang and Mr. Taylor ushered
in a soberly dressed man, whom he introduced as one
who could give much information on the methods of
thieves. The identity of the newcomer soon became
known, and an interesting hour of conversation followed.
Handy Andy survived his pardon but a short time, but
during that time he lived an honest life. It is claimed he
was a member of a fine family in Chicago.

A Dowie riot took place in 1870 in Fountain Square.
The followers of Dowie[3] began to hold meetings in
Fountain Square, to which Evanston citizens objected.
One night the Dowieites were ordered to disperse. Not
obeying, they soon found the fire hose turned on them.
The men immediately placed the women together and
locking arms formed a human fence around them. The
greater the deluge, the louder the fanatics sang! The
meeting was finally broken up by main force and the par-
ticipants were marched over to the police station to await
trial.

In the early days fishing in the lake was a worthwhile
pastime, and one that brought results. White fish, yellow
perch and trout that fed on small fish were plentiful, and
larger fish were caught occasionally. In 1872 Captain
Larson caught a sturgeon that weighed 165 pounds.

On Saturday afternoons in summer Lyman Gage,
later Secretary of the Treasury in President McKinley's
cabinet, Lloyd Gage, Frank Van Buren and E. S. Taylor,
all Evanston men, would walk out from Chicago to play
ball on the rough, unbroken ground that later became

---

(3) John Alexander Dowie was the founder of Zion City lace-making industry,
and the former head of the Zionites. He was born in Scotland.
28

Raymond Park. It was a long walk, but the train arrived too late to allow sufficient time for a good game.

In 1873 the Gross Point lighthouse tower was erected by the government. The contractor was W. F. Bushnell, a resident of Rogers Park at the time, and later of Evans-

GROSS POINT LIGHTHOUSE

ton. The tower,[4] ninety feet in height, stands on a bluff that has an eminence of twenty-five feet. It is constructed entirely of brick, steel and glass, no wood being employed,

(4) In 1914 a coating of concrete three and one-half inches in thickness was laid on the wall of the tower, making it appear bulkier than in former years.

and rests on a circular foundation of stone masonry, twenty-five feet in diameter. At the base of the lantern, the diameter of the tower is fifteen feet. At this place the tower is surrounded by a balcony. The lantern is a Fresnel lantern, one of the three the government bought

FRESNEL LANTERN IN GROSS POINT LIGHTHOUSE
KEEPER O. H. KNUDSEN

before the Civil War at a cost of $10,000 each. It is reached by a spiral staircase within the tower and its prisms are so arranged that the rays sent out in a horizontal direction waste none of the light. The lantern is

29

seven feet in height, octagonal in shape, with prisms and lenses in each of the panels. A clear white light is in the center which remains stationary, while a frame on the outside, containing two panels of red glass, revolves around it by means of clock work, which causes the red and white flashes. A sixty-pound ball, suspended from the center of the tower and wound up by hand power, forms the clock work, but soon electricity will be used as the motive power. During the revolutions, the light shows

Fog Whistle

white ninety-six seconds, partial eclipse thirty-nine seconds, red flashes six seconds, partial eclipse thirty-nine seconds, repeating in the same order. The light is visible nineteen miles from shore. It was first shown in March, 1874. When the light is obscured by a heavy fog, the big fog horn warning is sounded automatically, the blasts lasting five seconds each, with alternate intervals of twenty and forty seconds.

It was no less a hardship in the seventies for the students to forego Christmas at home than it is today. More than once during the holidays, the dormitory windows of the Evanston College for Ladies were quietly opened, and stockings attached to long cords were let down the high sides of the building to eagerly waiting Northwestern students, who filled them to overflowing with candy and cakes, to say nothing of hastily penciled notes, and then watched the bulging stockings make a safe return. Such adventures helped many a homesick youth and maid through a dull Christmas season.

On Chicago Avenue, a few doors north of Davis Street, a little house held a typical village store. Here the charming young women from the Fem Sem often met the dashing beaux from Northwestern University, although the store was forbidden ground to the young ladies. Many times the good-natured storekeeper hurried the girls back of the counter and hid them, while he politely waited on one of their teachers who happened in, thus preventing an unpleasant meeting.

Evanston's land values increased amazingly in a comparatively short time. The land Carney bought in 1840 from the government at $1.25 per acre, he sold to Andrew J. Brown and Harvey Hurd in 1854, fourteen years later, for $13,000. It was then divided into a subdivision and its best lots sold for $350 each. This land lay between Church and Dempster Streets and Chicago and Asbury Avenues.

The price of a lot, 70 by 215 feet, at the southwest corner of Davis Street and Maple Avenue almost doubled itself in the first sale, and more than tripled itself in each of the next two sales. In 1855 it brought $350; in 1865, $600; in 1870, $2,000; in 1889, $7,000. In less than thirty-five years there was an increase in price of $6,650.

Previous to 1870 land could be purchased at a very low price. In 1856 John Beck bought four lots on or near the site of the Davis Street L Station for $100 each. In 1857 the site of the Patten home sold for $52 an acre. In 1864 the corner lot at Chicago Avenue and Davis Street brought $65.

The following values were given on various pieces of property in Chamberlain's *Chicago and Its Suburbs,* published in 1874. General Julius A. White's home at 1028 Judson Avenue was worth $20,000; the Reverend George Noyes' home at Judson Avenue and Greenleaf Street, $10,000; A. L. Winne home at the corner of Hinman Avenue and Greenleaf Street, $12,000; Elijah Warren home on Chicago Avenue, $15,000; J. F. Keeney home on Wheeler (Michigan) Avenue, $13,000; S. Goodenow home on the Ridge, $45,000. Chamberlain says land near the railroad on Chicago Avenue commanded a price of $50 per front foot, selling rapidly at that price. Ridge lots sold at $40 per foot and upward. The following, quoted from his book, is interesting: "The frame depot already built for the Northwestern railroad (an impecunious corporation which cannot afford to build its own depots) is being replaced by a brick one, with a capacious side track, also donated to the company by private enterprises."

E. S. Taylor bought a lot with a three-room house on it at the northeast corner of Chicago Avenue and Grove Street, in 1870, for $300.

Mr. White's home at the Ridge and Church Street,

where Mr. Lincoln visited him, was cut in two in 1872 and one part moved to No. 1227 Elmwood Avenue and the other part to a lot just east of this location, facing Sherman Avenue. Mr. White's later home, at the corner of Davis Street and Chicago Avenue was moved to 1028 Judson Avenue, and a skating rink was built on the lot vacated. Mr. C. T. Bartlett owned the rink at the time when the roller skating craze was at its height. The building stood idle for ten years after the craze died out and was finally destroyed by fire.

Many of the houses constructed in the early days had cupolas, which were plastered and finished off like miniature rooms.

The Hamline house, 1742 Judson Avenue, contains twenty different kinds of wood in its interior.

In the late eighties came the Queen Anne style of architecture, with dormer windows, bay windows, balustrades and turrets, making busy days for the planing mill and jig saw. For a number of years Ben Peeney's saw and planing mill hummed its merry song at the corner of Church Street and Benson Avenue. It is said of Mr. Peeney that he was an able and industrious man, who did most of his work on credit, not keeping any accounts, but relying on his customers to make out their own bills. His faith in his fellow-men oftentimes spelled financial losses to him.

The first Evanston directory, 1879 and 1880, embraced the North Ward, Evanston and South Evanston, and in this, one notes that Joseph Hobbs was in the decorating business; D. P. Bowdish was the village blacksmith; James Wigginton, contracting mason; Charles F. Grey, Village Treasurer; J. J. Parkhurst, Village Trustee. In this early directory Thomas C. Hoag advertises on the first page that he is Notary Public and Fire Insurance Agent, and on the second page that he is Family Grocer. (Mr. Hoag started a bank in his grocery.)   M. F. Haskins kept a department store at the southwest corner of Davis Street and Sherman Avenue.   Mr. Haskins' store in time became The Enterprise, and later it was bought by W. S. Lord, who moved it to the sharp corner where Orrington and Sherman Avenues meet.   He afterwards moved it to the northeast corner of Davis Street and Sherman Avenue.   The latter place—the present site of the State Bank and Trust Company building—is of historic interest. This corner held the first store in Evanston, James B. Colvin's, in 1854.   The brick building erected on this corner was built in 1873 by Charles T. Bartlett for H. G. Powers.   Merrill Ladd's bank, the first bank in Evanston, was moved into the building about January 1, 1874, and remained until its failure.   The drug store of William C. Garwood, who was familiarly known as Deacon Garwood, was moved from east of this location into the corner store of the building in 1833.   Mr. Garwood paid a rental of $65 per month.   He said the profits from the sodas, which sold at five cents a glass, paid for all the drugs sold in the store.   He fitted up an electric bell over the edge of the sidewalk, in front of his door, so that anyone driving up could signal the clerks and he served with soda in the shade of the big tree, in front of the building, without getting out of his carriage.   W. J. Hamilton, later Evanston's postmaster, was prescription clerk at Garwood's store.   In 1894 Roscoe L. Wickes bought out Garwood.

The middle store in the brick building was occupied by George W. Muir's book store.   Later Henry Buhman had his barber shop in this store, and still later, it held William O'Flaherty's restaurant,—"O's."

The east room of the building was used by H. M. Angle, who sold sporting goods. His son Harry rode the first high wheeled bicycle in Evanston.

At the corner of Davis Street and Chicago Avenue, where Colwell's Drug store was located later, Erwin Ridgway tried to start a restaurant. Erwin Ridgway was later owner of *Everybody's Magazine*.

The directory of 1883 shows William H. Bartlett did practical horse shoeing; Powers and Schwall were in the livery business; Bailey and Company sold fresh and salt meats at 520 Davis Street; George Kearney was Justice of the Peace, Notary Public and Insurance Agent, at 601 Davis Street; Samuel Harrison had his place of business at 604 Davis Street. His illustrations showing cattle, pigs and sheep tell that he carried fresh meats.

Thomas E. Connor, born in Evanston in 1857, began work as a clerk in the grocery of T. C. Hoag. Later he went into the hardware business with his brother at 618 Davis Street, finally establishing his own store in 1895. (No. 618 was the old number.)

Two Evanston men were charter members of the Chicago Bar Association organized in 1874, William H. Holden and James S. Murray, the latter a resident of Evanston for sixty-seven years. Edwin Lee Brown paid Murray a high tribute, when he mentioned in his will that he desired his executors, in case legal advice was necessary in the settlement of his estate, to "counsel only with my friend (that rara avis, an honest lawyer) James S. Murray."

The early postmasters were as follows: Edwin A.

Clifford, who was appointed April 29, 1865, and continued in service until March 16, 1877; he was succeeded by Orlando H. Merwin; John A. Childs was appointed in 1885; George W. Hess received the appointment to office October 18, 1886, and Free Delivery was begun during his term. John A. Childs succeeded Hess September 16, 1889. David P. O'Leary was appointed February 1, 1894, when there was a political change in administration. Charles Raymond was O'Leary's successor, November 30, 1896. On May 10, 1897, John A. Childs was appointed

JOHN A. CHILDS

REBECCA ROLAND CHILDS

a third time and served until 1914, which made twenty-three years that he served as postmaster, a longer time than any other postmaster in the United States had served. The post office was moved from Chicago Avenue near Davis Street in 1874 to 617 Davis Street, where it remained many years. In 1889 it was moved to 810 Davis Street, remaining there until it was moved to the government building in 1906.

S. D. Childs, the father of John A. Childs, came to

Chicago in 1837, and was the first engraver in that city. He came to Evanston in 1868, but returned to Chicago in 1870, where he remained a couple of years, then came back to Evanston. John A. Childs married Rebecca Roland,[5] the first woman graduate of Northwestern University.

November 17, 1885, the Young Men's Christian Association[6] was organized in Evanston, with M. P. Aiken, president, in the Rink Building, at the corner of Davis Street and Chicago Avenue.

The idea of Saturday half-holidays originated with Frederick E. French, whose employment with John V. Farwell Company covered a period of nearly fifty years, dating from 1879. For many years he was one of the officials, as well as one of the directors of the company. One day in March, 1887, Mr. French spoke to Mr. Farwell in regard to giving the employes a Saturday half-holiday. Mr. Farwell discouraged him in the idea, saying that he thought the other merchants would not sign a petition to that effect. However, Mr. Farwell agreed to sign his name to the petition, and placed his signature on the second line, leaving the first line vacant for Marshall Field's name. After procuring Mr. Farwell's signature, Mr. French placed the petition in his desk, where it lay until an extremely hot day in June, when Mr. Farwell asked him how he came out on it. As the temperature had reached 95, with prospects of soaring yet higher, Mr. French decided that the psychological time

(5) Roland Hall, an infirmary for girl students, was named in honor of Rebecca Roland Childs about 1920, when it was moved into its present quarters at the southwest corner of Orrington Avenue and Clark Street.

(6) This association was originated in London by Sir George Williams, in 1844. The first association in North America was organized in 1851, and the first International Convention was held in Buffalo, June 7, 1854. In 1910 of the 8,000 Y. M. C. A. organizations in the world, 2,000 were in North America.

Miss Cornelia Lunt

Mrs. Elizabeth Harbert

had arrived to venture forth with the petition. In a few hours, Mr. French laid the petition before Mr. Farwell with every merchant's name affixed that he had desired, and Saturday half-holidays became an established fact.

The Evanston Woman's Club began with a small group of women whom Mrs. Elizabeth Boynton Harbert invited to her home early in the year of 1889. In March, 1889, the Woman's Club of Evanston was formed with Mrs. Harbert, President, and Mrs. Thaddeus P. Stanwood, Secretary. In 1890, the club's constitution was framed and regular officers were elected. In March, 1898, the club was incorporated according to the laws of the State of Illinois. The meeting place of the club continued to be under Mrs. Harbert's hospitable roof until 1894, when it accepted the offer of the attractive hall of the Evanston Boat Club, which it occupied for two seasons. The Country Club rooms were used for the next two seasons, after which time the members of the Woman's Club occupied their own suite of rooms in the Young Men's Christian Association building, remaining in this place until their own splendid building on Chicago Avenue and Church Street was erected several years later. In 1900 the membership numbered over three hundred. Mrs. Harbert served as president for eight years. Mrs. T. P. Stanwood was then elected to the office. She was succeeded by Mrs. Richard H. Wyman, who served two years. Mrs. H. H. Kingsley, a charter member, followed Mrs. Wyman in office and served until 1902.

Several departments developed out of the various activities of the members to further the objects of the club. Among these were Art and Literature Department,

Child and Home Department, Press Department, a French Study Class and a class in German.   Perhaps the greatest outside efforts of the club were in the interests of the Evanston Emergency Hospital and the Northwestern University settlement.

Mrs. C. O. Boring, formerly Miss Grace W. Jones, a teacher in the Noyes Street School, organized the first Mothers' Club in America at this school in 1897.   From this developed the present day Parent-Teachers' Associations.

The Evanston Hospital Association grew out of a meeting which the Evanston Benevolent Association— originated by Mrs. William Blanchard—held at the Avenue House November 17, 1891, where it was decided that "an emergency hospital is a necessity for the village of Evanston."   December 4, 1891, the Evanston Emergency Hospital was organized.   The organization began with sixty-three directors, which were soon reduced to thirty.   The hospital was opened for service March 27, 1893, in an eight-room cottage at No. 806 Emerson Street, with Miss Emily E. Robinson as matron.   The medical staff was composed of the following physicians: Isaac Poole, E. H. Webster, W. A. Phillips, Sarah A. Brayton, H. B. Hemenway, A. B. Clayton, M. C. Bragdon, O. H. Mann, E. P. Clapp, Mary F. McCrillis, I. V. Stevens and S. F. Verbeck.   Patients, both free and paid, were accepted.

In 1894 the little hospital needed money, but its friends were legion.   At one time these friends gave an entertainment in Bailey's Opera House (a building on the site of Rosenberg's store), which netted them $319 for the hospital.   An open-air performance of the opera,

The Mikado, in a vacant lot at the corner of Davis Street and Judson Avenue, by home talent, brought $2,000.

The new century approached with great promise for the young hospital, whose officers were striving for an institution that would compare favorably with any in the world. February 11, 1895, the name was changed from Evanston Emergency Hospital to Evanston Hospital Association. May 2, 1895, the purchase of 280 feet on

BAILEY'S OPERA HOUSE

Ridge Avenue for a hospital building was authorized. In 1897 a building was erected on the lot, capable of sheltering eighteen patients, and was opened for the reception of patients February 8, 1898.

Subscriptions in 1898 for four years, amounted to $25,418. In 1899 the city of Evanston made an appropriation of $300 to the hospital without specified obligations, and afterward continued to appropriate the same amount yearly. A thank offering gift of an ambulance came from Mrs. John M. Ewen. In 1900 came a great gift from Mrs. Herman D. Cable, who donated $25,000 for a needed addition, to be known as the Herman D. Cable Memorial Building, and gave an additional $25,000 to endow a children's ward that year. The outlook was good. The hospital had a fine board of directors, an efficient staff, staunch friends and a credit balance in the bank.

A co-operative housekeeping plan was started in 1891 by the Evanston Co-operative Household Association, Inc., with a capital of $5,000, and H. L. Grau was manager. The headquarters were at 711 Davis Street (old number). The weekly expenses far exceeded the income, and after a trial of six weeks, the association failed. A receiver was appointed, and the utensils and food were sold at auction.

About the year 1891 the first telephone station was erected in Evanston. This was at 612 Davis Street, with C. E. Wise as manager. In 1896 two booths were installed, two cabinet sets of telephones and two long-distance transmitters—a regular telephone exchange—the best known then. In the nineties, it was mostly the business houses that had telephone service. In 1898 there were 554 telephones in Evanston, the business men generally accepting the telephone as a necessity. Two years later the number of telephones installed was nearly doubled,— one thousand—and V. R. Lanestrom was manager of the plant.

On July 4, 1892, when the Evanston Boat Club was entertaining the public at Davis Street pier with fireworks and boat races, a rocket exploded near the bundle of fireworks, and instantly there followed confusion and uproar. An exploding rocket pierced the body of sixteen-year-old Tunis Isbester, who died instantly. Elsworth M. Board dropped through an opening in the pier to avoid being hurt, and David Noyes escaped by a miracle. That was the last time for many years there were fireworks for entertainment in Evanston.

J. Seymour Currey says Northwestern University was the first to recognize the sterling qualities of Theodore Roosevelt. On June 15, 1893, Theodore Roosevelt was invited by the faculty to make the principal address at the commencement exercises. At that time, he was but thirty-five years of age, and not extensively known outside of New York State. Following the conferring of degrees, the honorary degree of doctor of laws was conferred upon Mr. Roosevelt.

Fort Dearborn Chapter of the Daughters of the American Revolution was organized June 6, 1894. In response to an invitation from Miss Cornelia Lunt, forty ladies gathered at her home on this date. The stars and stripes waved gayly over the lawn and held places of honor throughout the house. Carnations of the national colors decorated the rooms, the blue carnations exciting admiring comment.

The State Regent, Mrs. S. H. Kerfoot, confirmed the organization of the chapter, and presented the charter. The charter, which hangs in the rooms of the Evanston Historical Society, contains the following names of charter members: Mrs. Sarah Welles Burt, Mrs. Laura Houston Wallingford, Mrs. Cornelia Augusta Gray Lunt, Mrs. Fanny Lincoln Kirkman, Mrs. Esther Stockton Cook, Mrs. Emily Huntington Miller, Mrs. Isabella Hunt

White Fuller, Mrs. Ellen C. Gillette Ward, Mrs. Maria Whipple Deering, Mrs. Maria Ford Holabird, Mrs. Laura Hurlbut Wilder, and Miss Estelle Frances Ward.

The officers elected were Miss Cornelia Lunt, Regent; Mrs. Sarah Welles Burt, Vice-Regent; Miss Sarah Watson Gillette, Registrar; Miss Lucy Elizabeth White, Secretary, and Miss Eliza A. Stone, Treasurer. Seventeen ladies became members, and eighteen became potential members. The name, Fort Dearborn, was chosen in memory of the old fort that gave protection to the gallant garrison, and to the early settlers of Chicago.

In 1897 Mrs. Julia R. Stone, whose father, Shubael Stone, enlisted in the Revolutionary War at the age of sixteen, was made an honorary member of the chapter. She was in her eightieth year.

Patriotic purpose is back of all the work of the Society. In one year alone the National Society spent over $74,000 in patriotic work among forty-four nationalities. The census of 1920 showed that of the 14,000,000 foreign-born, less than 43 per cent were naturalized, which proves that a tremendous amount of Americanization work is needed. The preservation of local records and traditions is one of the lines of the Society's work. Wherever a chapter of this Society exists, there will be found its members working earnestly and effectively "for Home and Country."

Dr. Oscar H. Mann, the city's first mayor, served three years, as he was re-elected. He was succeeded by William A. Dyche, who in turn, was succeeded in 1899 by Thomas Bates, who had been a Village Trustee for two years. Mr. Bates was nominated for the second term, but he declined a re-election.

Thomas Bates

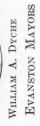

William A. Dyche

Evanston Mayors

Dr. O. H. Mann

It is interesting to know that Evanston had a share in politics in the early years, both in the state, and in broader fields. In Miss Willard's *Classic Town,* under *Evanston in Politics,* written by Honorable Edward S. Taylor, we glean the following: In 1861 Julius White was appointed by Abraham Lincoln collector of the port of Chicago, considered the most honorable of the presidential appointments in the northwest. General White was elected a member of the Board of County Commissioners under the constitution of 1870, and became its first president. In 1872 he was appointed by General Grant minister to the Argentine Republic.

In 1863 John Evans was appointed by President Lincoln governor of the Territory of Colorado.

In 1862 President Lincoln selected Professor W. P. Jones, founder and for many years president of the Northwestern Female College, consul to China.

For twenty-two years consecutively, with the exception of the thirty-third general assembly from 1883 to 1885, Evanston had a representative in the state administration, either in the executive or the legislative department. In 1866 Edward S. Taylor, who had for three years represented Evanston in the board of supervisors, was elected a representative in the twenty-fifth general assembly. During his term the park system of Chicago was inaugurated. He was re-elected to the twenty-sixth general assembly in 1868.

John L. Beveridge (sheriff of Cook County in 1868) was elected to the State Senate in 1870; in 1872 General Beveridge was elected lieutenant-governor. When Governor Oglesby was elected to the United States Senate, General Beveridge became governor, and served the unexpired term of three years. In 1882 he was appointed by President Arthur sub-treasurer.

Andrew Shuman, editor of the Chicago Journal for many years, was elected lieutenant-governor in 1876, and presided over the state senate during the terms of the thirtieth and thirty-first general assembly. General Oglesby appointed him commissioner of the penitentiary.

In 1880 John H. Kedzie, Esq., was selected as a representative in the thirty-second general assembly.

In 1884 Harry S. Boutell was elected to the thirty-fourth general assembly.

In 1886 C. G. Neeley was elected to the thirty-fifth general assembly.

George S. Baker, for several years head of the public schools in Evanston, was elected to the thirty-sixth general assembly in 1888.

Harvey B. Hurd, in 1869, was appointed by General Palmer one of a commission of three to revise the laws after the adoption of the state constitution.

Mr. Daniel Shepard was for many years secretary of the Republican State Committee.

Judge Walter B. Scates was at one time Chief Justice of the Supreme Court of Illinois. He, with another, compiled the statutes of Illinois, after the adoption of the constitution in 1848, known as the *Scates and Blackwell Revision*. In 1866 President Johnson appointed him collector of the port of Chicago.

Honorable Burton C. Cook was a member of the state senate from 1852 to 1860. He was a member of the peace conference in 1861 by appointment of his old friend President Lincoln. He was representative in the thirty-ninth, fortieth and forty-first congresses, from 1864 to 1870.

Evanston has produced such a great number of authors that it is impossible to do more than name those who have published books (previous to 1900). J. Seymour Currey, author of the history of Chicago, entitled *Chicago, Its History and Its Builders,* of which 30,000 sets were ordered before the book was put on the market, says in his article on Evanston authors, in Hurd's *History of Evanston,* "The literary life of Evanston began with the establishment of the Northwestern University in 1855. . . . This created an atmosphere that was favorable to the growth of every form of literary activity, and the book publishers, as well as those of journals and periodicals, soon became familiar with the names of Evanston people as authors and contributors." Mr. Currey goes on to say that both Edward Eggleston and Frances Willard began their literary careers in Evanston.

The following list, which Mr. Currey does not claim is complete, is of authors who have published books, and who, at some period of their lives, lived in Evanston: Isaac Emens Adams, A. T. Andreas, Mrs. Rena Michaels Atchison, Charles Beach Atwell, M. Helen Beckwith, Katharine Beebe, Charles Wesley Bennett, Henry Leonidas Boltwood, Lewis Henry Boutell, Frank Milton Bristol, Solon Cary Bronson, Walter Lee Brown, William Caldwell, Henry Smith Carhart, George Chainey, J. Scott Clark, Samuel Travers Clover, George Albert Coe, Lyman Edgar Cooley, Edwin C. Crawford, Henry Crew, Robert McLean Cumnock, Nathan Smith Davis, Sr., M.D., L.L.D., Nathan Smith Davis, Jr., Edward Eggleston, Finley Ellingwood, Frank Macajah Elliot, Joseph Emerson, Mar-

shall Davis Ewell, Charles Samuel Farrar, Randolph
Sinks Foster, Francis Gellatly, Anna Adams Gordon,
Ulysses Sherman Grant, John Henry Gray, Evarts
Boutell Greene, Mrs. Elizabeth Morrisson Boynton Har-
bert, James Taft Hatfield, Erastus Otis Haven, Henry
Bixby Hemenway, Newell Dwight Hillis, Rosa Birch
Hitch, Jane Currie Hoge, Thomas Franklin Holgate,
George Washington Hough, Mary Hess Hull, Harvey
Bostwick Hurd, Edward Janes James, James Alton James,
William Patterson Jones, John Hume Kedzie, Daniel
Parish Kidder, Homer H. Kingsley, Nellie Fitch Kings-
ley, Marshall Monroe Kirkman, Samuel Ellsworth Kiser,
Loren Laertes Knox, John Harper Long, William C.
Levere, Arthur Wilde Little, Charles Joseph Little, Wil-
liam Sinclair Lord, Mrs. Catherine Waugh McCulloch,
William Smythe Babcock Matthews, Samuel Merwin, Mrs.
Emily Huntington Miller, William Dick Nesbit, Mary
Louise Ninde, Mrs. Minerva Brace Norton, Samuel Nel-
son Patten, Charles William Pearson, William Frederick
Poole, Miner Raymond, Henry Bascon Ridgaway, Charles
Humphrey Roberts, Henry Wade Rogers, Robert Dickin-
son Sheppard, Matthew Simpson, Alice Bunker Stock-
ham, Charles Macaulay Stuart, Milton Spenser Terry,
David Decamp Thompson, Edward Thomson, Charles
Burton Thwing, Henry Kitchell Webster, David Hilton
Wheeler, Mrs. Irene Grosvenor Wheelock, John Henry
Wigmore, Mrs. Caroline McCoy Willard, Frances Eliza-
beth Willard, Josiah Flynt Willard, S. R. Winchell,
Erwin E. Wood, Abram Van Eps Young, Jane Eggleston
Zimmerman, Charles Zueblin, Frank Grover.

The publications of the authors mentioned include
books on Bibliography, Political Economy and Law, Phi-

lology, Science, Art and Music, Fiction, Essays and
Poetry, Biography and History, and are not all confined
to the English Language.

In 1900 Evanston, a residential City Beautiful, had a
population of over 20,000. Not quite three-quarters of a
century before, the first white man had built his cabin
along the shore—Stephen J. Scott. John Quincy Adams
was then the president of the United States. During his
administration, the first edition of the most used book in
the country was published, Noah Webster's dictionary.
In 1832 the first lake steamers reached Chicago from Buffalo. In 1833, when Andrew Jackson was president, the
nation did not owe a dollar—the national debt was paid!

About 1835 John Frink, later of the Frink and
Walker Stage Line, wrote from Illinois to Major John
Morgan in Massachusetts, "John, come out here. This
is God's country. Leave the rocks and come where you
can plow a straight furrow a mile long without striking a
stump or a stone."

In 1836 when Arunah Hill came to the Ridge, Chicago streets were full of Indians and its river was filled
with their canoes. Thousands of yellow canaries built
their nests in the bushes along the shore, north of the
white birch trees that grew on the former site of Rogers
Park. Deer roamed at will over the ridges and waded the
swamp.

The end of the century saw a far different picture.
In a short space of time an up-to-the-minute city had
risen, where once grew swamp grasses and forest trees.
Dr. D. H. Burnham, Director of Works at the World's
Fair in 1893, said, "Evanston is the most beautiful city
in the world." William C. Levere went a step further in

his assertion at the time of the death of a pioneer in 1898, "He found the place a wilderness, and when he died, Evanston was the most civilized city in the world." And so we leave Evanston in 1900, Evanston—to all Evanstonians—the gem suburb of one of the greatest cities in the world.

ADDENDA

John Evans

EVANSTON may well be proud that it owes its existence to such men as John Evans and Orrington Lunt,
and, because it commemorates the name of the former, a
brief sketch of his life is here given.

John Evans was born on a farm near Waynesville,
Ohio, of sturdy Quaker stock, March 9, 1814. Edgar
Carlisle McMechen says: "The Evans family is of Welch
extraction, and traces its descent to Eylstand Glodrydd,
founder of the fourth royal tribe of Wales."

John Evans' grandfather, Benjamin Evans, married
Hannah Smith in North Carolina about 1790, and became
a member of the Society of Friends. He removed in 1802
to Ohio, as his conscience would not allow him to dwell
in a slave-holding state. John Evans' father, David,
married Rachel Burnet, who is spoken of in McMechen's
book as a stern Quakeress. David, after his marriage,
became a farmer, but continued in his father's occupation
as a manufacturer of tools, and was rated as a wealthy
man. His son John was the oldest of eleven children.
John's Quaker mother, Hannah, found time, besides caring for her eleven children, to sing her hymns before
saloon doors and exhort the saloon-frequenters to abjure
the "poisonous concoctions of the Evil One," occasionally following a "tippler" home, where, in the presence
of his wife and children, she would fervently pray for his
redemption. Such was the background of John Evans'
youth, whose whole life reflected his religious training.

A cousin, Benjamin Evans, influenced John in his
choice of a medical career. The two boys were employed
in the merchandise store of John's father, "counter-hop-
pers," they called themselves. Benjamin had already

decided on entering a medical school, while John had a literary career in mind and had gained a reputation of being a "poemster"—an accomplishment regarded with contempt by the elder Quaker generation. The younger generation, especially the young lady cousins, declared he wrote beautiful verses.

Before his twentieth birthday John persuaded his parents to send him to the Academy at Richmond, Indiana, as he had had only a common school education. His letters to his cousin, Benjamin, are filled with "thys" and "thees." They are preserved by his descendants and are of more than ordinary interest. He ends his letters asking for a "sheetful" in return. With postage at twenty-five cents per letter, and transportation by stagecoach, failure to answer a letter was a grievous offense, and a good letter-writer's sheetful consisted of the sheet written full in black ink, then criss-crossed in red.

John's year at the Academy at Richmond, where there were but eight young men, was followed by his enrollment at a Quaker school at Philadelphia, the Gwynedd Boarding School for boys. From this school John wrote to Benjamin that he had taken up chemistry to fit himself for the study of medicine. In regard to algebra and philosophy he wrote: "They are both pleasing studies, and I would rather read philosophy than eat peach pie."

The father and mother were not in sympathy with John in his ambition to learn the "doctoring trade," as they did not consider it a high calling. One brother wrote him: "It is true it is not the top-gallant of education."

The Quaker school proved a disappointment to John, which was revealed in a letter to Benjamin, in which he boyishly says: "I am all the time mad at old Gwynedd School. The old fellow is as dumb as a goat."

Benjamin continued to urge John to study medicine, and answered, refuting the arguments of John's family: "The character of the humane, moral, Christian, scientific physician proximates the Diety more closely than the character of any other man," and derided the man who entered the profession for mere livelihood. This letter decided John in his choice. However, he wrote to his father that he would not persist in the study of medicine if his father did not consent, saying: "Thy word is sovereign, and I hope to be dutiful." So the father "reckoned John would have to be a doctor," and John was jubilant. After studying two winters at Lynn Medical College in Cincinnati, he graduated in 1838. The death of his favorite cousin, Benjamin, some time before this, was a great blow to him. After his graduation, John left Ohio with a pony, a saddle, and a ten-dollar bill, which were presented to him by his father. Crossing the rough frontier country of Indiana, he settled in Hennepin, Illinois, where he did not remain long. In 1839 he married Hannah Canby. After residing a short time in Milton, Miami County, Ohio, the young couple removed to Attica, Indiana, a place largely settled by friends from John's old neighborhood. Within two years, John built up a large practice, and was one of the town's most influential citizens.

John Evans' long friendship with Bishop Simpson commenced in Attica in 1841.

The reputation of dreamer had already been given to John Evans by his friends in Attica. One day he remarked that before he died he "intended to build a city, found a college, become governor of one of the states of the Union, go to the United States Senate, amass a fortune, and make himself famous." Step by step this prediction came true, and his Attica friends in later years often repeated his words.

Dr. Evans, while residing in Attica, began to publish articles in regard to founding hospitals for the care of the insane, who, in Indiana, were then kept in jails and poorhouses. Widespread interest in the subject was aroused, and in 1848 two wards of an insane hospital were completed, five patients were accepted, and Dr. Evans was made the first superintendent. The two wards

were the nucleus of the Central Indiana Hospital for the
Insane, located at Indianapolis. About 1845 Dr. Evans
became a faculty member of Rush Medical College in Chicago. For three years he taught as a professor, and
later he was elected to a chair in that institution. He
edited the *Northwestern Medical and Surgical Journal*
until 1852.

John Evans was one of the founders of Mercy Hospital, which had its beginning as the "Illinois General
Hospital of the Lakes." Great difficulty was encountered
in securing women as nurses. In 1849, during the cholera
epidemic, the Sisters of Mercy served with devotion and
sacrifice, and Dr. Evans and Dr. N. S. Davis petitioned
the Bishop of Chicago to permit the Sisters to take over
the work. On February 22, 1851, the control of the hospital passed into the nuns' hands.

In 1849 Dr. Evans wrote his famous "Observations"
on cholera in the *Northwestern Medical and Surgical
Journal,* asserting it was a communicable disease. However, not until 1866 was this theory accepted by the profession, at which time the National Quarantine Law (for
which he was largely responsible) was passed.

In 1850, two years after moving to Chicago, Dr.
Evans' wife died, leaving a half-grown daughter, Joseph-
ine. Mrs. Evans' body was taken overland by wagon to
Attica for burial.

Dr. Evans' connection with the founding of Northwestern University has already been related. This institution, to use his own words, was to be a place "where
Christian education could be dispensed without money
and without price." His gifts to the University totaled
approximately $181,000.

He built the Methodist Church Block and was one of
the projectors of the *Northwestern Christian Advocate*
and the Methodist Book Concern.

In 1850 he and his partner, Dr. Daniel Brainerd,
erected the Evans Block in Chicago. Among its first
tenants were the Chicago post office and the *Chicago*

Tribune. The four lots, on which this building was erected, were located on the east side of Clark Street, south of the alley, between Randolph and Lake Streets. The partners took a twenty-year lease at $1,000 a year and taxes. The building was crowded with tenants from the first and the owner of the lots soon sued for annulment of the lease. Dr. Evans, with his father, who had become reconciled to his son's profession, bought out the partner, fought the suit and compromised on a rental of $3,000 a year. The property brought an annual rental of $50,000, which at the end of the twenty-year lease amounted to $1,000,000. This was Dr. Evans' first great real estate transaction.

In 1853 Dr. Evans organized a Board of Instruction in Chicago. Up to that time Chicago had never been placed educationally on a systematic basis. Dr. Evans was elected alderman on a school-advancement program, and was immediately appointed chairman of the Committee on Schools. During his term as alderman, 1853 and 1854, three schools were established, one of them Chicago's first high school. The doctor nominated and secured the election of the first superintendent of schools in Chicago, John C. Dore.

During the time Dr. Evans was a member of the Board of Aldermen, he recommended establishing street grades and sidewalks. The City Council ordered the work of grading done, which forced owners to fill many lots. Dr. Evans raised the entire Evans Block several feet. This was the "first lakeshore reclamation, and the beginning of the great improvement which gave Chicago adequate drainage and a firm foundation."

In 1853 he married Margaret Patten Gray, sister of Mrs. Orrington Lunt.

While living in Evanston, Dr. Evans became interested in electricity and had a workshop fitted up in his basement for the study of it. In later years, in Denver, he helped his son organize one of the first electrical railways in the world.

About 1850 Dr. Evans took his initial step as railroad promoter and builder. He became a director of the Fort Wayne and Chicago railroad, and procured the right-of-way through the streets and through Illinois to the Indiana state line, paying for the forty-acre site for the station $35,000. One-half of this terminal site was sold the next year to the Burlington and Quincy railroad for $140,000. The Chicago Union Depot now occupies the grounds, and the Pennsylvania System operates the right-of-way.

Dr. Evans was a pronounced abolitionist, "a conductor on the underground railway," attacking slavery in a public controversy with Judge Skates of the Supreme Court of Illinois, the controversy being carried on through the columns of the *Chicago Evening Journal.*

President Lincoln, almost immediately after his inauguration, offered Dr. Evans the governorship of Washington Territory, as he recognized the value of sound judgment for the territories at this critical period. Dr. Evans decided Washington Territory was too far removed from his Chicago business interests and declined the office. The governorship of Nebraska territory, which he was offered later, had been requested by a son-in-law of a cabinet member. Before giving his answer to President Lincoln in regard to the Colorado Territory gubernatorial post—the third post of its kind offered him,—Dr. Evans made the trip to Colorado from Chicago by stage-coach. After a trip across the plains that took thirteen days he reached Denver, "a sprawling town of frame houses with its three thousand-odd inhabitants," saw the prairie-schooners of the immigrants, the patient oxen, the red-shirted horsemen passing through the town, leading pack animals upon which were tied the gold-seekers' picks and pans; he breathed in the dry atmosphere and recognized its healing properties to affected lungs. Believing it would benefit his daughter, Josephine, he decided to accept the President's offer. He began his duties as governor of the Territory of Colorado May 18,

1862. McMechen says that no war governor in the Union was called upon to meet a more trying situation. Schuyler Colfax, Speaker of the House, wrote a letter to President Andrew Johnson June 2, 1865, in which he said he did not think any of the territories had a better governor.

One of Governor Evans' first acts was the emancipation proclamation which resulted in the freeing of the women and boys of the Ute and Navajo tribes, who had been taken by the enemy tribe and sold as slaves to the Mexicans and Spaniards. He solved the Indian problems wisely, and the treaty, signed October 7, 1863, was considered from the white standpoint the most successful ever concluded in Colorado. Governor Evans said that singing hymns and parading school books around were not good ways to civilize the Indians. He tried a new method, showing them how they could obtain a subsistence. He used the appropriations of the tribes to buy sheep and cattle, of which he gave a certain number to each family, instructing them not to kill the animals.

In Denver, as in the Middle West, Governor Evans surrounded himself with men of proven ability and firm character, which, his biographer says, was one of the most consistent traits of his life.

From the day Dr. Evans became governor, his life was filled with big endeavors and big results. His daughter said: "My earliest recollections of father are filled with an atmosphere of expectancy. Some 'great scheme' was always pending or about to be realized." At these times conversation at dinner was carried on in an unobtrusive manner.

The organizations of the Rocky Mountain Conference, and later of the First Methodist Episcopal Church of Denver, were due to Governor Evans' efforts.

Governor Evans' connection with the railroad in the west is made interesting reading by his biographer, but can only be touched upon here. Denver, within a six months' period, lost nearly half of its population to Cheyenne, where the Kansas Pacific railroad had reached.

Denver was apparently doomed to an inconspicuous future. T. C. Durant, Vice-President of the Union Pacific Railroad, said Denver was *too dead to bury*, which so enraged the Denverites that its leaders decided to "make a city." The result was the organization of a Board of Trade, which in turn organized the Denver Pacific Railroad and Telegraph Company. The first train over this road to reach Evans, Colorado,—a town half way between Cheyenne and Denver—was on December 16, 1869, and by acclamation of the assembled business men from Denver and Northern Colorado the name of the peak known as Rosalie was changed to Mount Evans, in honor of the governor, and in grateful acknowledgment of their appreciation of his bringing the railroad to them. Mount Evans is situated midway between Pike's Peak and Long's Peak, and is 14,260 feet in height.

The Denver Pacific Railroad was completed and opened for traffic June 24, 1870, to the cheerful clamor of the Colorado Seminary bell, and the first locomotive owned by the Union Pacific drew a special train into Denver. To Governor Evans was assigned the honor of driving the silver spike, on which was an engraving commemorating the event. The Georgetown mayor who was to bring the spike was delayed, and Governor Evans took an ordinary iron spike, wrapped it with tin-foil and "hammered it home." The silver spike arrived soon afterward and it is now treasured in the Evans family. The construction of the Denver Pacific Railroad saved the town from disaster. In ten years Denver's population grew from 4,000 to 34,000. The success of this railroad venture, and of others later, was largely due to the work of Governor Evans. His last venture as a railroad promoter was made after he had passed is eightieth birthday.

Governor Evans resigned his office August 1, 1865. Change in administration and mis-statements of fact by his political enemies caused him to take this step.

December 18, 1865, John Evans and Jerome B.

Chaffee were elected senators from the State of Colorado.
The first movement toward statehood for Colorado was
defeated.   The second bill for statehood was passed by
Congress, but vetoed by President Johnson.   Governor
Evans and Mr. Chaffee were assigned seats in the senate,
but they could not exercise their rights as senators until
the statehood bill was passed.   Both men resigned September 25, 1866, "to clear the way for statehood," which
did not come until 1875.

The University of Denver, beginning as the Denver
Seminary, and later having the name of Colorado Seminary, sinking into "a state of coma for twelve years,"
owed its birth in 1864 and its rejuvenation in 1876 to
Governor Evans.   The University is, in truth, the "people's university," having been assisted financially by
more than forty thousand persons.

It was the governor's invariable custom to contribute
not less than one hundred dollars to every church started
in Colorado, regardless of denomination.   These donations were not always confined to his state; sometimes
churches as far east as Washington were benefited.

Governor Evans, high-minded, open-hearted, toler-
ant, charitable—always working for the betterment of his
fellow-men, with no motive for personal gain—passed
away July 2, 1897.   President Walter Dill Scott of Northwestern University said of him: "Not even John Harvard
or Eli Yale contributed more to the cause of higher education than did John Evans."

While those associated with John Evans in his business ventures deserve credit, there is no doubt that his
was the "controlling spirit that guided the destinies of
the institutions," which were started by him.

(The data for the foregoing sketch were obtained from the LIFE OF
GOVERNOR EVANS by Edgar Carlisle McMechen.)

REFERENCES

AMERICAN INDIAN, HAINES'. Elijah Middlebrook Haines.

AMERICAN INDIANS. Frederick Starr.

BATTLES AND LEADERS OF THE CIVIL WAR, Volume I. The Century Company.

CHARLEVOIX'S LETTERS TO THE DUCHESS OF LESDIGUIERES, published in London in 1721.

CHICAGO AND ITS SUBURBS. Everett Chamberlain.

CHICAGO AND NORTH WESTERN RAILWAY SYSTEM, A HISTORY OF THE. W. H. Stennett.

CHICAGO'S HIGHWAYS, OLD AND NEW. Milo M. Quaife.

CHICAGO, ITS HISTORY AND ITS BUILDERS, Volume VII. J. Seymour Currey.

CHICAGO, THE STORY OF. Jennie Hall.

CLASSIC TOWN, A. Frances E. Willard.

COOK COUNTY, ILLINOIS, HISTORY OF. A. T. Andreas.

CRAIN, MRS. CHARLES, MEMOIRS OF.

DISCOVERY AND CONQUESTS OF THE NORTHWEST, THE. Rufus Blanchard.

DOMESTIC ECONOMY. Catherine E. Beecher.

EARLY NARRATIVES OF THE NORTHWEST. Louise Phelps Kellogg.

ECONOMIC HISTORY OF THE UNITED STATES. Ernest Ludlow Bogart, Ph. D.

EVANSTON, HISTORY OF. Harvey B. Hurd.

EVANSTON PUBLIC SCHOOL PAMPHLETS ON THE COURSE OF STUDY, 1879, 1884, 1892 AND 1915.

GEOGRAPHY OF CHICAGO AND ITS ENVIRONS, Bulletin No. 1 (Geographic Society of Chicago). R. D. Salisbury and W. C. Alden.

GEOLOGICAL AND NATURAL HISTORY SURVEY, Bulletin No. 2. Frank Leverett.

GLIMPSES OF FIFTY YEARS. Frances E. Willard.

GREAT EVENTS OF OUR PAST CENTURY, THE. Published 1881. R. M. Devens.

HANDBOOK OF AMERICAN INDIANS, Volumes I and II, U. S. Bureau of Ethnology.

HISTORICAL ENCYCLOPEDIA OF ILLINOIS AND HISTORY OF CHRISTIAN COUNTY. Newton Bateman, L.L.D., Paul Selby, A. M., Henry L. Fowkes.

HISTORIC ILLINOIS. Randall Parrish.

ILLINOIS, THE LAST OF THE. John Dean Caton.

ILLINOIS AND INDIANA INDIANS, THE. (Fergus Historical Series.) Hiram W. Beckwith.

ILLINOIS CATHOLIC HISTORICAL REVIEW. Joseph Thompson.

ILLINOIS HISTORY, CHAPTERS FROM. Edward G. Mason.

ILLINOIS, THE MAKING OF. Irwin F. Mather, A. M.

ILLINOIS, PIONEER HISTORY OF. John Reynolds (Governor of Illinois 1832-1834).

INDIANS OF THE NORTHWEST, HAINES'. Elijah Middlebrook Haines.

INDIAN TRIBES OF THE CHICAGO REGION, THE. William Duncan Strong.

JENNINGS, CHARLES E., MEMOIRS OF.

LASALLE AND THE DISCOVERY OF THE GREAT WEST. Francis Parkman.

LEADING FACTS IN AMERICAN HISTORY, THE. David H. Montgomery.

LETTERS ON FILE IN THE EVANSTON HISTORICAL ROOMS. From old residents.

LIFE OF GOVERNOR EVANS. Edgar Carlisle McMechen.

NEWSPAPER ARTICLES. J. Seymour Currey.

NEWSPAPER ARTICLES. William C. Levere.

NORTHWESTERN UNIVERSITY, ALUMNI RECORD OF 1903.

NORTHWESTERN UNIVERSITY, THE STORY OF. Estelle Frances Ward.

OFFICIAL RECORDS OF THE UNION AND CONFEDERATE ARMIES IN THE WAR OF THE REBELLION.

OLD FORT DEARBORN, STORY OF. J. Seymour Currey.

OLD RECORD BOOK OF DISTRICT NO. 2 (now District No. 76).

OLD RECORD BOOKS OF THE FIRST METHODIST EPISCOPAL CHURCH.

PAPERS. By Frank R. Grover.

PHYSICAL GEOGRAPHY OF THE EVANSTON-WAUKEGAN REGION. (Illinois State Geological Survey Bulletin No. 7). Wallace M. Atwood and James Walter Goldthwait.

PHYSIOGRAPHY. R. D. Salisbury.

RAMBLER IN NORTH AMERICA, THE. Charles Joseph Latrobe's *North America*, Volume VII, published in London 1835.

RECOLLECTIONS OF BENJAMIN FRANKLIN HILL, given in a talk before the Evanston Historical Society May 21, 1902.

RECORDS ON FILE AND MAPS AT THE EVANSTON CITY HALL.

RECORDS ON FILE IN THE EVANSTON HISTORICAL ROOMS.

SOURCE BOOK FOR SOCIAL ORIGINS. William I. Thomas.

WAU-BUN, THE EARLY DAY. Mrs. John H. Kinzie.